SCOTLAND
A New Study

SCOTLAND
A New Study

EDITED BY CHALMERS M. CLAPPERTON

Contributors:

Ian H. Adams
J. B. Caird
Keith Chapman
Chalmers M. Clapperton
James R. Coull
Michael Cross
J. H. Farrington
Valerie Haynes
William Kirk
A. S. Mather
E. A. Smith
Joy Tivy

DAVID & CHARLES
Newton Abbot London North Pomfret (Vt)

British Library Cataloguing in Publication Data

Scotland.
  1. Scotland—Description and travel—1951-
  I. Clapperton, Chalmers M.
  914.11   DA867

  ISBN 0-7153-8084-2

Photoset in Baskerville by
Northern Phototypesetting Co Bolton
and printed in Great Britain by
Butler and Tanner Limited Frome and London
for David & Charles (Publishers) Limited
Brunel House Newton Abbot Devon

Published in the United States of America
by David & Charles Inc
North Pomfret Vermont 05053 USA

Contents

83-7471

List of Illustrations

Plates

Figures in Text

Introduction

Chalmers M. Clapperton

SCOTLAND has always been a land of contrasts and conflicts, a theatre of action on whose stage physical and human processes have acted out the drama of geological and geographical evolution from distant times. It is not surprising that there are so many descriptive and narrative accounts of the country, not to mention the romantic and historical fictional treatments. Much less, however, seems to have been written in explanation of the equally fascinating patterns formed by the various elements of its geography. This book offered an opportunity for leading authorities to contribute expertise based on their research and teaching skills in compiling a new geographical account of Scotland with *explanation* as the central theme. The following paragraphs review and justify the thirteen chapters composing this book, all of which are designed, as far as possible, for a wide audience.

In view of the remarkable variety and complexity of rocks in Scotland and because of recent advances in our understanding of the earth's large-scale geological processes, it was thought that a separate chapter summarising Scotland's geological evolution would be a new and helpful contribution. This opening chapter also lays the foundation for a review of the main geomorphological processes that have operated on the geological framework to create the natural landscape surrounding us today. For example, it is now known that Scotland lay in the southern hemisphere (and possibly in polar latitudes for a time) when some of the oldest rock sequences were being formed. It is equally exciting to imagine the active volcanic landscape in west Scotland little more than 55 million years ago – just the other day geologically speaking – as the Atlantic ocean basin opened up; ash from many explosive eruptions was probably scattered eastwards over the land by the prevailing westerlies, rather like that from the recent eruption of Mount St Helens in the western United States.

The chapter on landforms draws attention to the length of time that has been available for landscape evolution and reviews the most plausible theories explaining the plateau surfaces at different levels, the pattern of major river valleys, and the intriguing basins, isolated hills and tors in the Central Highlands and north-east Scotland. Now that we understand better how glacier ice behaves, more accurate explanation can be offered for the distribution and characteristics of glacially eroded terrain and glacial deposits. The age-old myth that Scotland once had Alpine mountains which were ground down to rounded summits by the ice sheets can surely be laid to rest; glaciation had a rather superficial effect on much of the pre-glacial landscape. This chapter ends with the implication that a great deal has still to be discovered about the rate at which the present-day landscape is evolving.

Because weather affecting Scotland is very much a British and West European phenomenon, it was decided that a chapter bringing together the relationships between climatic factors and plants that grow on the varied physical landscape was of greater value than a chapter purely on Scotland's climate. Chapter 3 explains the interaction of major factors, such as the variety of air masses from different sources and the relatively high latitude and altitude, in affecting the growth and success of both natural and cultivated vegetation. This background is most important for the appreciation of points raised in later chapters dealing with agricultural development and the present-day economics of agriculture and forestry.

The physical landscape, with its variety of forms, natural vegetation and animal life, and vagarious climate, was the stage on which the human drama began many thousands of years ago. Chapter 4, in its approach to the historical colonisation of the land, emphasises the regional identities that had developed by the Dark Ages – a regionalism which partly reflected the natural environment and partly the varied pattern of colonisation by different culture groups, and which still pervades Scotland's geography in modern times.

Through time, the potential of the rural landscape was increasingly realised, and distinct patterns of settlement evolved between the medieval period and the mid-nineteenth century. Chapters 5 and 6 are devoted to this foundation period, during which the basic framework of the present-day rural geography became established. With the growth of agricultural wealth and technological innovations through the eighteenth and nineteenth centuries came industrial development and the mushrooming of towns and cities. Chapter 7 provides an insight into the reasons underlying the manner in which urban growth, and particularly the Scottish tenement landscape, occurred. This background aids an appreciation of the dreadful deprivation problems that have existed in Scotland's major towns and cities for a hundred years, and that have led to the various efforts aimed at urban renewal since World War II.

With such escalation in economic and urban growth, heavily focused in central Scotland, the development of transport systems was crucial to its success. The evolution of transport networks, from the early drove roads to present-day motorways, therefore merits a separate chapter. With the recent expansion in air travel, largely as a result of the impetus of North Sea oil, it can be seen how important transport development is to the country's future welfare.

With 98 per cent of the land officially designated as countryside, it is obvious that an overwhelming amount of Scotland's geography involves rural land use. This topic is pursued in Chapter 9, in which the characteristics of the major land uses and their current trends are outlined. Trends in agriculture are particularly significant with respect to British agricultural policies within the broader framework of the European Economic Community. Developments in forestry, the economics of hunting and shooting in vast deer forests and grouse moors, and the potential of outdoor recreation and nature conservation, are other highly topical themes. Contemporary, often controversial, issues such as land transfer to urban use, the effect of afforestation programmes on hill farming and deer enterprises, and the ownership and control of rural land (particularly in the Highlands and Islands), conclude the chapter.

Fishing has been of vital importance in many parts of Scotland since the earliest human settlement, and because the country's fisheries – supported by one of the most advanced fleets in the world – are of major importance in the European context, a short separate chapter explains their evolution and present trends. But in addition to land and sea, Scotland is also endowed with considerable energy resources. Historically, water power laid the foundations for factory-based industry, but the main phase of industrial development used coal for fuelling steam engines and generating electricity. Such themes have been well documented in geography books over the years and so the chapter on Scotland's energy resources considers trends exclusively since 1945. Since that time the exploitation of primary resources such as coal and the oil–natural gas couplet have dramatically declined and grown respectively, while the generation of electricity from nuclear reactors and from natural elements like wind and waves is still a controversial issue. Ten years ago a book on Scotland's geography would have had little to say about oil and natural gas as indigenous energy resources. Today they are profoundly influencing patterns of population movement and the location of manufacturing industry in some parts of Scotland; and locally they are creating a new geography.

Despite the asset of considerable energy resources, Scotland's manufacturing industry is in the doldrums. The penultimate chapter of the book provides an insight into the processes which have brought about fundamental industrial change since 1945. The decline of industries in the major cities is well-known, but another critical change has been the increase in the level of external (ie non-Scottish) ownership of industries in Scotland. Following a concise historical perspective, the chapter focuses particularly on the structure of manufacturing industry in the 1970s and the change in manufacturing employment, and concludes by outlining prospects for the future. This logically leads into the final chapter, which looks ahead to Scotland's future geography. From the physical point of view one can say that both natural and, increasingly, man-made processes will continue to modify the landscape. Another ice age will almost certainly develop within the next 10,000 years unless technological development leads to the artificial control of climate. On the human time-scale, however, by the end of the century most major changes in Scotland's geography will be taking place on the economic and political stages.

1

Scotland's Geological Evolution

Chalmers M. Clapperton

To understand the remarkable diversity in Scotland's geological basement (Fig 1.1) and hence the variety of landscape etched out of it by denudational processes, it is necessary briefly to trace the country's geological or palaeogeographical evolution. This assumes that readers will be familiar with the concept of plate tectonics which has revolutionised geological interpretation during the last twenty years or so. With this concept in mind, it is worth stressing that present-day Scotland is an assemblage of bits of the earth's crust separated by more than 2,500 million years of time and that much of it had lain and/or originated in the southern hemisphere before arriving in its present geographical position perhaps no more than 40 million years ago (Fig 1.2, Table 1.1).

The story begins in the realm of great uncertainty when we consider the oldest rock, the Lewisian gneiss of the north-west mainland and the Outer Hebrides. This is a tough grey crystalline rock which was once volcanic ash and sand deposited around a volcanic island chain, possibly 3,000 million years ago. During the next 2,000 million years, such sediments were buried, melted, pressurised and injected with hot igneous rocks on more than one occasion; all this tectonic activity altered or metamorphosed the entire sequence of rocks into the gneisses we now see on the surface. The last event to affect them was uplift and erosion to a gently rolling plain-like landscape with higher hills in places – this had happened by 1,000 million years ago. Part of this landscape is now on view as it appears from beneath the cover of rocks (Torridonian) that buried it after its formation; the low-lying coastal plateau of Wester Ross and Sutherland is thus largely an ancient re-exposed or exhumed landform of Precambrian age. Much of the adjacent North-west Highlands are composed of a thickness of about 10km of younger Precambrian metamorphic rocks known as the Moine series. Originating as limestones, sandstones and mudstones mixed with volcanic ash and other igneous rocks, the Moine series is now a complex of schists, granulites and gneisses. They were probably formed

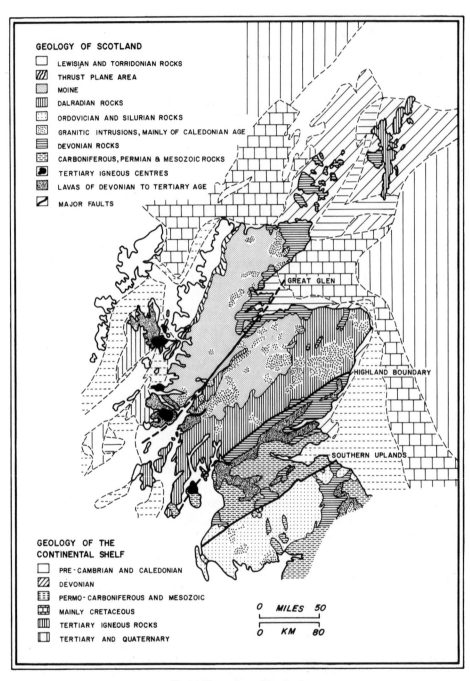

GEOLOGY OF SCOTLAND

- ☐ LEWISIAN AND TORRIDONIAN ROCKS
- ▨ THRUST PLANE AREA
- ▨ MOINE
- ▥ DALRADIAN ROCKS
- ▨ ORDOVICIAN AND SILURIAN ROCKS
- ▨ GRANITIC INTRUSIONS, MAINLY OF CALEDONIAN AGE
- ▤ DEVONIAN ROCKS
- ▨ CARBONIFEROUS, PERMIAN & MESOZOIC ROCKS
- ▨ TERTIARY IGNEOUS CENTRES
- ▨ LAVAS OF DEVONIAN TO TERTIARY AGE
- ▨ MAJOR FAULTS

GREAT GLEN

HIGHLAND BOUNDARY

SOUTHERN UPLANDS

GEOLOGY OF THE
CONTINENTAL SHELF

- ☐ PRE-CAMBRIAN AND CALEDONIAN
- ▨ DEVONIAN
- ▤ PERMO-CARBONIFEROUS AND MESOZOIC
- ▨ MAINLY CRETACEOUS
- ▥ TERTIARY IGNEOUS ROCKS
- ▯ TERTIARY AND QUATERNARY

0   MILES   50

0   KM   80

Fig 1.1 The geology of Scotland

DIRECTION OF MOVEMENT OF CONTINENTAL MASSES

Fig 1.2a The position of Scotland in the southern hemisphere: during Ordovician times *c*475 million years ago

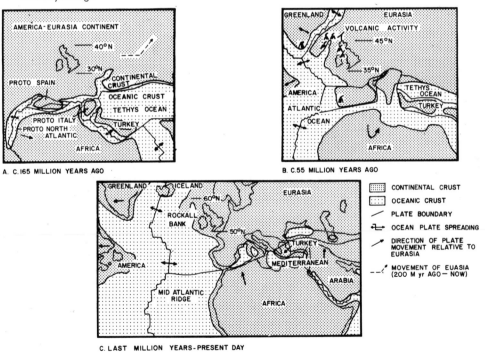

Fig 1.2b The position of Scotland in the southern hemisphere: from *c*165 million years ago to the present day

at the edge of a continent being underthrust by a segment of ocean floor, like western South America today.

The next sequence, the Torridonian Sandstone, which is the youngest (and undeformed) of the Precambrian rocks, was deposited at the base of high mountains in a tectonic environment that had become stable. The sandstones and conglomerates are still only gently dipping after more than 700 million years, and in places have developed into spectacular isolated mountains like Quinag, Suilven and Canisp. These rocks survive only west of the Moine thrust, a major geological fracture line along which older Moine rocks from the east were moved tectonically westwards to lie on top of younger Cambrian rocks. Beyond the shoreline of the Torridonian land mass and its river systems, the continental shelf and a contiguous ocean trough began a long history of almost continuous sedimentation, lasting from the late Precambrian, about 700 million years ago, to the end of the Silurian period about 415 million years ago. During this time typical marine sediments such as muds, silts, sands, limestone and volcanic ash from island arcs accumulated to a thickness of 15km.

Around 570 million years ago, a distinctive boulder bed (the Portaskaig-Schiehallion bed) is believed to have been deposited by an ice sheet, implying that the land mass carrying Scotland must have been in sub-polar or high-temperate latitudes (probably in the southern hemisphere). Two major tectonic disturbances affected these rocks. An early phase in pre-Ordovician times metamorphosed and thrust Precambrian and Cambrian sediments known as the Dalradian series, forming the widespread schists, quartzites and migmatites of the Central Highlands between Kintyre and Buchan. The later phase, which affected marine and volcanic sediments of Cambrian, Ordovician and Silurian age, did not metamorphose them but compressed and folded them into the highly cleaved structures widespread in the Southern Uplands. These events occurred at a time when Scotland lay at the south-eastern edge of a continent separated by an ocean basin from a more southerly land mass bearing Wales and England. The two masses ultimately joined as the ocean basin was consumed and this all happened in sub-tropical latitudes of the southern hemisphere. The folding, fracturing and faulting – caused by crustal compression, thrusting and uplift during the Caledonian orogenic episodes – have imparted the distinctive 'grain' to most of the Scottish land mass, which in Scotland's present geographical position is aligned roughly south-west to north-east.

Thus by 400 million years ago the whole of Scotland was part of 'Euramerica', one of the three large continents of the Devonian or Old

Red Sandstone period; it initially had high mountains and volcanoes and lay in the tropics. Between the Highlands and Southern Uplands lay a large basin elongated with the Caledonian 'grain' and into which torrential streams carried vast quantities of sands, pebbles and cobbles. (The 'pudding rock' exposed in cliffs at Stonehaven harbour is of this material.) Temporary lakes appeared and chains of andesitic volcanoes poured out lavas and ashes, and the environment must have resembled parts of the present-day Andes. Lavas and ashes forming the Ochil and Pentland Hills, for example, belong to this period and remain upstanding in today's landscape because of their relative resistance to weathering and erosion. These rocks were then gently folded and down-faulted between the Highland Boundary fault and the Southern Upland fault, creating the tectonic trench of the Midland Valley; this happened in Lower Old Red Sandstone times. Most of the so-called 'Newer Granites' which are widespread in the Grampian Mountains were intruded during this period of magmatic activity, and many now form prominent massifs such as the Cairngorms. Ben Nevis, Lochnagar and the Cheviot lie on the sites of what were large central volcanoes of the time. The Younger Old Red Sandstone period followed the disturbance, and in north-east Scotland and the Orkneys sequences of sands and limy muds were poured into a large but shallow inland sea (Lake Orcadie), which was teeming with fish. The monotonous plateau of Caithness and much of the gentle relief of Orkney is underlain by the flagstone rocks of this period. Like the Torridonian sandstone, the Old Red has promoted the development of spectacular cliffed scenery, particularly at the coast (eg Old Man of Hoy).

At the beginning of the Carboniferous period 370 million years ago, southern Britain lay across the equator and a warm shallow sea similar to parts of the Caribbean gradually spread northwards. It covered the Old Red Sandstone continent as far as the Scottish Highlands, but some areas, such as the Southern Uplands and perhaps the Pentland Hills, stood as islands in this sea. The most characteristic rocks laid down as sediments in this area are limestones, typically containing fossils such as stem fragments of sea lilies (crinoids), brachiopod shells and corals. Other sediments such as sandstones derived from the Northern continent, and muds settling out slowly in lagoons in the vicinity of today's Edinburgh, were rich with algae and forest plant fragments, thus forming the well-known oil shales. Volcanic activity was rife and great volumes of basaltic lava poured out from fissures to form plateau country and several hundred individual central volcanoes developed. Because of their resistance to erosion, these lavas and volcanic rocks form many prominent hills in central Scotland, such as the Clyde plateau, the Campsie and Kilpatrick Hills, and the well-known volcanic hills of Edinburgh. As the Carboniferous period progressed, through the next 100 million years, the mountains of the Old Red Sandstone continent were eroded to low-lying land, and adjacent basins – such as the Midland Valley, the Merse, and northern England – became choked with sediment. Thus much of the Scottish landscape became an ill-drained lowland covered with vast swamps rich in plant and animal life. Repeated rises and falls in world sea level, possibly in response to the repeated growth and decay of large ice sheets covering continents close to the south polar region, caused the periodic drowning of the plant life. As plants rotted and became buried by sand and other sediments, they gradually compacted into the coal seams exploited today.

These sedimentary events came to an end about 280 million years ago, when a major tectonic disturbance affected the southern part of Britain and much of southern Euramerica. A likely explanation is that a large southern continental crustal plate or group of plates moved northwards to collide with Euramerica, compressing sediments and other rocks along the line of collision; these were thrust up to form ranges of young mountains known as the Hercynian or Variscan system. Scotland lay too far north to be seriously disturbed by these tectonics and only minor folds developed in the Midland Valley, but many east–west trending volcanic dykes and large sills of quartz dolerite were injected as a result of crustal fracturing and associated magmatic activity; prominent landforms like Stirling Castle Rock and crags in the Lomond Hills have developed from such resistant rock.

The Variscan mountains in a sense welded two super-continents together (Laurasia in the North and Gondwanaland in the South) to form the remarkable cluster of conjoined continental plates called Pangea. Somewhere in the midst of this, lying just north of the Equator and swept by dry easterly trade winds, Britain lay in a hot arid climate. Desert sands from the Permian and succeeding Triassic periods now crop out in only a few parts of Scotland. Preserved in down-faulted basins in south-west Scotland (Nithsdale, Annandale, Stranraer) and in Arran, the cross-bedded red sandstones are typical of desert sand dunes; alluvial sandstones and conglomerates indicate the erosion of adjacent uplands. Creamy-coloured sandstone of this age in the Elgin district has been extensively used as an attractive building stone; reptilian remains and footprints found in these rocks indicate the beginning of the dinosaur era about 200 million years ago. For over 150 million years, shallow shelf seas fluctuating in level and areal extent through the Jurassic period penetrated from a southerly source; presumably it was a great gulf of the Tethys ocean which penetrated westwards between parts of the great northern and southern continents.

Great populations of dinosaurs roamed the continents at this time, particularly in tropical latitudes, but since Jurassic rocks are only present in a few scattered localities in Scotland (eg North Skye, Raasay, Brora), not much is known about the Scottish environment and its inhabitants. Considerable sedimentation occurred in the adjacent and subsiding North Sea basin, where Jurassic sandstones became major oil reservoirs (eg the Brent and Piper Fields). Dense 'clouds' of planktonic organisms in the narrow, shallow warm seas annually lived and died, sinking into stagnant mud on the sea bed. The natural distillation of this organic substance beneath overlying sediments has formed petroleum which migrated to accumulate in porous sand (hence sandstone) formations. Faulting and igneous activity in the North Sea heralded the beginning of a period of crustal fracturing in the super-continent which ultimately formed the Atlantic Ocean. Uprising plumes of thermal energy from the earth's upper mantle, bringing masses of partially melted rocks (magma) to upwarp and fracture the crust, initiated the series of mega cracks (rifts) west of Britain which developed into the Atlantic spreading centre and ocean basin. This process uplifted the west of Scotland in particular, tilting and warping the land mass in an easterly direction. By this time the land mass on which Britain lay had moved to about 40°N where the climate may have been warm, humid and monsoonal.

During the Cretaceous period 135 to 65 million years ago the Atlantic Ocean began opening between North Africa and eastern North America, but the fracturing spread to the area between Greenland and north-eastern North America and then to the line between the Outer Hebrides and the Rockall Bank. The crustal tensions and compressions associated with sub-crustal magmatic activity (thermal circulation), related to ocean-floor spreading and mountain building (the collision of Africa with southern Europe–Asia), led to much basin subsidence around the Scottish land mass. An ever-changing geography of land and river basins discharging to seas and lakes began the final episode in shaping today's scenery. As the global sea level rose as a result of the development of massive mid-ocean ridge systems, it is possible that in Upper Cretaceous times a low rolling Scottish landscape may have been covered by a shallow (chalk) sea, as was most of Europe. Thin beds of chalk lie protected beneath younger lava flows on Skye, and Cretaceous chalk is found all round Scotland in the marine basins, but there is no firm evidence for a former complete cover. Approximately 58 million years ago a great thermal plume caused an outburst of volcanic activity in west Scotland, more or less at the time when the main mid-ocean ridge of the North Atlantic caused 20km of oceanic spreading every million years.

The youngest hard rocks in Scotland were created at this time by three main styles of volcanism over a period of probably 3.5–5 million years. Initially, north–south tension cracks in the crust caused by the opening of the Atlantic basin permitted the mobilisation of tholeiitic basalts probably from a linear zone of partially melted magma at shallow depths. Such basalts were mostly erupted from fissures and because of their fluidity, due to low silica content, high temperature and fast rate of extrusion, they covered wide areas of terrain. Successive outpourings over the same region, but always from different fissures, piled up the lava beds to thicknesses exceeding 2,000m in places. Long intervals of time between one lava flow being covered by a succeeding one are indicated by intervening red beds. These are lateritic soils developed by weathering of the iron and aluminium-rich basalt under a warm and humid climate. The wholesale production of fissure basalts was accompanied by the development of large central volcanoes, in Skye, Rum, Ardnamurchan, Mull, Arran and St Kilda. That in Mull began possibly as a basaltic shield volcano, but as the magma became progressively differentiated, to leave a silica-rich (acidic) residue, the volcano became explosive and ash-producing. Nothing remains of the super-structure of these volcanoes but they must have been imposing mountains, rising to perhaps well over two to three thousand metres. They probably formed the highest land in Tertiary Britain.

The former magma reservoirs and concentric ring dykes and cone sheets intruding the volcanic centres are now exposed in today's landscape, giving rise to impressive mountain scenery amidst gently tilted basaltic plateaux. The basic gabbro of Skye has weathered distinctively into the jagged Cuillins, whereas acid granite and granophyre have weathered into the rounded and smooth Red Hills. On Ardnamurchan, concentric rock structures and ridges of land developed on resistant outcrops trace the outlines of the former central volcano. The magmatic activity was accompanied by considerable crustal tension in west Scotland, which permitted the intrusion of myriads of basic dykes, many of which now crop out as small ridges or trenches, depending on relative resistance. Although the dyke 'swarms' seem closely linked with the central volcanoes, the overall north–west to south–east alignment and length (extending into northern England) indicate regional tension and widespread mobilisation of basic magma.

It is clear from the volcanic stratigraphy that the lavas were erupted on to a low-lying landscape, and fossil plants indicating a warm temperate climate have been taken as evidence that the British land mass may have been located in more southerly latitudes at this time.

For at least the last 58 million years, possibly longer, most of Scotland has been above sea level, thereby exposed to the agents of denudation which create landforms. Exactly how the present-day landscape evolved during this long period and before the first glaciers formed is difficult to assess, since there are no sedimentary deposits containing indicators of environmental conditions, such as fossils and pollen grains. However, it is estimated that 1,000–2,500m of rock were removed from parts of west Scotland by Tertiary denudation. Since a few thousand metres of sediment accumulated in the North Sea and other surrounding basins during the same period, it may be inferred that uplift, bedrock weathering, stream incision and the development of slopes proceeded to evolve the present landscape by removing vast amounts of material. Calculations indicate a rate of landscape removal of 1cm/220–600 years in west Scotland, where the wetter climate promotes more rapid operation of processes. Meanwhile, during this period, Britain moved farther north into cool temperate latitudes and the global climate cooled in response to the build-up of permanent ice and snow in the polar regions. Repeated glaciation by ice sheets and local glaciers over the last 2.5 million years (possibly) has added the final, distinctively glacial, touch to some of the Tertiary landforms. For the last few thousand years human beings have increasingly changed the superficial appearance of the natural landscape.

Notes to this chapter are on page 301.

Table 1.1 Pre-Quaternary geological and geomorphological development of Scotland in relation to Plate Tectonics (*Compiled by V. Haynes*)

Geological periods	Millions of years	Tectonic events	Latitude and climate	Possible traces in the present landscape	Geomorphological events
Precambrian Lewisian Moine Torridonian Mid Dalradian	1,000	An ocean basin (*Iapetus*) gradually opened up between England and most of Scotland	Not much known	The irregular sub-Torridonian landscape in the far North West may form the oldest landforms in Scotland though they only cover a small area	Scotland forms the fringe and continental shelf of a mountain region (Greenland) with outlet canyons over the Outer Hebrides. Vast amounts of erosion are recorded in screes and alluvial fans (up to 7,000m of deposits). The deltaic portions have subsequently been metamorphosed into the Moinean rocks
	570		Possibly in polar position		
Palaeozoic Cambrian		*Iapetus* at its widest			The sea encroaches. All Highland Scotland flooded
Ordovician Early Mid	500	Moine and Dalradian metamorphosed and folded because of plate collision and subduction	Probably in Southern Hemisphere – moving generally northwards		Highlands now mountains – deposits in S. Uplands contain material eroded from the Highlands
Late		Midland valley now a down-faulted trench			
Silurian	430	Still metamorphosis at depth. Large intrusions – because of plate subduction			S. Uplands now mostly upland and Midland Valley more obvious
	395				

CALEDONIAN OROGENY

Period	Events	Latitude / Climate	Location	Description
Devonian (Old Red Sandstone)	Ocean now closed because of collision of two continental plates and original marginal sediments form part of mountain range. Some volcanicity – lavas in Ochils, Sidlaws & Lorn	25°S Sub-tropical	Large basins in S. Uplands, eg Lochmaben Merse, in Nith and Annan Valleys and Lauderdale. Highland edge of Midland Valley. W. coast of Kintyre. The main traits of the relief of much of the Grampians between Lochnagar and Mt. Keen & S. of Elgin & N. Scotland – the low plateau of Caithness and E. Sutherland has Old Red Sandstone outliers, some only a few metres across, scattered widely over it. Particularly significant is Scaraben – Devonian breccias, representing fossil screes, cling to the quartzite spine of the mountain implying that it is essentially pre-Devonian	Highlands and S. Uplands form part of a large mountainous continent, actively eroded. Vast amounts of deposits collect in fringing structural basins. Rock fragments and pebbles in alluvial fans form breccias and conglomerates on mountain edges, grading to inland lakes (Caithness Flags). Even at this time part of the North Sea forms a major indentation in the continent – marine limestone occurs in Central Graben opposite the Forth. Gradual reduction of the relief shown by the gradual fining of the sediments up the series
345				
Carboniferous Dinantian	Volcanicity – lavas and many volcanic necks in Central Valley	15°S–10°N Equatorial, hot swampy climate (bauxites and laterites)		
Westphalian (Coal Measures)			Solway Firth coast from mouth of Nith to Abbey Head, Stranraer and L. Ryan area and Luce Bay basin	Highlands and S. Uplands still possess considerable relief, shedding debris into surrounding basins, at first estuarine and lagoonal – ie non-marine. Highlands now a pulsating upland with less severe erosion – Midland valley has finer deposits
Variscan (Hercynian)	Another large continent and mountain range formed through plate collision farther south in Europe – no great effect in Scotland except folding and faulting (E–W) in Midland Valley. Caledonian faults reactivated			
280				

V A R I S C A N O R O G E N Y

Geological periods	Millions of years	Tectonic events	Latitude and climate	Possible traces in the present landscape	Geomorphological events
Permian	225		20°N Desert climate due to latitude and large Caledonian and Variscan continents	Large parts of S. Uplands. The Annan (especially the Devil's Beeftub) and the lower Nith are re-excavated along a line of basins filled with Permian sediments, and their wide form contrasts with the narrow Esk valley which does not appear to have had a Palaeozoic precursor	Continued erosion of upland. Deposition similar to Devonian. Basins infilled with alluvial fans, braided river deposits and limited wind action. Continental shelf (Forth Approaches basin) at first dry then later restricted marine deposition. Source in N. North Sea is to W. and N.W.
Mesozoic Triassic		Large N. Atlantic continent	30–40°N Seasonal – wet and dry		Still relatively rugged relief (pebbly deposits in very large braided rivers)
Jurassic Liassic	190		Warm, monsoonal climate, like S. China due to large continent + Tethys ocean over S. Europe and Asia 20–25°C (68–77°F) (isotopic temperatures)		Much drowning. Highlands probably a series of islands with sea invading from Minches. W. coast and Inner Hebrides under the sea. North Sea only shallow.
Mid Jurassic (Gt Estuarine Series)		N. and C. Grabens of North Sea developing Widespread uplift		Whole major outline of upland block N. of Great Glen and its steep faces to W. and E. eg E coast of Black Is. and Sutherland and the steep 200km long mountain front of N.W. Scotland.	Long low land mass from Scotland to Pennines. Quiet warm lagoons in Inner Hebrides (like Gulf States and Florida Everglades) surrounded by hills mantled in deep weathered soil and thick forest (much plant debris in deposits). North Sea marine with extensive fluvial and deltaic interludes. Sea excluded from Britain
Late		Rockall trough opening			
Cretaceous	135				
Cenomanian (Lower chalk)		Separation of N. America from Greenland/Europe caused widespread subsidence, flooding much of Britain Rockall trough stopped developing			Extent of submergence in Scotland is contentious. The surrounding shelves and troughs contain extensive thick chalk (eg 1370m in N. North Sea)
Senonian (Upper chalk)					Scattered chalk remnants in Inner Hebrides

Tertiary	Epoch	Age (Ma)		Climate	Relief	
Tertiary	Palaeocene Eocene	63	Separation of Greenland from Norway/Scotland Uplift in W. rejuvenated erosion. Subsidence in C. North Sea (marine) Volcanic activity in west Scotland	40–47°N Flora and fauna types now found in India and Mexico. Red deep weathered lateritic soils		Deep weathering. Low lying broad flat basins with fluviatile and laccustrine silts and swamps in Inner Hebrides before and during lavas. Continental shelf to W. has fresh water deposits and so was still land
	Oligocene	38	Intrusions in Hebrides Widespread subsidence of shelf to N. & W. (eg Rockall Platform submerged)	(Rocks in Devon suggest N. Mediterranean/Portuguese type of climate)		
	Miocene	26	Crustal instability continued. Mild folding and faulting of igneous rocks. Reactivation of major previous faults		? Major elements of relief – surfaces, basins etc	No rocks formed on land. Much of continental shelf land also. Presumably erosion active creating erosion surfaces and exhuming older landscapes
	Pliocene	7	Continued uplift	Possibly Mediterranean at first, and changing to cool temperate by c. 3.5 million years ago	Lowest erosion surface (most extensive in N. Scotland) coastal platforms eg in Arran and benches along main valleys. Also valley incision, giving narrow deep valleys prior to glaciation	Denudation
		2.5				

2

Scotland's Landforms

Valerie Haynes

CHAPTER 1 looked at the influence of Scotland's geology and geological history on the scenery. This chapter aims to explain how Scotland's landforms have evolved and how the main contrasts in scenery have arisen. To do this a broad landform classification is first provided. Then the main variables which have inter-acted to develop such a kaleidoscopic variety of landforms are considered. Opinions are reviewed on the origin of the river system and ancient landforms (palaeoforms) such as planation surfaces, weathering basins, inselberg-like features and deeply weathered bedrock. Next there is the impact of successive glacial and interglacial periods when at different times the land was occupied by various scales of glacier, from full ice sheets to small corrie glaciers. This is followed by an assessment of post-glacial and current processes operating on the land and on the shoreline.

Landform Classification

Scotland is usually considered to be an upland country (Fig 2.1). In fact, although 65 per cent lies above 120m (400ft), only 6 per cent is above 600m (2,000ft) and 20 per cent is below 60m (200ft). Thus the absolute altitudes are not great – it is the close interweaving of high and low land which gives rise to the overall mountainous appearance of the landscape (Fig 2.2). An attempt is made in Fig 2.3 to divide the country into broad areas with different categories of relief, thereby providing a framework for discussion and explanation.

A backbone of deeply dissected mountains (category 1) runs down the west of the country from Durness to Loch Lomond. Here the valley network is much denser than elsewhere and a greater volume of the terrain has been consumed by agents of erosion (Fig 2.4). This is largely the result of the steeper drop to the sea (giving greater scope for slope movement and stream power), the wetter climate and more intense glaciation. East of the highland backbone and over most of the

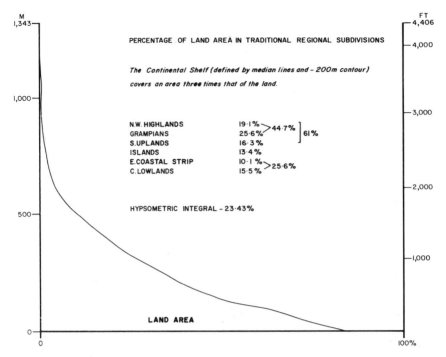

M
1,343

FT
4,406

4,000

PERCENTAGE OF LAND AREA IN TRADITIONAL REGIONAL SUBDIVISIONS

The Continental Shelf (defined by median lines and - 200m contour)
covers an area three times that of the land.

1,000

3,000

N.W. HIGHLANDS	19·1 %		
GRAMPIANS	25·6 %	44·7 %	61 %
S.UPLANDS	16· 3 %		
ISLANDS	13·4 %		
E.COASTAL STRIP	10· 1 %	25·6 %	
C.LOWLANDS	15·5 %		

2,000

HYPSOMETRIC INTEGRAL - 23·43%

500

1,000

LAND AREA

0

0   100%

Fig. 2.1 Hypsometric curve for Scotland. This indicates a considerable degree of dissection of the original landmass

Southern Uplands lie extensive rolling plateaux, sometimes as high as the mountains to the west (category 2). Indeed Geikie[1] remarked that there is more flat land on the hilltops in the eastern Grampians than in the valley bottoms. Here, dissection may still be deep, but it is less dense and, on the longer slope to the North Sea, the rivers have more opportunity to gather into larger systems; the Tay, for example, has the largest discharge in Britain. Large areas of the North-east and South are occupied by broad subdued plateaux at intermediate levels and a lowland fringe exists round much of the country (categories 3, 4, 5, 6, 7 and 9). This is more extensive in the east and south, though even the so-called Central Lowlands are discontinuous, being interrupted by steep-sided hill masses like the Pentlands, Ochils and Campsies which rise to heights of over 600m.

Small areas are occupied by other types of relief. Especially in the Northern Highlands impressive isolated hills (category 11) rise abruptly from lower, more subdued terrain. Such areas have been likened by some authors to typical savanna landscapes of more tropical climates. In other areas there are partially enclosed basins (category 8), as at Glenmore and Abernethy which have been etched out of the northern Cairngorms. Such features are common in the eastern Grampians

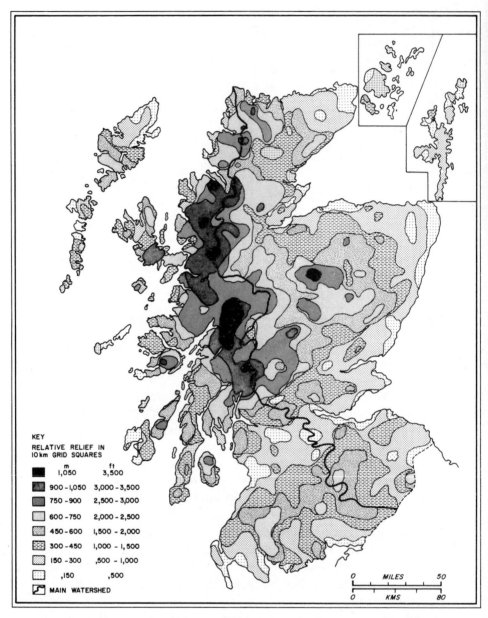

KEY

RELATIVE RELIEF IN
10 km GRID SQUARES

	m	ft
■	1,050	3,500
	900 - 1,050	3,000 - 3,500
	750 - 900	2,500 - 3,000
	600 - 750	2,000 - 2,500
	450 - 600	1,500 - 2,000
	300 - 450	1,000 - 1,500
	150 - 300	,500 - 1,000
	,150	,500

MAIN WATERSHED

MILES 0 — 50

KMS 0 — 80

Fig 2.2 Ruggedness of the terrain. Greatest relative relief occurs where highest ground lies close to coast (e.g. Lochaber) or where it is deeply dissected (e.g. the Cairngorms). High levels of ruggedness have an overwhelmingly western distribution, while areas with a relief of less than 300m (1,000ft) are extensive only in the east and the Central Lowlands. Enclaves of higher values are found on the isolated igneous hill masses of N.E. Scotland, and of lower values in the basins (e.g. Rannoch Moor) and also on monotonous upland watersheds (e.g. Slamannan plateau – Lanarkshire and the Ladder Hills – Aberdeenshire). (Data kindly provided by K. J. Lea)

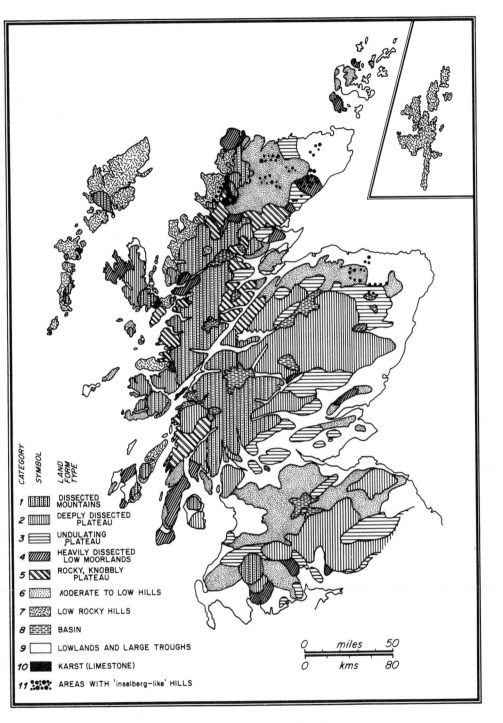

CATEGORY	SYMBOL	LAND FORM TYPE
1		DISSECTED MOUNTAINS
2		DEEPLY DISSECTED PLATEAU
3		UNDULATING PLATEAU
4		HEAVILY DISSECTED LOW MOORLANDS
5		ROCKY, KNOBBLY PLATEAU
6		MODERATE TO LOW HILLS
7		LOW ROCKY HILLS
8		BASIN
9		LOWLANDS AND LARGE TROUGHS
10		KARST (LIMESTONE)
11		AREAS WITH 'inselberg–like' HILLS

Fig 2.3 Landform classification and distribution

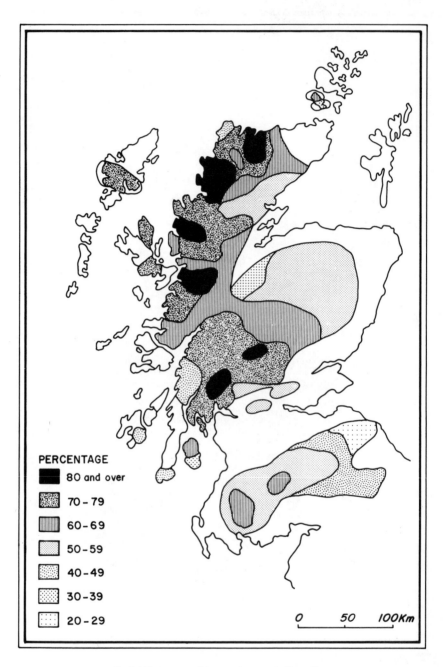

Fig 2.4 Percentage of the terrain occupied by valleys

Page 33 *(top)* Typical 'palaeo' landscape of north-east Scotland. Open basin of the western Garioch with gently rolling, glacially moulded topography at c180–250m above sea level. Steeper slopes rise to higher plateau surfaces on Tap O Noth at c600m in the middle distance. View towards the north-west; *(above)* Gruinard Bay, Wester Ross. Raised fluvio-glacial outwash delta in the foreground at c15m, backed by heavily ice-scoured (mamillated) bedrock of Lewisian gneiss

(Overleaf) Page 34 *(top)* Thick blanket peat from a period of cooler and moister climate about 4,000–2,000 years ago; now being eroded into 'hags'; eastern Grampian mountains; *(centre)* southern slopes of the Campsie Fells; a series of parallel glacial meltwater channels slope diagonally across the hillside in the middle distance; *(bottom)* view from Goat Fell, Arran. One of the intensely dissected Tertiary igneous centres. Two different types of granite produce a contrast in hill forms. A finely jointed granite produces smoothed hillslopes (left middle distance) while a granite with wider spaced joints gives rougher mountains (foreground). Prominent glacial forms include corries and a horn-shaped peak

where they may be related to weaker rocks in places, but in others have little obvious link with rock type, suggesting that the pattern of denudation history may be important in their explanation.

On a local scale geology exerts a considerable control on morphology (eg category 10, karst limestone terrain), but the distribution of the landform types, such as the uniform plateaux (planation surfaces) at different altitudes, tends to disregard geological boundaries and so is largely the result of tectonics and erosional history.

Landform Evolution
Geomorphological Processes

The landforms classified in Fig 2.3 have evolved through the operation of geomorphological processes on the varied bedrock. The most important processes have been and still are: bedrock weathering (physical disintegration and chemical decomposition); mass downslope movement of weathered materials; and erosion, transportation and deposition by streams, the sea, wind and periodically by glacier ice. Because bedrock varies in its properties such as chemical composition, mechanical strength, joint density and arrangement, it has often been weathered or eroded differentially. Since Scotland has moved from warm sub-tropical to cool-temperate latitudes over the last 70 million years, the intensity and nature of denudational processes have changed through time, so that processes dominant say 40 million years ago may be less significant now and newer influences like glaciation have developed. Whatever the climatic system, denudation is dictated by gravity and its effect on an uplifted land surface is generally to remove bumps and fill in hollows; so that varying tectonic events may also influence the rates of processes.

Accepting the tectonic uplift of the Scottish land mass to roughly its present altitude and shape sometime during the last 70 million years, the main geomorphological processes that have operated are as follows. Weathering has broken up and decomposed bedrock to form a loose regolith (disintegrated bedrock of which soil is the upper layer); rivers have cut down to form valleys; and the sea has etched the margins of the land mass to form cliffs and rock platforms. Under the influence of gravity the mass downslope movement of regolith has widened out valleys and lowered hill tops; much of such movement is achieved by slow imperceptible creep of individual particles and by more rapid processes such as slumping, landsliding, mudflow and rockfall. The intensity of the different mechanisms has varied over the millions of years of exposure to atmospheric processes; for example, deep chemical weathering of the bedrock was probably dominant when Scotland experienced warm humid conditions, whereas physical shattering of bedrock predominated in the intensely cold phases when ice sheets were developing. Debris from the slopes ends up in rivers, the principal transporting agents. These either deposit the sediment load on their flood plains and as alluvial fans, or transport it to lakes or to the sea where it is redistributed to form beaches and continental shelf deposits. Such processes are normal during non-glacial periods like the present, but are replaced during glaciation, when the erosional, transportational and depositional processes associated with glacier ice and meltwater streams predominate. Thus both the relative importance and absolute rates of different processes have varied over time.

Glaciation is probably the most effective agent of all on hard rocks, but in sub-aerial environments, processes, especially chemical ones, are usually speeded up by warmer climates. Taking the last 70 million years of Scotland's evolution, the climate was warmer at first. The main effect of climatic cooling towards the end of the Tertiary era would probably have been to slow down the rate of landscape development, as cool temperate regions seem in general to be areas of slow landform change. Chemical weathering is usually still the most significant geomorphological process, though it is slower than in warmer climates. Deciduous woodland provides a great deal of protection to soils on slopes, making their removal slow, so this would allow the retention of any pre-existing deep-weathered regolith. It may well be that tectonic events like pulsed uplift would have had more effect on erosion rates than climatic change, by speeding up valley incision, thereby creating steeper slopes. We can identify a number of landforms which evolved through the action of all these processes before glaciation.

The River System

A number of different views exist on the origin of the present river valley patterns. A tendency for rivers to flow in one general direction, especially if unrelated to geological structure, is interpreted as showing the inclination of the land surface on which they developed. Some authors[1] believed there was an overall south-easterly trend to the proto-drainage system in Scotland, while others[2,3] favoured an eastward flow. It has been suggested that the initial rivers rose on a land mass west of the present west coast. This can only have been east Greenland, and any such river initiation would have to predate the opening of the Atlantic. Bremner[2] and Linton[4] believed that the drainage was

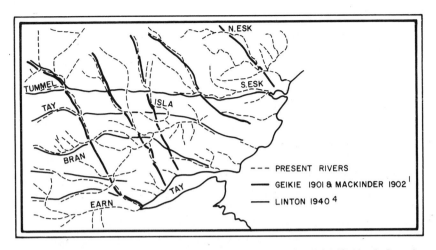

Fig 2.5 Different reconstructions of the original drainage pattern of the S.W. Highlands. It can be seen how by linking together different elements of the present drainage pattern very different reconstructions can be made; this leads one to doubt the validity of the idea

initiated on a mantle of Cretaceous rocks uplifted with a general eastward tilt. As the Minch developed, the headwaters were gradually captured by new active west-flowing streams, to leave many east-west gaps through the mountains. Problems with such an interpretation include the existence of *two* main views on the direction of slope of the original land surface (suggesting that there is no one main river direction) and rather tenuous river reconstructions based on linking together widely separated and unrelated valley segments. An example is shown in Fig 2.5. Many of the peculiarities of the river pattern have been re-interpreted as glacial diversions. George[5] totally rejected the idea of a Cretaceous cover and suggested instead a series of late Tertiary marine surfaces on which the rivers were initiated in short sections varying in direction with local tilt and progressively extended as uplift proceeded or as sea level fell. Sissons[6] argued against this concept and proposed instead a more piecemeal model with rivers flowing away from the main axis of early Tertiary uplift, which coincided with the present main watershed (Fig 2.2). The discordance of some rivers with the geology may be explained by their having developed over slight extensions of the various fringing sedimentary rocks, including those of Cretaceous (chalk) age.

A possible alternative explanation of the superimposed drainage exists, however. Land surfaces in moist tropical and warm temperate climates are normally deeply mantled with weathered regolith, whose characteristics after a long period of chemical weathering often do not vary greatly even over different rocks. Rivers could be superimposed

from such a mantle on to the rocks beneath. Such a view seems
attractive, not least because there actually is evidence in Scotland for
deep weathering.[7] Also, superimposition of rivers from deep regolith
can be verified in present-day humid tropical areas,[8] and other features
of the Scottish landscape can readily be fitted into this model for the
evolution of pre-glacial landforms.

Erosional Basins

It is not easy to explain why rivers alone should open out wide,
almost enclosed basins in the midst of higher ground. Nor can these
basins be explained tectonically, as some of the most striking are quite
unrelated to downfaulting; the Glenmore and Abernethy basins in the
Spey valley, the Tarland, Lumphanan and Feugh basins in the Dee
valley, and the high level Cabrach basin in the Ladder hills are
particularly fine examples. Deeper weathering in zones of weaker rocks
may begin to develop basins, however, as illustrated by the Rannoch,
Tarland and Alford (Don) basins, which roughly coincide with granite
outcrops amid metamorphic rocks. In the tropics there is a tendency for
valleys to be widened rather than deepened. This is because, in humid
areas, chemical decomposition is more active on gentle slopes because
there is slow seepage of the fresh water needed for weathering, and by
the time it reaches the flatter valley floors it is often saturated with
weathered products and unable to attack the rocks further. In drier
parts, weathering becomes more restricted to moist sites such as slope
foot areas, and produces a similar, but much more pronounced, effect of
undercutting and steepening valley sides. Thus, by a combination of
weathering and slope processes, one can envisage wide basins
developing with fairly gentle floors and steeper sides. They will perhaps
be especially well developed if the climate varies between wetter and
drier so that the regolith is alternately weathered and stripped.
Godard[9] suggested that the floors of many basins in northern Scotland
are formed by his 'Scottish surface' (Fig 2.6), which he thinks evolved
under a dry climate. Basins would be characteristic of the east rather
than the west, because the greater uplift in the west meant that incision
by erosional agents dominated over weathering.

Planation Surfaces

The widespread existence in Scotland of plateau surfaces and hill
summits at accordant levels and at several different altitudes has led to
considerable speculation about their origin. Some of the main views on

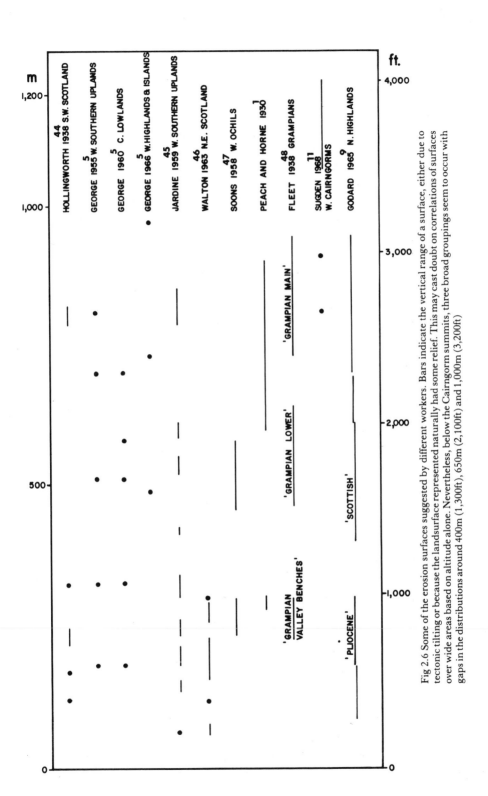

Fig 2.6 Some of the erosion surfaces suggested by different workers. Bars indicate the vertical range of a surface, either due to tectonic tilting or because the landsurface represented naturally had some relief. This may cast doubt on correlations of surfaces over wide areas based on altitude alone. Nevertheless, below the Cairngorm summits, three broad groupings seem to occur with gaps in the distributions around 400m (1,300ft), 650m (2,100ft) and 1,000m (3,200ft)

the levels represented are shown on Fig 2.6. As can be seen, each postulated surface varies in altitude across the country and since the surfaces are now fragmentary because of subsequent erosion this can lead to various different correlations. Some authors, George for example,[5] have interpreted them as being uplifted and tilted surfaces of marine planation, but this seems unlikely (there is no other independent evidence for overall marine inundation since the Cambrian), and the extent of the erosion seems too great for the sea to have accomplished. Others, such as Sissons,[6] have regarded them as sub-aerial in origin – resulting from such long continued denudation that the landscape is reduced to low relief (peneplains) close to the prevailing sea level – or as having a mixture of both origins. The definite levels would have resulted from uneven rates of uplift, each level representing a long period of constant sea level.

Postulating an evolution in climates warmer than the present adds another dimension. A variety of processes in both the wet and dry tropics seem to widen valleys rather than deepen them, creating widespread gentle surfaces surmounted by steep hillsides, thus providing a means of perfecting or even developing the so-called erosion surfaces at a variety of levels not necessarily wholly related to the sea level prevailing at the time.

Residual Hills (Inselbergs and Tors)

During the extensive development of erosion surfaces, residuals of higher land are generally left in areas which are less actively attacked – either by virtue of their position near watersheds or because of more resistant geological make-up. Sometimes this simply means the survival of an area of higher erosion surfaces (eg the Cairngorm and Ben Nevis summit levels), but in other areas attention has been drawn to the inselberg-like character of some hills. Inselbergs are the characteristic steep-sided residual hills which rise abruptly from savana plains, as a result of the enhanced slope foot weathering mentioned above. Parts of Caithness and East Sutherland are extraordinarily reminiscent of such areas. Again Godard particularly associated such hills with his 'Scottish surface'. Care needs to be exercised over this interpretation, however, as isolated hills in glacial environments may also acquire over-steepened slopes. A pre-glacial origin involving deep weathering has also long been suggested for the tors (small rock residuals left on patches of less jointed rock on hill tops) which exist on a number of the broad hill tops in the Eastern Highlands (eg the Cairngorms).[10,11] Although they can develop by frost shattering and solifluction of regolith, they are widely found as a result of the partial removal of a weathered mantle of variable depth in climates ranging from sub-tropical to tropical.

Age of the Landscape

This view of the evolution of many of Scotland's landforms gives a coherent picture, but since Scotland has been in warmer latitudes than the present for most of geological time (Table 1.1), the timescale over which the present landscape has evolved is still uncertain. One could think in terms of a few million years (Miocene-Pliocene), of tens of millions of years (Tertiary era) or of hundreds of millions of years (post-Caledonian times). If there is a continuous chain of geomorphological inheritance, with landforms of one phase influencing the processes of the next, perhaps only large-scale geological events like folding or burial by thick marine sediments are able to interrupt the continuity of evolution. This leaves the question wide open as there has been no large-scale folding since the Caledonian orogeny, and only the lower margins have been buried by sediments (this took place particularly in the Old Red Sandstone, Permo-Triassic and Cretaceous periods). Even here, provided the overlying sediments are much weaker than the underlying hard surface, fragments of previous landscapes preserved by such burial can still be uncovered (exhumed) to form very ancient elements in the relief. The most ancient landforms in Scotland are believed to be in the rocky knolls of the sub-Torridonian surface in the North-west. Some authors have ascribed much larger parts of the Scottish relief to exhumation, especially popular being surfaces of pre-Old Red Sandstone, pre-Permian and pre-Cenomanian (ie Upper Cretaceous chalk) age.

The main difficulty is the lack of any definite way of dating erosion surfaces. They must be younger than the youngest component rocks, and since Tertiary dyke swarms in western Scotland are cut by summits as high as 900m (3,000ft), the high surfaces here must be younger than the dykes. In the Inner Hebrides, there have been vast amounts of erosion since the early Tertiary, as originally deep-seated (by many kilometres) plutonic rocks now form the highest land. This led George[5] to reject any idea of survival of widespread Mesozoic (and thus earlier) surfaces. Folding and faulting of the igneous rocks, thought to be of Miocene age, predate the evolution of the landforms and thus imply that all surfaces and valleys in the area are mid-Tertiary or later, in other words younger than c26 million years. If surfaces of the same or similar height are regarded as contemporaneous, this argument can be extended to the whole of Scotland.

Another way of tackling the dating problem is to compare the volume of erosion needed to produce the present landscape with the volume of sediment of different dates derived from such erosion. There are thick Mesozoic, Tertiary and Quaternary deposits on the continental shelf which may shed light on the age of the Scottish landscape, but at the moment such studies are difficult and rather speculative. In the meantime, extrapolation backwards in time using the measured rates of present-day processes, although by no means providing an accurate estimate of long-term erosion rates, may give a very crude idea of which broad timescale is appropriate.

Consider a notional uplifted block of land, whose top is represented by an extension of the summits of Ben Nevis and the Cairngorms. (This is represented by the whole rectangle shown in Fig 2.1.) To allow for the violent climatic oscillations of the last 2 million years, half of this period will be assumed to be glacial and half temperate. The current rates of chemical and mechanical processes in drainage basins of moderate relief in southern Scotland will be taken as representative of cool temperate conditions, and erosion rates during the glacial periods as ten times faster. (This is suggested by sedimentation rates in the North Sea.[12]) In order to consume the whole block of land down to its present volume (23.43 per cent remaining) a period of approximately 9–13 million years would be needed. This would take landscape evolution back beyond the cool temperate period at least into the late Miocene when the climate was probably warm temperate. One must not, however, discount entirely the inheritance of some landforms from pre-Miocene times, not only because of the possibility of exhumation but also because subsequent erosion often seems to have occurred along lines progressively established from Caledonian times: for example, the general distribution of uplands and lowlands.

The late Tertiary landscape may thus be reconstructed as having most of the broad outlines of the present relief. It was a landscape of dissected plateaux, already displaying a contrast in degree of dissection between west and east, with many closely spaced valleys in the former but with basins and fewer valleys in the east. Recent uplift had caused the valleys to be deeply incised. The landscape probably still retained characteristics due to its warmer past, being mantled by a variable depth of chemically weathered regolith, with some hilltops surmounted by tors. The modification of this, substantial in some places but slight in others, into the present landscape was largely accomplished by glaciation which may have begun in Scotland between 2 and 1.5 million years ago.

Glaciation
The Glacial Sequence

Glaciation in Scotland must have occurred many times, but it is not known how many of the seven to ten major cold periods detected in deep sea cores[13] caused ice to form here, since later glaciations have swept away depositional evidence for earlier ones. Whereas the scale of the erosional features suggests that they took several glaciations to form, most of the depositional features only date from the last glaciation, particularly from the last phases of it. Only three truly interglacial sites (ie with sediments containing temperate vegetation sandwiched between glacial deposits) are known, two in Shetland and one in north-east Scotland.[14] In several localities, however, deposits dated to around 27,000 BP (years before present) suggest that areas outside the main mountain centres were ice-free at that time, which was prior to the maximum build-up of the last ice sheet. This is generally regarded as having been around 18,000 to 17,000 BP when the Scottish ice sheet extended offshore all around Scotland and south to the English Midlands. Other dated deposits relate to the decay of the ice sheet, a topic which has provided some of the greatest contention in Scottish geomorphology. Some believe that Scotland was wholly ice-free by about 13,000 BP when the climate seems to have been about as warm as it is now.[15,16] This implies a rapid rate of retreat of the ice sheet (80–100m per year[17]). The climate then became colder again, perhaps even by about 12,000 BP, culminating in the Loch Lomond Advance which reached its maximum extent around 10,800 BP. This glacial event was curtailed by a sudden climatic amelioration around 10,300 BP. The ice cap which developed at this time was most spectacular and extensive in the west, reaching to sea level in places (Fig 2.7). Great piedmont lobes pushed down Loch Lomond and over Aberfoyle into the Forth valley around Menteith, where large terminal moraine complexes were developed. Elsewhere were smaller ice caps and corrie glaciers, particularly in the more continental climate of the Cairngorms and Eastern Grampians.[16]

At a scale most easily appreciated by people travelling through the landscape, glaciation has left a more striking imprint on Scottish scenery than any other geomorphological system. It performed enormous feats of erosion and plastered quantities of drift over many areas of the lowlands. On some parts of the continental shelf, the Quaternary deposits exceed 1,000m (3,300ft), though they thin near the coast.[12] Despite its huge impact, glaciation has nevertheless been very selective in its effects, sometimes eroding deeply but elsewhere

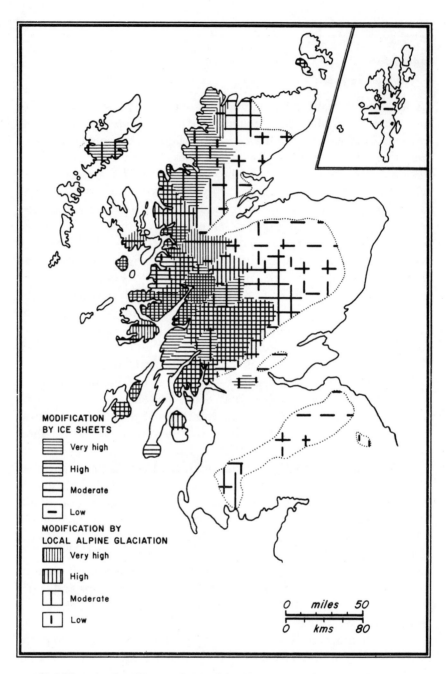

MODIFICATION
BY ICE SHEETS

Very high

High

Moderate

Low

MODIFICATION BY
LOCAL ALPINE GLACIATION

Very high

High

Moderate

Low

0   miles   50

0   kms   80

Fig 2.7 Intensity of modification of the landscape by ice sheets and mountain glaciation

apparently leaving quite delicate pre-glacial forms unscathed. Some of the reasons for the variety of glacial effects are described below.

At glacial maxima an ice sheet possibly 2,000m (over 6,000ft) thick covered the whole country, including the continental shelf. In the west it extended at least to the Flannan Isles and in the east it merged with the Scandinavian ice sheet. The Scottish ice sheets were not simple in form but consisted of a number of domes occupying the areas of greatest accumulation, and great streams of ice within the general mass radiated from these as they do in Antarctica and Greenland today. An elongated dome was centred to the east of the Northern Highlands and a very important centre lay over Rannoch Moor. Smaller centres of outflow seem to have overlain important upland blocks like the Cairngorms and Eastern Grampians, Galloway, the Southern Uplands and the larger of the Western Isles.

As each glaciation waxed and waned, each area experienced varying glacial conditions with ice sometimes flowing across them in a different direction at different times. Not all areas would have experienced the same sequence of glaciation and, as can be seen from Table 2.1, the western mountains probably had the most varied glacial history,

Table 2.1

A general model of the sequence of glaciation during the build up and decay of an ice sheet in a west to east transect across the Highlands. Phases I and II are well exemplified by the conditions of the Loch Lomond Advance (Fig 2.10)

	Climate	West Highlands	Eastern plateaux	Eastern lowlands
I	Cool	Corries and valley glaciers Frost shattering of ridges	Limited corries and plateau ice caps Patchy solifluction lobes on mountain sides	Periglacial
II	Cold	Transection glaciation Nunataks	Plateau ice caps and outlet glaciers Solifluction	Severe periglacial permafrost
III	Very cold	Ice sheet Nunataks	Ice sheet	Ice sheet
IV	Cold	Transection glaciation	Downwasting ice sheet	Downwasting ice sheet
V		Corries and valley glaciers	A few corries and plateau ice caps	Severe periglacial permafrost
VI	Cool	Corries	A few corries	Periglacial

whereas lower peripheral areas, particularly eastern Scotland, had only the ice-sheet type of glaciation. The latter areas probably experienced severe periglacial conditions with permafrost before and after inundation by the ice sheet. Transitional conditions obtained in the Central and Eastern Highlands where, in general, these plateau areas lacked suitable terrain for the development of alpine glaciation, though a number of corries formed. However, there were still extensive areas sufficiently high for early accumulation of snow, possibly permitting plateau ice caps to form before and after main ice-sheet phases.

Differences in ice temperature at the bottom of the ice sheet in different places were another cause of subsequent variety in the glacial landscape. Glaciers may be either frozen to their beds or sliding on them like a skater or curling stone gliding over an ice rink. Glacial erosion is caused by sliding, and this only occurs if the temperature at the base of the ice sheet is close enough to melting point for fluctuations in pressure to cause melting and refreezing as ice flows over bedrock roughnesses. This is known as 'warm-based' ice. When the basal temperature is well below 0°C, the lowest ice layer is frozen on to the underlying surface and much less erosion takes place.

Types of Glaciation

1 *Mountain glaciation*. Corries, the most typical glacial landforms of the mountains, are cut by small independent glaciers. Because these require large volumes of drifting snow to develop, they are more common, and occur at lower altitudes, in snowier climates. During glacial periods in Scotland this meant the west. Sissons,[16] however, also found a drop in corrie floor altitude from the Cairngorms south-eastwards, suggesting the existence of snow-bearing winds from the south-east. Because corries generally favour shady north- and east-facing sites in the lee of mountains, many ridges are asymmetrical, as corries have steepened their north and east faces while the south-western slopes remain more gentle. On the whole, corries show little sign of attack by ice sheets, and their sharp-crested back walls may be contrasted with the convex valley heads where outlet glaciers spilled off plateaux, like, for example, the head of Glen Avon in the Cairngorms.

2 *Ice sheet glaciation*. One of the most distinctive ways in which the ice sheets modified the terrain was by altering the valley pattern, changing the dendritic river-cut system into an interconnected one. Ice sheds (ie the highest area of the ice sheet from which flow diverged) did not

always coincide with the underlying pre-glacial watersheds. In the Northern Highlands, for example, the ice shed lay east of the high ground, so that westward flow from this had to cross the mountains, creating breaches – probably by deepening existing cols. Several such 'through valleys' have been used as easy routes for roads. Radial outflow from major accumulation domes is also apparent in the Rannoch basin – one can now travel easily through the glacially breached mountain rim north into Glen Coe, west into Glen Etive, south towards Tyndrum, as well as east along the pre-glacial route of the Tay. The existence of such major watershed breaches indicates that ice must have been thick enough to over-top the whole country. The pattern of the breaches not only outlines centres of accumulation not wholly related to the topography below, but also explains how ice could cut deep valleys across the highest land, like the Lairig Ghru in the Cairngorms.

Effects of Glaciation

1 *Glacial erosion.* Because of the varied pre-glacial topography and sequences of glacial events, different parts of the country display different assemblages of landforms and intensities of erosion (Figs 2.8 and 2.9). In Fig 2.8 the intensity of ice-sheet glaciation is shown by using an index based on the extent to which valleys have become interconnected by breaches; the intensity of alpine glaciation is based on the percentage of valleys which are corries.[18] It can be seen that both are at their maximum in the western mountains, where precipitation is highest. The deepest lakes in the country are found here and some valley floors are now below sea level, forming long sea lochs. Sometimes the influence of both types of glaciation is marked (eg in the Ben Nevis area), while some areas show low valley connectivity but intense local glaciation. Here the corrie phase was followed by local centres of strong radial outflow which prevented external ice from crossing the ridges. Thus the Cuillins have been reduced to a set of skeletal, yet virtually unbroken, arêtes. In other areas ice-sheet activity has been dominant because there were relatively few sites in which corries could form. There is a general fall-off in both types of glacial modification eastwards, where there was less precipitation and a colder, more continental regime, in which the land was covered by ice that was probably frozen to its bed over wide areas for long periods. This different activity has produced three main types of glacially eroded landscape: landscapes of areal scouring; landscapes of selective linear erosion; landscapes of little or no glacial erosion.

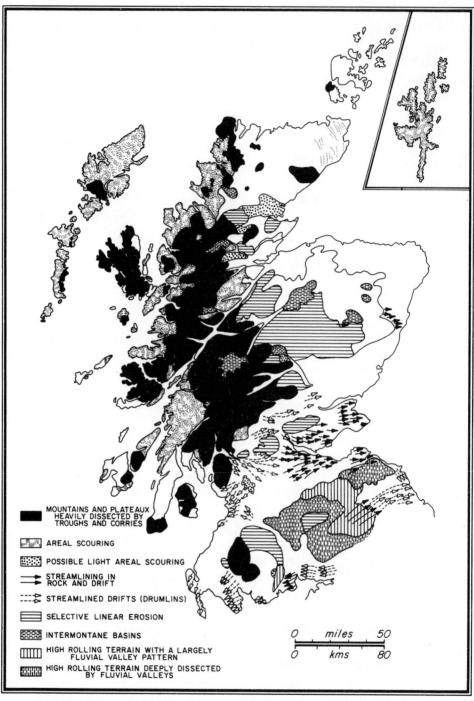

MOUNTAINS AND PLATEAUX
HEAVILY DISSECTED BY
TROUGHS AND CORRIES

AREAL SCOURING

POSSIBLE LIGHT AREAL SCOURING

STREAMLINING IN
ROCK AND DRIFT

STREAMLINED DRIFTS (DRUMLINS)

SELECTIVE LINEAR EROSION

INTERMONTANE BASINS

HIGH ROLLING TERRAIN WITH A LARGELY
FLUVIAL VALLEY PATTERN

HIGH ROLLING TERRAIN DEEPLY DISSECTED
BY FLUVIAL VALLEYS

0   miles   50

0   kms   80

Fig. 2.8 Regional patterns of types of glacial erosion. Blank areas have indeterminate relief or are drift covered

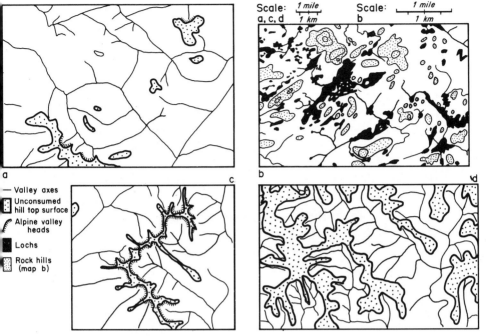

Fig 2.9 Examples of different types of glacial terrain. (a) Area of heavy ice sheet modification with a very interconnected valley pattern and a few residual mountains with corries from phases of mountain glaciation (Wester Ross); (b) Region of areal scouring (Sutherland); (c) Area of dominantly mountain glaciation. The valley pattern is dendritic, but the ridge is skeletal yet unbroken due to the intense development of corries (Cuillins, Skye); (d) Relict fluvial landscape. The valley pattern is dendritic and much unconsumed upland remains (Moorfoot Hills, East Lothian)

(a) Landscapes of areal scouring (Figs 2.8 and 2.9). Where the ice is warm-based (ie close to 0°C) erosion takes place over the whole landscape (areal scouring), streamlining the bedrock from the scale of large hills down to small knolls. This may be done without accomplishing any great *depth* of erosion, so that pre-glacial erosion surfaces can still be recognised. Detailed forms vary with the geology. The Lewisian gneiss of the North-west supports classic features, called 'knock and lochan' topography,[19] with roches moutonneés smoothed on their up-glacier faces and plucked on their lee faces, interspersed with myriads of rock-basin lakes. Although the landscape looks chaotic from ground level, the ice has picked out geological structures which show clear patterns on air and satellite photographs.

A wide zone of such areal scouring fringes and even impinges upon upper slopes of the Scottish mountains, especially in the west, where ice flowed actively into a relatively warm maritime environment. Many possibly scoured lowland areas in the north, in the Central Lowlands and in the east are obscured by drift. Very subdued forms have been described in Caithness[20] and small patches of scouring have been reported from Aberdeenshire,[21] but the extent of such moulding is unknown. More extensive streamlining of rock and drift occurs in the Central Valley where ice converged from the Highlands and Southern Uplands. In the Lothians and Fife[22] erosion of the bedrock is sometimes comparable with the classic scoured areas of the west. Resistant volcanic necks in the Edinburgh area have protected sedimentary rocks in their lee, forming crag and tails, while deep curving depressions have been gouged around their flanks. In the eastern Borders also there is a gradation of forms, from linear rock ridges on well-scoured Silurian rocks on the plateau between the Ettrick, Yarrow and Teviot valleys, to large crag-and-tail features on the volcanics and Old Red Sandstones near Melrose and St Boswells, to streamlined glacial deposits from the vicinity of Kelso eastwards.

(b) Landscapes of selective linear erosion (Fig 2.8). This type of landscape occurs where thinner parts of the ice sheet were cold-based, making it relatively protective over the high ground but warm-based and erosive where it was channelled into valleys. A typical result is seen in the Cairngorms, where deep glacial troughs like Glen Avon lie side by side with an undulating plateau topped by tors and pockets of rotted rock (features which were unlikely to survive beneath a sliding, actively eroding ice sheet). This type of glaciation has been favoured by the more continental climate and the broad plateaux of the Central Grampians.

(c) Landscapes of little or no glacial erosion (Figs 2.8 and 2.9). In peripheral and still more continental areas, the ice sheets seem to have been cold and sluggish even over the valleys, so there is little or no evidence of severe glacial erosion. Here are smooth, rolling uplands, in which the normal pre-glacial valley systems have survived almost untouched in form and pattern as dendritic networks of deep V-shaped valleys. Such landscapes are present in the very eastern parts of the Southern Uplands and in much of the Eastern Grampians and contiguous Buchan.

2 *Glacial deposition.* Some of the debris incorporated by the ice was deposited in the mountains, but most was transported towards the lowlands where it was laid as a layer of glacial till (boulder clay) of variable thickness, smoothing and subduing the landscape. Although it may contain some far-travelled erratics, the bulk of any till is very locally derived with colour variations reflecting the local bedrock. Indeed, the quantity of erosion on soft rocks in lowland areas, although producing less spectacular landforms, may rival that of the channelled

Page 51 Raised marine platform cut into bedrock, Isle of Islay, west Scotland. The platform may have been developed during cold episodes of the last glacial period (c75,000–10,000 years ago) when the adjacent mainland was depressed by the weight of an overlying ice sheet

Page 52 *(left)* Upper Glen Dee, southern Cairngorm mountains, a classic glacially eroded valley with prominent truncated spurs such as Devil's Point (centre top); view towards the south west; *(below)* impressive cliff scenery and isolated sea stack surmounting an abrasion platform; gently dipping sandstone flags of upper Old Red Sandstone age, Latheronwheel, Caithness

trough-cutting and scouring ice in the highlands.

Active warm-based ice builds up 'lodgement' tills on the ground surface, and over a long period of glaciation may achieve great thicknesses. In some places the till forms featureless sheets but elsewhere has been moulded into a variety of streamlined forms. The most distinctive features are drumlins. Typically these are egg-shaped hills about 1km ($\frac{1}{2}$ mile) long and 30m (100ft) high, but they range in shape to elongated cigar-like forms, as in the centre of the Tweed valley around Kelso. The main areas of drumlins are around Glasgow, in the Ayrshire and Solway lowlands and in the Merse (Fig 2.10), though smaller drumlins occur in many localities. Drumlins nearly always occur as clusters known as drumlin fields, with each hill forming a distinct feature separate from its neighbours – as in the Glasgow area – or with the hills merging with each other to form a more rolling terrain – as in parts of the Merse.

Because of its high debris content in areas of intense erosion, the ice sheet probably also let down a considerable blanket of melt-out till as it gradually melted away on becoming stagnant. In the broken terrain of many highland glens close to the main (western) centres of ice accumulation, the final phase of deposition apparently caused widespread 'dumping' of hummocks of 'ablation' moraine, eg in Glen Torridon. Terminal moraine ridges laid down at the margins of the ice seem largely restricted to the last phases of local glaciation (Loch Lomond Advance) in the Highlands (Fig 2.10). At the glacial maxima the ice margins lay well beyond the present coastline and were probably often floating and subject to calving into icebergs. Thus terminal moraines from this phase are lacking, but ridges present below sea level on the Wee Bankie between Aberdeen and the Forth estuary may be a terminal moraine.[23]

3 *Glacial meltwater*. Glacier ice is always accompanied by meltwater, and wherever the ice sheet was warm-based an extensive hydrological system existed under the ice. Thus, although traditionally meltwater is associated with the decay of ice sheets, it is also produced in great quantities in periods of active glaciation.

The flow of meltwater moves generally in the same direction as the ice, so – where this coincided with major valleys – meltwater streams probably discharged down them and contributed to their erosion. This would have happened especially in the highly dissected west, but also occurred in the eastern Southern Uplands and Grampians (Fig 2.10). Completely new channels formed where the ice crossed the grain of the topography[24] and in places multitudes of meltwater channels furrow

Fig 2.10 Some aspects of glacial deposition and deglaciation

hillsides at all altitudes. They vary in size from only a few metres in depth to those big enough to site villages (at Carlops), roads (Slochd Summit on the A9) and railways (south of Stonehaven). Major meltwater rivers may have cut the buried channels under the drift cover of the Central Lowlands and the 'tunnel valleys' on the continental shelf,[12] some tens of kilometres long and about 100–150m (300–500ft) deep. Many channels are not related to current drainage conditions, being dry and having anomalous courses and 'up-and-down' long profiles. The latter means that the water had to flow up hill, indicating that they have a subglacial origin and the water was driven by hydrostatic pressure. There is often a preferred orientation over wide areas, as water flow was driven by the hydraulic gradient under the ice, which was related to its surface slope. Thus a north-eastward pattern occurs between the upper Clyde, Forth and Tweed, and a series of large channels sweeps round the north edge of the Moorfoots and Lammermuirs (Fig 2.10).

On a smaller scale, sets of channels run diagonally down hillsides, eg in Strathallan. Water making its way through the ice has been superimposed onto the landscape beneath often creating channels in positions where no normal stream would form, eg across spurs or hilltops as in the Menteith Hills, to quote only one of countless examples. The origin of such channels is betrayed by their two, open ends, formed as the water left and then rejoined the ice. Many channels are located in cols and valley heads,[24] because subglacial streams were directed by pressure at the ice-sheet base to follow such lines of less resistance.

Meltwater also laid down a great variety of coarsely stratified sands and gravels, which are of tremendous economic significance as the main source of aggregates for the construction industry. These sediments tend to be concentrated in complexes where debris-rich ice stagnated during the period of ice-sheet decay. There are two broad types of deposits: those accumulated beneath and in decaying ice; and those accumulated at the margins. The former are hummocky, as a result of the irregular opportunities for deposition. Sinuous ridges (eskers) sometimes mark the former courses of individual rivers. One of the best known systems is at Carstairs, but other conspicuous esker complexes occur near Dinnet in the Dee valley, at Loch Flemington near Nairn and in many parts of central Scotland (Fig 2.10). The largest esker in Britain is probably that on the south-west outskirts of Inverness.

Marginal deposits form gently sloping spreads in the form of kame terraces (between the ice and valley walls), outwash plains and occasionally the strandlines of ice-dammed lakes, the best known being in Glen Roy. By volume the largest amounts of fluvioglacial deposits occur in vast outwash plains and contiguous ice-contact mounds and ridges along the eastern edge of the Highlands, as around Blairgowrie, in the North Esk valley and in valleys like the Spey. Sometimes the outwash rivers flowed into the sea to form deltas merging with raised beaches, eg at the mouth of the River Naver in Sutherland and in many places in the Forth and Tay valleys. As downmelting of the ice sheet exposed hilltops, the terrain and more continental climate of the Eastern Highlands and Southern Uplands caused the separation of quite large masses of ice from active accumulation centres, particularly in basins and the wider lower reaches of valleys. As such ice masses stagnated, they provided ideal 'dead-ice' receptacles for meltwater deposits. Thus there is an almost continuous belt of ice-contact landforms along the north edge of the Southern Uplands, and massive accumulations of eskers and kames in sites like the Glenmore basin in the Cairngorms and in many parts of central and north-east Scotland (Fig 2.10).

4 *Sea level change*. Much of the Scottish coastline is backed by raised shorelines. Although the largest areas occur in the eastern estuaries, the most spectacular forms are in the west. Raised rock platforms with cliffs in Islay and large spreads of shingle storm beaches in Jura occur at 14–38m (50–120ft) above sea level.[25]

Two types of sea-level change are involved. One is a world-wide change (eustatic) caused by ocean water abstracted to build ice sheets (lower sea level) and returned when they melt (normal sea level). The other is a regional or local change (isostatic) resulting from the land being depressed by the weight of the overlying ice. At the end of each glaciation, as the ice melted, both the sea and the land were rising, but at different rates. The result was that sometimes the sea overtook the land, flooding in to give marine deposits, and at other times the rise of the land gained the upper hand, raising the previous shorelines above the sea. In areas of quiet sedimentation, like the Forth estuary, a very complex series of events can be detected from the numerous raised and buried beaches. The final phases were the flooding of the area by post-glacial mudflats and then, as the world sea level rise slowed down after about 5,000 BP (when the big North American and Scandinavian ice sheets had finally melted), the continuing isostatic rise of Scotland raised these mudflats to give wide areas of carseland.[16] The land is still rising at rates of around 52mm (0.17ft) per century at Dunbar.

Because the land rises most where the ice was thickest, shorelines, which are horizontal at the time of their formation, become tilted on uplift. The highest shorelines are in the West Highlands and the Stirling area, around 30–40m (95–130ft), but this drops to 18m (60ft) around Ullapool and they are absent or at very low altitudes in the north-east, the Outer Hebrides and Shetland, where the ice was thinner. Because of the multiplicity of glacial events, the sea has been at the same level against the land many times over, so features cut in rock probably have a composite origin and their age is often controversial. Some of the raised rock platforms, even some at present sea level, seem previous to at least one glaciation since they are striated or till-covered. One of the most fascinating raised marine features is the rock platform and intricate cliffline occurring extensively in the South-west Highlands, in narrow sheltered straits where the wave-fetch seems insufficient to allow the erosion of a wide platform in hard rocks. Sissons has suggested that inter-tidal erosion here was enhanced by freeze-thaw during the cold late-glacial period.

Post-glacial Changes

By extrapolating the measured rates of present-day processes it seems that an average of about 0.15m of material has been eroded from the ground surface in the whole of post-glacial time; this cannot have altered the glacial landscape very much. Reasons for the lack of change include the short time interval since glaciation and the slowness of most post-glacial processes. Sub-aerial processes were only re-established in those areas covered by the Loch Lomond Advance about 10,000 BP, and elsewhere up to about 3,000 years before that.[15] Probably the greatest changes occurred immediately on deglaciation, as a result of the still severe climate and the need for readjustment to new environmental conditions. At first there would have been no soil and no protective vegetation cover. Many major landslips on newly oversteepened slopes probably date from this period (Fig 2.10), although the most spectacular landslips in Scotland, the Storr and the Quirang in Skye, probably have a much longer history.[26]

Late Glacial Periglacial Features

Landscape change has been greatest in those areas first uncovered from the ice sheet (mountain tops and lowland fringes in the east and south), as the climate was still severe close to the retreating glaciers. Frost shattering created screes and blockfields on many Highland valley walls and summits. Screes are often sparse in those corries

Table 2.2
Measured rates of current erosion in a variety of catchments[29,49,50,51,52,53]

| | Tonnes per km² per year | | |
	sediment load	dissolved load	total load
Tay		53–100	110–295
Earn (between L. Earn and Forteviot)	197–235*		
Nith	178.9		
Clyde (at Daldowie)	58.8		
tributaries:			
White Cart	132.3		
Kelvin	35.9		
Leven	35.4		
Deugh (Galloway)	42.4		
Kelly reservoir (nr. Greenock)	41		
North Esk (Pentlands)	26**		
Comparative data from elsewhere			
Av. Europe	35	42.6	
Exe (Devon)		29–108	
Kärkevagge (Swedish Lappland)		22–35	

* The range shows years with different amounts of runoff
** The values are low despite visual evidence of accelerated erosion of hillslope soils

Table 2.3
Measured rates of transport by chemical[28] and mass movement[29] processes averaged over drainage basins to give an average rate of landscape lowering by each process. Both drainage basins are of moderate relief and rainfall

	Average denudation rate mm per 1,000 years
Chemical weathering, Eden valley, Fife:	
Calciferous sandstone	47*
Lavas and tuffs of Lower Old Red Sandstone age	19*
Deugh valley, Galloway:	
Shallow landslips on undercut river bluffs	14.99
Gullying	0.79
Soil creep	0.18
Rockfalls	0.15
Soil wash	0.04

* These rates are based on summer measurements only, so they may be overestimates as rates of weathering may be ten times slower in the winter. If the latter were the case the landscape lowering values would be reduced to about 26mm and 10mm

occupied by ice during the Loch Lomond Advance but abundant outside the glacier limits, suggesting that this was an important period of periglacial activity. Slopes in the Southern Uplands, where the rocks are fissile and clay-rich, are often mantled by several metres of angular soliflucted debris.[27] Solifluction involves the downslope sludging of the regolith and is particularly associated with tundra conditions, where meltwater often saturates the ground in summer, especially if ice layers (permafrost) in the soil inhibit drainage. It has also probably redistributed much of the till into the valley bottoms – for example 4–5m (12–15ft) of till collected at the base of a drumlin in Glasgow after 11,200 BP.[17] Over much of the Highlands solifluction produced features known as stone-banked lobes, particularly good examples of which are present on Mt Keen, Lochnagar, and in the Cairngorms where they are up to 5m (15ft) high. The lack of vegetation and the concentration of snowmelt in a short summer season led to active soil erosion. Alluvial fans and much of the sediment in the valley bottoms can probably be attributed to this period (though much is also attributable to meltwater during deglaciation).

Present-day Processes
Rivers and Slopes

Some idea of contemporary gross erosion rates can be derived from the amount of material being transported by the rivers in solution and as sediment. Unfortunately, very few studies of this have been undertaken in Scotland and they are too restricted in location to be fully representative. Nevertheless they do provide some insight into the relative importance of chemical weathering (which provides the dissolved load of streams) as against the mechanical processes of mass movement and erosion (which provide the sediment load).

Table 2.2 shows that sediment transport is marginally greater than chemical transport in the Tay basin, and both are a little above European averages. The greater sediment load is probably a consequence of the recent glacial history, as the Tay contains masses of easily eroded fluvioglacial materials. Rates of sediment transport are nearer to the European average in smaller catchments of moderate relief. Data on water chemistry are very few but seem within the same range as other European catchments. However, rates averaged over whole drainage basins conceal tremendous local variations in weathering. In the Eden valley (Fife) estimated rates of lowering of the landscape by chemical weathering vary from almost nothing to over 80mm per thousand years, depending on the rock type[28] (Table 2.3).

Although generally subsidiary to chemical weathering, a variety of mass movement processes operates on slopes and contributes to micro-landforms, with apparently some regional variation in their order of importance. Probably the most ubiquitous of these processes are shallow landslips, especially on undercut river bluffs in glacial materials. In the Deugh basin in Galloway they account for 93 per cent of the sediment moved.[29] Debris flows also seem to be important in many Highland valleys, eg Glen Coe, the Lairig Ghru and the Pass of Drumochter, where their characteristic tracks can be seen below gullies. No systematic study of them has been made in Scotland but, as in Scandinavia, they probably occur mainly during periods of intensely heavy rain and occasionally snowmelt. On steep rocky slopes the most significant mass movement may be rockfalls, as on Edinburgh Castle rock. Climbers must be aware of the rockfall hazard on many mountain walls in winter and early spring. Particularly large landslides and falls may occur during colder climatic phases – for example, a large landslide occurred in Arran some 250 years ago during the Little Ice Age. Avalanches occur on slopes over 30° in snowy areas like the Cairngorms where several hundred may occur in one winter alone.[30] Some of these are of dirty slushy snow and so transport debris downslope. Mild periglacial conditions are still to be found at higher levels. Frost action, ice lenses in the soil, and wind cause vegetation erosion which can be exacerbated by animal treading – including tourists! Frost action causes small active soil polygons and stripes which may be found in scattered locations from Tinto Hill[31] to Skye and the Cairngorms. These may reach down to quite low altitudes in the north, eg in Shetland they can be found at only 60m (200ft).[32] Occasionally solifluction lobes have been found to be still moving, but as a rule soil creep and wash are quantitatively unimportant.

Exceptionally heavy storms are probably the main cause of rapid change in the Scottish landscape. Rainfalls of over 100mm (4in) in a day are likely at least once a century over about half of Scotland, and there are quite extensive areas in the heart of the West Highlands where such rainfalls may occur at least once a decade.[33] There is also a high frequency of intense summer thunderstorms in the Eastern Grampians, where twelve such events affected the Findhorn basin between 1829 and 1962, several occurring within three or four years of each other.[34] Rainfalls of this nature will cause gullying,[34,35] trigger off many soil slides and flows, particularly on walls smoothed by ice action,[36] and cause extensive flooding and deposition of debris over fields and roads. Certain conditions encourage such effects: for example, field drains increase the likelihood of flooding by allowing rapid runoff and gullies are often initiated at their outlets; indurated soil horizons, thought to have been caused by a permafrost layer during the Ice Age, are widespread in north-east Scotland[37] and may encourage saturation of the topsoil. Another exacerbating factor is vegetation damaged by sheep or moor burning.

Coastal Processes and Forms

Some of the most rapid and persistent present-day geomorphological changes occur on the coasts. Marine action is both destructive and constructive. Although some cliffs seem to have developed over a series of interglacials and not just in the present period, marine erosion is currently active in exposed situations, eg in the Shetlands, where blocks have been torn off the cliff face and flung on to the cliff top.[38] Cliffs occur as a result of marine erosion on both hard and soft materials, the only prerequisite being that the land should stand at sufficient height above the sea. Thus rock cliffs form quite long sections of the Scottish coast in most areas outside the western sea lochs.[39] Cliffs cut in glacial deposits have formed entirely in post-glacial times and can be very actively developing by mass movement processes, like slumping, as well as by marine undercutting.

Where the offshore zone is gently sloping and the sediment supply large, waves are constructive rather than destructive, and build beach complexes. This occurs mainly in the east coast estuaries and embayments and on parts of the Ayrshire and Solway coasts. On the steeper rocky shores of the west, beaches are much more restricted (only 3 per cent of the coastline of Wester Ross has sandy beaches),[40] although some of the shorelines facing the open Atlantic are swathed in sands formed largely of pulverised shells (the machair of the Hebrides). Blown sand covers almost the whole of Tiree, for example.

Most of the sediment which builds sand and shingle beaches has been derived from glacial meltwater and present rivers, especially where they are eroding glacial deposits. Such material is distributed along the shoreline by longshore drifting. Where both sand and pebbles occur, the latter are usually heaped in ridges at the back of the beaches by storms and the sand occupies the foreshore. As well as simple bay-head beaches, other features such as river mouth spits exist, often formed by a complex balance between fluvial and marine processes.[41] The mouth of the Spey in particular fluctuates violently, because of its heavy load of pebbles and its variable regime, and its spit has undergone three cycles of breaching and growth since 1829.[42] The latter causes river deflection and erosion problems, so the spit has been artificially cut through several times but with no great success.

Dunes fringe many beaches (eg 75 per cent in Fife[43]). These are a very fragile environment, being easily upset by over-use. The recent history of the dunes at Gullane in East Lothian is a classic example of what happens if careful control of use is not maintained. Increased numbers of visitors from the 1930s together with Army use during World War II resulted in rapid vegetation destruction and, in the centre of the bay, the fore-dunes were completely swept away. Since the 1960s attempts have been made to restore the situation by trapping a new foredune with fencing and planted marram grass. The two most fascinating dune systems in Scotland are undoubtedly at Culbin and Forvie. In both, sand blowing has continued for many centuries on account of natural and man-made conditions, resulting in large complex dune areas. The sand has been progressively swept inland over previous agricultural land, and in the case of Forvie a church inundated in 1413 has subsequently been uncovered by the inland march of the sand. The area is still evolving actively, though Culbin has now been stabilised by afforestation.

Conclusion

Through a long period of time erosional processes of various kinds, from tropical weathering to glaciation, have acted selectively on the complex geology to create Scotland's varied landscape. A number of overall themes can be identified. First, the tectonic history of the country controlled the broad division of Scotland into Highlands, Southern Uplands and Lowlands. It has also thrown the rocks into particular arrangements which have profoundly influenced the type of landscape in each area. Tectonic events connected with the opening of the Atlantic ocean caused conspicuous differences in scenery between west and east Scotland. Differences in amount of uplift and exposure to oceanic climatic conditions have led to differences in the intensity of dissection, first by rivers and then by glaciers. In the West Highlands the valley network is much more closely spaced and steep mountains of 'alpine' form have developed. To the east plateaux are more typical and, rather than active dissection, the influence of pre-glacial chemical weathering in the form of near-enclosed basins is evident. On the whole, glacial erosion has also been less intense here, so there is also greater preservation of evidence for weathering under pre- and inter-glacial conditions, in the form of deeply rotted regolith and tors.

Secondly, the landscape evident at any one spot often shows the influence of different factors when viewed at different scales. The

Merse, for example, is a large-scale topographical basin occupying a pre-Old Red Sandstone tectonic basin, within which at the medium scale the effects of glaciation are apparent in a great sweep of drumlinoid and fluvioglacial forms swinging round the northern margin of the Cheviots. On the scale of an individual slope, on the other hand, present-day processes like shallow landslips or river erosion and deposition may be dominant.

Thirdly, the final modifier of the landscape has been man. Great tracts of the Highlands have scarcely been altered; changes in the rates of present-day processes are negligible in comparison with the scale of the landforms, though the ski slopes of Cairngorm and the grouse moors of the Eastern Grampians have been scarred by bulldozed access tracks and by runoff on trampled and compacted footpaths. The natural forms of some lowland areas, especially around Glasgow and in parts of Fife, have been all but obliterated by mining subsidence and dumping of waste. The other main area of human impact is in the fragile environments of coastal dunes many of which are now cluttered permanently or periodically with holiday caravans and scarred with eroded paths.

Landscape can thus be seen to be dynamic, changing through time, sometimes apparently slowly as perceived at present in a human life span, and sometimes relatively rapidly as during glaciation; its evolution is everlasting.

Notes to this chapter are on pages 301–3.

3

The Bio-climate

Joy Tivy

SCOTLAND shares with the rest of Britain what is generally described as a cool, humid, temperate climate. It is, however, distinguished by a somewhat greater change of climatic conditions and more variable weather than elsewhere in the country. This is a consequence of three important interacting factors. First, Scotland occupies a particularly critical position in relation to the interplay of the three principal conflicting air masses (cold Polar, cool Continental and North Atlantic, and warm Tropical maritime) and of oceanic currents off the north-west coast of Europe. Second, it lies at a higher latitude than the rest of Britain. And, third, it is a largely upland and montane area.

The marked regional variation in climate is reflected in the varying ecological conditions and the associated patterns of vegetation and land use within Scotland. However, the problem of analysing and describing the *bio-climate* (ie those climatic conditions relevant to a full understanding of biological processes and distributions) is difficult, some would say impossible, as yet. This is because of the lack of climatic data for a large part of the country. Some two-thirds of the mainland lies above 152m but few long-term records other than for precipitation exist, and at present there is only one first-class Meteorological Station sited above this altitude. It is at Eskdalemuir, Dumfriesshire (350m). Also, there is a paucity of data for ecologically significant climatic parameters such as solar radiation, evaporation, evapo-transpiration, atmospheric humidity and, particularly, soil climate. Finally, there is the inherent difficulty, indeed artificiality, in all bio-climatic studies of trying to isolate the effect of one from a set of closely interacting climatic parameters; or of trying to isolate climatic conditions from those other dependent (soil) or independent (geology, landforms) variables which also influence biological processes. This chapter therefore will not so much attempt to correlate biological with climatic distributions as to analyse the range of climatic advantages or limitations, as the case may be, to which plant and animal life in Scotland is exposed. In some cases these can be expressed in

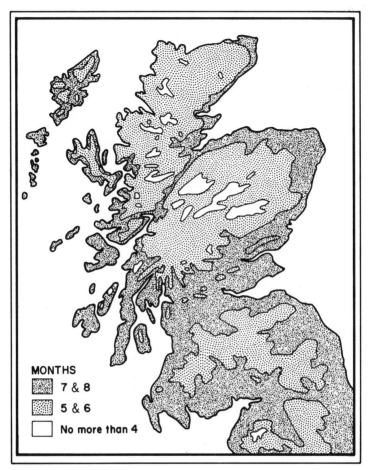

MONTHS

7 & 8

5 & 6

No more than 4

Fig 3.1 Length of growing season defined by number of months with a mean temperature above 6°C (42.8°F). From Miller, R. (1973) 'Bioclimatic Characteristics' Chap. 2 in *The Organic Resources of Scotland.* (Ed. Joy Tivy), Oliver and Boyd, Edinburgh

quantitative terms; in many others qualitative judgements based on experience or knowledge accumulated over a long period of time are all that is available at present.

The Growing Season

Of paramount importance to all biological processes is the length of the *growing season*, or that period favourable to the completion of the life cycle and hence the survival of an organism; or, in the case of many crops, for the maximum production of that part of the plant for which it is cultivated. The growing season has long been determined by using the standard of a mean daily or mean monthly *threshold temperature* of 6°C (42.7°F) – the average temperature for the commencement of

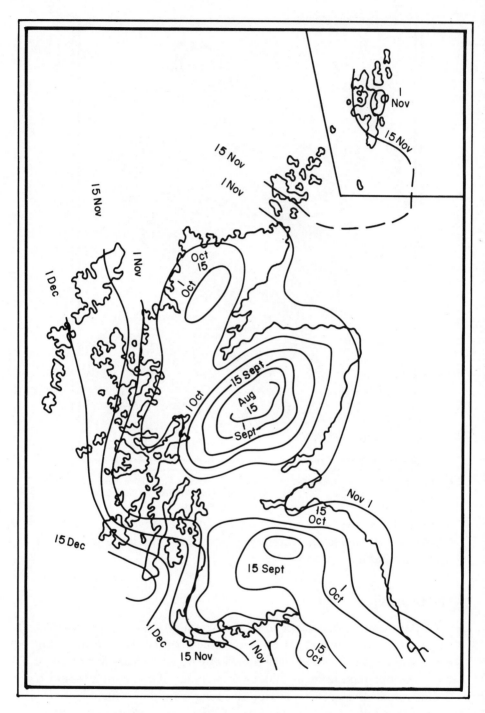

Fig. 3.2a Average dates of first air frost from period 1911–1940

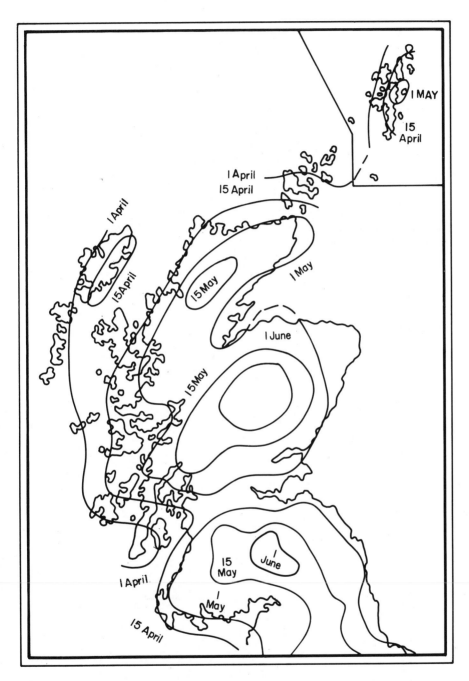

Fig 3.2b Average dates of last air frost for period 1911–1940. (After Green, F. H. W. 1964) 'The Climate of Scotland' Chap. 2 in *The Vegetation of Scotland*. Ed. John Burnett, Oliver and Boyd, Edinburgh

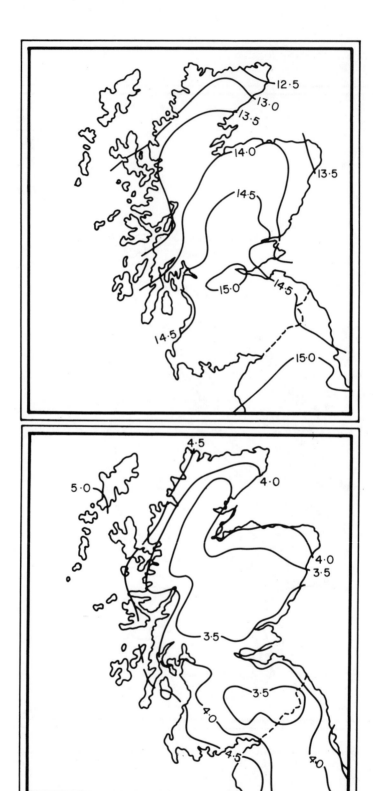

Fig 3.3 (a) Mean seasonal temperature in winter, °C (1931–60). Reduced to sea level; (b) Mean seasonal temperature in summer °C (1931–60). Reduced to sea level. From Booth, R. E. *Climatological Memo* No. 43A, Meteorological Office

growth of temperate cereals (Fig 3.1). Scottish foresters have used thresholds of 6.1–7.2°C (43–45°F),[1] as more applicable to coniferous trees. Recent work, however, has revealed that grasses and cereals in Scotland can maintain growth, albeit slowly, down to 0°C (32°F).[2] In this case, the length of the frost-free period, long used to determine the agricultural growing season in the United States, would seem to be a more realistic measure for Scotland too (Figs 3.2a and 3.2b). According to Green,[3] the area with the longest frost-free period – from just before the beginning of April to just after the beginning of December – is the southern part of the Outer Hebrides. Indeed, only the Scilly and the Channel Islands have significantly longer growing seasons, and attempts to introduce commercial bulb-growing in Tiree and elsewhere in the Outer Isles in the 1960s were biologically, if not always economically, sound. The comparatively long frost-free period in the South-west and along the west-coast lowlands of mainland Scotland is an important factor in the production of early potatoes on the light, warm soils of the raised beaches of Ayrshire and Wigtownshire. It also permits the successful establishment of gardens (such as Logan Gardens on the Rhins of Galloway) characterised by frost-sensitive exotic trees and shrubs. The date palm (non-fruiting) is a common garden plant and an exotic indicator of the mild winters of coastal Galloway.

The length of the growing season in lowland Scotland in general is comparatively long, by Scottish standards, varying from five to eight months (Fig 3.1).[4] Mean summer, sea-level temperatures, however, rarely exceed 15°C (59°F), with a small daily range of 3–5°C (Figs 3.3a and 3.3b). In terms, therefore, of *accumulated temperature* (total day- or month-degrees above a selected threshold), the growing season is cool, particularly when compared with southern England or continental locations at the same latitude.[5] On the basis of a 6°C threshold, the warmest areas in Scotland, with accumulated temperatures over 1,300 day-degrees Centigrade, occur – as might be expected – in the southern, particularly the south-western, lowlands (Fig 3.4). Northwards the decline in length and warmth of the growing season is compensated by long day-length in the summer months. This is one of the most important factors contributing to the successful cultivation and relatively high yields of wheat and barley in the lowlands of Aberdeenshire, Nairnshire and around the Moray Firth. In fact, Scottish wheat and barley yields are on average higher than those from England and Wales[6] (Table 3.1).

Scottish-bred cereals are very tolerant of cool summer temperatures. They mature late and hence can take advantage of the whole growing

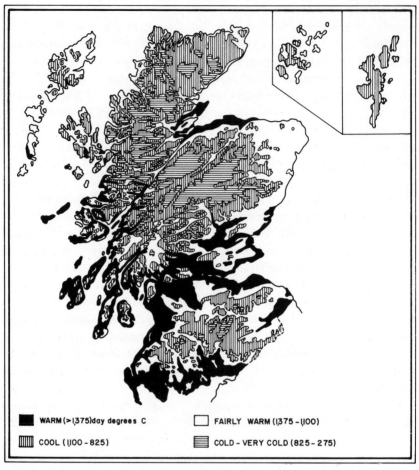

WARM (>1,375)day degrees C   FAIRLY WARM (1,375 - 1,100)

COOL (1,100 - 825)   COLD - VERY COLD (825 - 275)

Fig 3.4 Accumulated temperatures. Adapted from *Assessment of Climatic Conditions in Scotland*. 1. Based on Accumulated Temperatures above 5.6°C. Birse, E. L. and Dry, F. T. (1969). Macaulay Research Institute for Soil Research, Aberdeen

season. They are not limited by high late-summer temperatures which, in southern Britain, increase evapo-transpiration and water-stress in the plants and hence accelerate leaf-senescence by raising respiration rates, both of which make for lower yields than further north. For certain crops it would appear that the cooler, more humid Scottish summer is also an advantage. This is particularly true for barley, which is now one of the major cereals in Britain, but which has a considerable variability in yield. The variations in yield mainly result from variations in climatic conditions, which in turn are consequent upon the passage of depressions forming at the junction of the cool North Atlantic and the warm Tropical maritime air masses at this season of the year. The same is true for turnips and swedes,[7] and for soft fruits such as raspberries and strawberries, whose yields and quality are higher in Scotland than

Table 3.1
Yield of barley in tonnes per hectare

	East Midlands	Scotland
1971	3.66	4.38
1972	3.99	4.67
1973	3.85	4.42
1974	4.07	5.00
1975	3.23	4.79
1976	3.49	4.11
1977	4.21	5.09
1978	4.30*	—

* = estimate yield
Source Lyall, I. T. 'The growth of barley and the effect of climate', *Weather* 35(9)
1980

in England and Wales. In the latter areas, high summer temperatures increase the rate of respiration and, hence, of the breakdown of the sugar content of the fruit.

Another agricultural advantage of the cool growing season is that summer temperatures are near the lower range of tolerance for many insect pests and pathogenic organisms. The potato, a widely cultivated and important cash crop, is particularly susceptible to disease because it is propagated vegetatively. Scottish seed potatoes are less susceptible to green-fly infestation in the cool and windy summer weather. As a result, Scotland is a major producer of disease-free seed potatoes, with production highly concentrated in the lowlands of the East and North-east, from Berwickshire to Aberdeenshire.

In contrast, it has been demonstrated[8] that the shortness of the growing season, combined with the rapid growth rates promoted by the long day-length, can and does create peculiar problems for intensive grass farming. Light and temperature are thought to be the most important climatic parameters affecting the productivity of a grass crop. Grasses have a characteristic growth pattern whereby 50 per cent of the total annual production occurs over the eight-week period in May and June; 25 per cent in the four-week period July/August; and 25 per cent in early spring, mid and late summer. Even the use of special grass mixtures or varieties with different production peaks can only lengthen the period of maximum growth from eight to twelve weeks in mid-summer. Productivity is closely related to light duration. Although this increases northwards, and in the summer period generally exceeds that which the grass leaves can effectively use, in early spring and autumn – with less growth – productivity is related to light intensity, which decreases northwards. This results in a severe reduction in productivity northwards in the autumn, and more particularly in the spring, leading to a greater reduction in the grass-growing season than might otherwise be expected. Day-length (or photo-periodicity) influences grass productivity in that it determines the time of change from the vegetative to the flowering phase of the plants. Grass species and varieties vary in their photo-periodic requirements; hence dates of flowering in the same species are progressively later with increasing latitude. As the optimum grass-cutting stage also becomes later, so the climatic problems of hay-making at the end of the summer increase.

Another biologically significant characteristic of the growing season in Scotland is its variability in length and, particularly, the variability in its date of commencement in spring. Critical also is the marked changeability of weather at this period, when temperatures may fluctuate for longer or shorter periods above and below freezing-point or the growth threshold. Characteristic of late spring are protracted periods of cold weather, resulting from the incursion from the north of Polar maritime or Arctic air, often brought about by an extension of a continental high pressure system over the whole country. Lateness or retardation, particularly of grass growth, constitutes a major climatic hazard for the majority of Scottish farmers. All produce some livestock and so a fresh supply of grass before the stocks of winter feed are depleted is economically crucial. In this respect they would probably agree with T. S. Eliot that 'April is the cruellest month'. The inherent 'fickleness' of the spring weather also creates a biological hazard for all plants not adapted to these conditions. It particularly affects the introduction of continental species adapted to climates where the transition from winter to summer is more abrupt and its timing more consistent. Exotic trees, which 'flush' almost as soon as critical temperature thresholds are crossed, are more likely to suffer frost damage than native species or those introduced from a comparable climatic regime, which normally start producing new leaves later.

Atmospheric Humidity

In contrast to the situation for temperature and light, however, a surplus rather than a deficit of water is the main biological problem associated with Scotland's characteristically humid climate. Mean annual rainfall varies from 500–700mm (20–28in) in the Eastern to over 1,000mm (40in) in the Western Lowlands (Fig 3.5). Seasonal variation is not high, though on average a higher percentage of the total rainfall occurs in the winter months. July and August often have a secondary maximum associated with the warm humid air-flow from the south-west, while dry spells associated with calm continental air are more

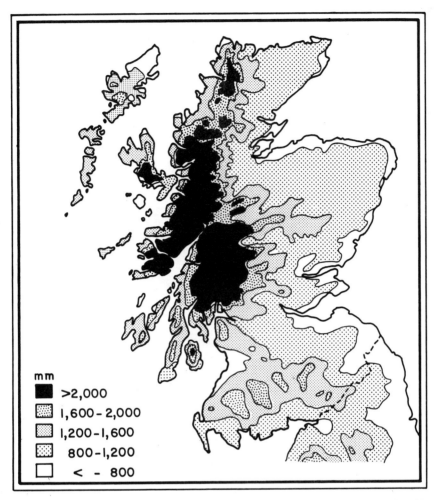

Fig 3.5 Average annual rainfall (mm) for the 30 years 1930–61. From *Hydrological Memo* No. 37, Meteorological Office

frequent in spring and, to a lesser extent, in the autumn months. Wetness, or the frequency of wet (1.0mm or 0.04in+) or rain (0.2mm or 0.01in+) days, is considered, however, to be biologically more significant than rainfall. The average number of rain days varies from approximately 175 in East Fife to well over 250 in parts of the West and in the Western Islands. However, rainfall amount alone is an inadequate index of biological wetness or rainfall efficiency. In the absence of evaporation or evapo-transpiration data, various methods of expressing absolute humidity in terms of the relationship between rainfall and either the saturation deficit or potential evaporation or the potential evapo-transpiration of the atmosphere have been employed. Green[9] has estimated that the average annual potential evaporation in

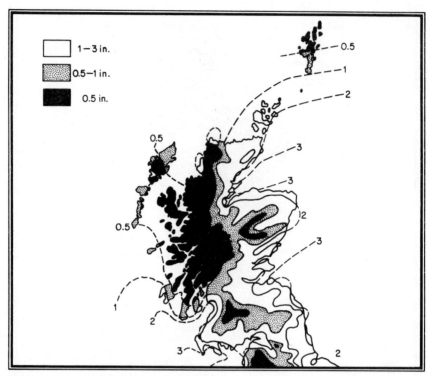

Fig. 3.6Annual average potential water deficit (soil moisture deficit). From Green, F. H. W. (1964) A map of annual average potential water deficit in the British Isles. *J. applied Ecol.* 1 : 151–158

Scotland is, with Scandinavia, the lowest in Europe (Fig 3.6). Also, it increases from east to west, as does the frequency of fog, mist and low cloud, features characteristically associated with high climatic humidity. A local but distinctive phenomenon is the east-coast sea-mist (*fret* or *haar*), formed when warm continental air is cooled on its passage over the cooler North Sea. It can extend the length of the coast from Aberdeen to Berwick and, depending on atmospheric conditions, may penetrate several miles inland, particularly in the lowlands of Central Scotland. Most pronounced in summer, its biological advantages in lowering water-stress in plants probably outweigh the disadvantages of lowered temperatures and amounts of sunshine.

Soil-water Conditions

The biological significance of high atmospheric humidity is related to the associated soil-water conditions. Mean annual potential soil-water deficits (PWD) are either absent or very low. Even the highest values of 75mm (*c*3in) around the inner shores of the Moray Firth, in the lowlands of East Lothian and Berwickshire, and in some small coastal areas in Ayrshire rarely signify a serious shortage of soil water.[9] Nevertheless, it is in areas such as these where protracted periods of low rainfall may, particularly on light, well-drained soils, result in deficits,[10] with effects such as retarded growth at the beginning of the growing season and reduced crop yields. For instance, the average summer rainfall in East Lothian from April to September gives less water than growing crops could profitably use.[11] The chief cash crop on areas of light soil, as in other coastal areas in south-west Scotland, is the shallow-rooted early potato which has been shown to give large increases in yield and mature more quickly when irrigated. In fact, past weather records indicate that in four years out of ten irrigation was not only profitable but essential. Today there are few early-potato-growing areas in Scotland which do not use spray-irrigation at the beginning of the growing season.

Grass-growing days have been defined[12] as those with a soil-water deficit of not less than 25mm. While response to irrigation in parts of Scotland might be expected in four years out of five, it has been demonstrated that similar results could be obtained more economically by fertilisers. Most of Scotland has more than sufficient moisture throughout the growing season for grass production. In fact, it is excess rainfall in spring and from August onwards that can limit grassland productivity, because of the leaching of soil nutrients (particularly nitrogen), soil saturation and consequent oxygen deficiency, and the susceptibility of heavier soils to puddling (poaching) by livestock. More recently attention has been drawn to the agricultural significance of the *accessibility period*.[13] This has been defined as the number of days in the year when machinery can work on the land without detriment to soil structure, or when animals can use pasture without causing sward damage. Excess of soil moisture and poor natural drainage are a characteristic of the heavier Scottish soils which, in certain areas and particularly in wetter years, can seriously curtail the length of the growing season, as well as making the harvesting and drying of hay and grain crops as problematic as spring or autumn cultivation.

High humidity, low evapo-transpiration and soil-water surpluses are among the main factors responsible for the widespread development of poorly and imperfectly drained soils, particularly surface-water gleys, peaty soils and peat. The widespread development of blanket-bog in Scotland owes much to high atmospheric humidity which can be absorbed directly from the atmosphere by that most important peat-former – the bog moss (*Sphagnum* spp). Various attempts have been made to express the relationship between humidity (or wetness) and the distribution and formation of peat quantitatively. Pearsall[14] suggested a mean annual rainfall of 1,200–1,400mm (48–56in) as a measure of 'effective humidity', and that above this limit there is an increasing tendency to soil saturation and peat formation. Fraser[15] expressed the same boundary in terms of a precipitation:saturation deficit (N/S) ratio of 1,000mm (40in). The area of Scotland with an insignificant potential water deficit is in fact the greater part; and Jowsey[16] has illustrated cartographically that most peatlands in the country occur within an area with a PWD of less than 15mm (0.6in). However, the difficulty of correlating existing climatic variables and peat distribution is that other relevant factors such as soil type, surface gradient, sub-surface materials and climatic change through time, are ignored. Thus the extent to which existing distributions are a function of current or past processes can never be fully assessed.

Climatic Oceanicity and Vegetation

Humidity, wetness and precipitation, together with cloudiness, increase from east to west in Scotland. This is an important climatic gradient, which is paralleled by a decrease in the amount of sunshine received at the ground surface, and in the annual temperature range; and by an increase in the length of the frost-free period, and in the exposure to high wind force (Fig 3.7). This reflects the east–west transition from a less to a more maritime or oceanic type of climate. Ecologists, in particular, have attempted to express this climatic gradient in terms of an index of either continentality or oceanicity. Conrad[17] has computed a *continentality index* for the whole of Britain on the basis of the mean annual range of temperature (°C) and the angle of latitude. This gives a range of relative magnitude from 12.5 near London to 1.3 at Cape Wrath and 0 in the Faeroe Islands. Norwegian ecologists have calculated *indices of oceanicity* (such as Kotilainen's Index) based on annual precipitation or the number of wet days, the number of days with temperatures between 0°C (32°F) and 10°C (50°F), and the difference between the mean temperature of the warmest and coldest months. This is thought to give the best correlation with the distribution of biological phenomena.[18]

On a regional scale increasing oceanicity of climate is reflected in some distinctive floral and vegetational trends.[19] For instance, certain species have a more continental, others a more oceanic, range of distribution. Decreasing insolation westward increases the rate of growth and the competitive advantage of certain mosses, particularly *Sphagnum* spp, *Rhacomitrium* spp and *Hypnum* spp. On the other hand,

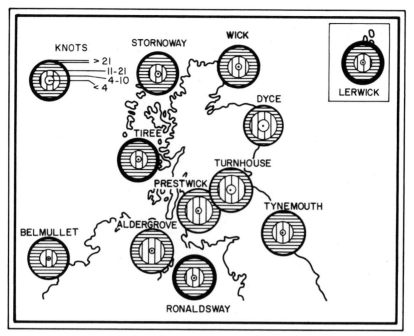

Fig 3.7 Annual percentage frequency of mean wind speed from all directions. Radius of outer circle = 100 per cent. From Chandler, T. and Gregory, S. J. (1976) *The Climate of the British Isles.* Lowe and Brydone Printers Limited

lichens play a more prominent role in the East. In addition, some particularly frost-sensitive species are confined to the West Highlands where, in coastal areas, temperatures are more equable than in the East, and there is also freedom from competition. The purple moor grass (*Molinia caerulea*) and bog myrtle (*Myrica gale*) are distinctive components of western and south-western moorlands. And the greater vigour and luxuriance of growth (up to 2m or more) of bracken (*Pteridium aquilinum*) in the lowlands of the West Highlands is thought to be a function of the milder, frost-free winter, which allows the survival of more over-wintering buds on the underground rhizomes than in the severer winters of the East.[20]

Increasing oceanicity is also reflected in the greater development of wet moorland communities (Fig 3.8); deer sedge (*Tricophorum caespitosa*), bog-cotton (*Eriophorum* spp) and purple moor grass (*Molinia caerulea*), together with the cross-leaved heath (*Erica tetralix*), are more common co-dominants in the West than the East of the country. The widespread occurrence of blanket-bog on slopes of less than about 15° and of peaty soils is also a characteristic feature of the more oceanic West. The distribution of plant species and communities undoubtedly follows this east–west climatic gradient so closely as to suggest a causal relationship.

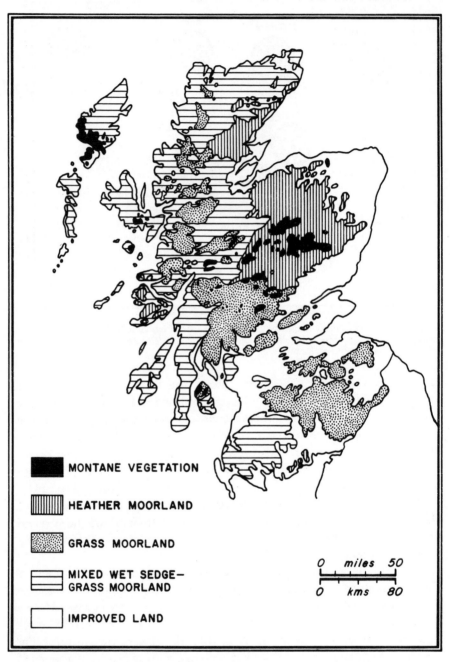

MONTANE VEGETATION

HEATHER MOORLAND

GRASS MOORLAND

MIXED WET SEDGE–
GRASS MOORLAND

IMPROVED LAND

0   miles   50

0   kms   80

Fig 3.8 Major types of Scottish moorland vegetation. From Tivy, Joy (1973) 'Rough Grazings' Chap. 6 in *Organic Resources of Scotland*. Oliver and Boyd, Edinburgh

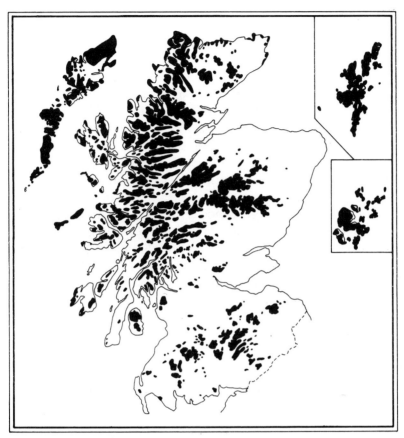

Fig 3.9 Areas exposed to very high wind force (6.2–▷8.0m/s). Adapted from *Assessment of Climatic Conditions in Scotland. 2. Based on Exposure and Accumulated Frost.* Birse, E. L. and Robertson, L. (1970). Macaulay Research Institute for Soil Research, Aberdeen

In some localities one climatic factor can have such extreme values that it becomes the dominant limiting factor. In Scotland, wind and high-altitude snowfall come into this category. Scotland is one of the most exposed countries in the world, with wind forces and frequencies greater than elsewhere in Western Europe and comparable only to the coasts of North West America, Tierra del Fuego, the Falkland Islands, and other high latitude islands. Around the coasts high wind force, combined with salt spray, can limit all but the hardiest species, and curtail productivity by increasing evapo-transpiration and lowering temperatures. Wind-sheared trees are a characteristic feature of all coastal areas and they extend well inland, particularly along valleys and lowlands open to westerly and south-westerly influences. The need to provide shelter for both crops and livestock is reflected in the widespread use of shelter belts on both lowland and upland farms[21] (Fig 3.9).

Effect of Altitude

The other, and probably even more ecologically significant, climatic
gradient in Scotland is that related to increasing altitude, which
strongly influences upland and montane bio-climatic conditions. As
stated earlier, two-thirds of the mainland surface lies above 152m
(500ft), and a third of this is above 305m (1,000ft). However, despite
this extent of upland and mountain, and the growing need to optimise
the use and conserve the values of such areas, few meteorological
stations are located above 305m (1,000ft). Records, other than of
rainfall, are relatively short-term and are generally of parameters
chosen for particular requirements, such as those of ski-centres (wind
and snow conditions); forestry and agricultural research centres; high-
level radar stations (for air traffic as on Lowther Hill, Lanarkshire); or
academic research projects. Analysis of climatic conditions in the
uplands is still dependent on estimates based on differences between
low-ground stations and the station which operated from 1883–1904 at
the summit of Ben Nevis (1,344m), the highest peak in Scotland, as well
as on assumed (but not always proven) relationships between climate
and dependent variables such as vegetation and soil.

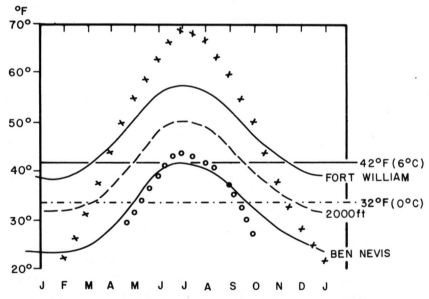

Fig 3.10 Mean monthly temperature in °F at Fort William and at the summit of Ben Nevis (4406ft)
– continuous lines. The broken line gives calculated figures at 2000ft. Circles = summer
temperatures in West Greenland and the crosses mean monthly temperatures for Vermont
(USA). Horizontal lines at 42°F and 32°F represent the two critical *thresholds* or base lines for plant
growth. After Pearsall, W. H. (1950) *Mountains and Moorlands*. New Naturalist Series, Collins,
London

There is a very rapid deterioration of bio-climatic conditions with altitude, consequent upon the inherently high lapse-rate of temperature in the maritime air masses which dominate Scotland's weather patterns. According to Manley[22] the lapse-rate in Polar maritime air, with a typical decrease of 6.5°C per 1,000m, is the steepest in the world. Moreover, soil temperatures usually decrease with altitude even more rapidly than does air temperature.[23] This temperature gradient is accompanied by a concomitant increase, with altitude, in rainfall, wetness, humidity, cloudiness and, particularly, wind speed (Fig 3.9). In an oceanic climatic regime, characterised by a low mean seasonal range of temperature, the consequent reduction in the length of the growing season is much more drastic than under a continental regime (Fig 3.10).

The rapid altitudinal decrease in the length and warmth of the growing season is one of the main factors responsible for the comparatively low limits of improved agricultural land, while increased leaching consequent upon higher rainfall and lower evaporation makes it even more costly to preserve soil nutrients at levels necessary to raise and maintain the biological productivity of improved grassland. The Meteorological Office has estimated a decrease in the growing season, in Britain as a whole, of 13 days per 1,000m increase in altitude. This means that for inland areas at an altitude of only 120–140m the harvest may be two weeks later than at coastal sites; and at 200–300m, on many upland stock-rearing farms in Scotland, it is three to four weeks later. As a result, the harvest becomes increasingly prone to interruption by wet autumn weather and gales. In eastern Scotland the floral development of grasses is delayed on average by 43 days per 1,000m increase in altitude, and annual yields fall by 2 per cent for every 30–31m rise.[24] The fall in spring could be by 5 per cent as compared with 1.8 per cent in autumn. Summer trends, however, are less constant and can occasionally be reversed because of the compensating factor of greater day-length, depending upon the aspect of a particular hill slope.

Effect of Wind Exposure

The biological disadvantage of insufficient warmth is exacerbated by increasing severity of exposure, and this is reflected in an exceptionally low *tree-line* in Scotland (Fig 3.11). The climatic exposure of many hill summits can equal or exceed that around the coasts. Experiments have indicated that wind force at altitudes around 610m in the Cairngorms are comparable to the highest values recorded along the west coast of Ayrshire. An anemometer attached to the most exposed chair-lift pylon

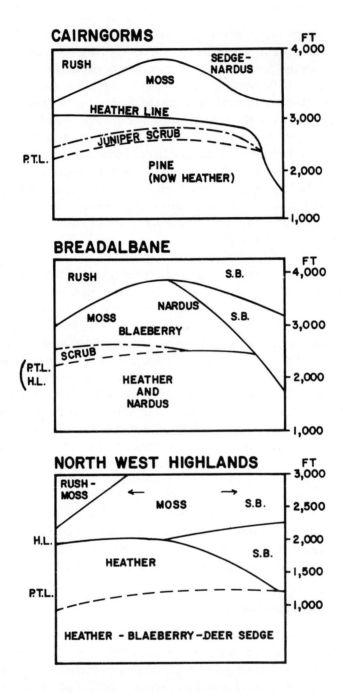

Fig 3.11 Vegetation diagrams showing altitudinal decline in vegetation zones from south-east to north-west in the Scottish Highlands. SB = Snow Beds; PT-L = Potential Tree Line; HL = Heather Line. Adapted from Poore, M. E. D. and McVean, D. N. (1957). 'A new approach to Scottish Mountain Vegetation'. *J. Ecol.* 45 : 401–439

at Cairngorm in March 1967 recorded the highest gust ever measured instrumentally in Britain (145mph).[25] As well as causing physical damage to trees – by wind-throw and stem-breakage – wind has a desiccating effect which, together with lowered temperatures, severely curtails tree growth and makes the establishment and survival of seedlings precarious. The latter, near ground-level, are also particularly susceptible to abrasion by hail and fine sand. Pears[25] has shown that there is evidence for a 'natural tree-line', which probably attains the maximum possible altitudes at 609–820m in parts of the Cairngorms. Elsewhere in Scotland the tree-line has generally been depressed, normally to about 457–487m, by sheep grazing and/or moor burning. Exposure to high wind-force is the most important factor inhibiting a re-advance of the existing degraded and open forest or woodland to its former potential limits. It has also influenced the altitude to which economic reafforestation may proceed. The upper altitudinal limit of the Forestry Commission's plantations – the so-called *planting-line* – is lower in Scotland than elsewhere in Europe: 500m in the South and East of the country, 300m in the North and North-west, and on particularly exposed sites, as low as 200m or even sea level in places.[26]

From a maximum in the East, the altitudinal limits between the forest and montane zones decline markedly towards the North-west and North of the country (Fig 3.11).[27] Increasing oceanicity alone could account for the westward altitudinal descent of vegetation zones, of which the most ecologically and economically significant is the tree-line. However, when the latitudinal decline in temperature is combined with severe exposure, the effect becomes even more marked – as in Shetland and along the extreme north and north-west coasts of Scotland. The gradual decline in the upper limit of sub-montane scrub has been traced by Spence[28] from the Central Highlands to the Outer Hebrides. In fact, on most of the exposed coasts of north-west Scotland, Orkney and Shetland, the forest and tall shrub zones disappear completely and the climax vegetation at sea level is thought to be a dwarf shrub-heath. Any trees that do grow are normally stunted and severely sheared by the combined effect of high wind force and salt-spray. Wind is a dominant bio-climatic factor in Shetland, where exposure is severe all the year round. The average annual wind speed on the top of Sandness Hill is almost half as high again as at Lerwick Observatory (94m), twice that in any month at Eskdalemuir, and only slightly less (80 per cent) than on the summit of Ben Nevis; it is therefore believed[28] that at least on the higher parts of Sandness Hill bare ground is the direct result of high wind-force and salt-spray.

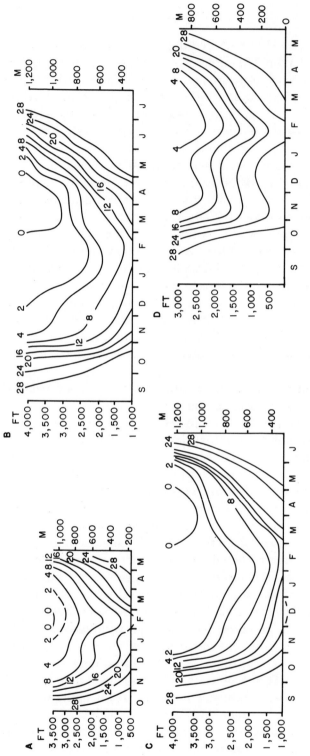

Fig 3.12 The snow line on: (1) South of Ben Wyvis, viewed from Fairburn, Black Isle, Easter Ross. 1964–5 – 1970–1. (2) South face of Derry Cairngorm, as viewed from Derry Lodge, Aberdeenshire. 1965–1973 (calendar years). (3) Northern face of Braeriach, as viewed from Achnagoichan, Strathspey, Inverness-shire, 1965–73 (calendar years). (4) Eastern face of Beinn Eighe, as viewed from Anancaun, Kinlochewe, Wester Ross. 1965–73 (calendar years). From Green, F. H. W. (1975) 'The transient snow-line in the Scottish Highlands'. *Weather* 30(7) : 226–235

Effect of Snow

Another important bio-climatic feature is the rapid and effective increase, with altitude, in the frequency, amount and duration of snowfall and snow-cover (Fig 3.12). Snow-cover is ecologically important because it shelters dormant vegetation and insulates the ground from frost penetration. It shortens the growing season; it provides, on thawing, soil-water surpluses (while snow-free areas which are most subject to temperature variation tend to suffer from water deficits in the growing season); and it acts as a trap for wind-blown mineral and plant debris which accumulates and enriches the underlying soil.

The only reasonably long records of snowfall and snow-lie in upland Scotland are the annual Meteorological Office Snow Survey Returns. These record the snow-lie visible to observers on specified hills. Among the longest records are those for Ben Wyvis (from 1946–7) and on the Western Cairngorm (from 1955). The average number of days with snow falling varies from 10 in the South-west to 40 in the North-east, and with snow lying between 12 to 36 days in the same direction; and between 5 days at the coast to a maximum of about 70 inland at

Fig 3.13 Average annual number of mornings with snow cover 1931–60. From Chandler, T. and Gregory, S. G. (1976) *The Climate of the British Isles*. Lowe and Brydone Printers Limited

Braemar. Table 3.2 gives an indication of the increase in length of snow-lie with altitude. Manley[29] noted that at an altitude of 610m the annual snow-cover varies from 50 to 170 days (average, 100 days). The '*transient*' *snow-line*, in general, occurs at a lower altitude in the East than in the West and on north-facing rather than on south-facing slopes (Fig 3.13). Green[30] suggested that the pattern of snowfall distribution during the season has been changing and that, in recent decades, there has been more snow at the beginning and the end than in the middle of the winter.

Table 3.2

Average number of days snow cover observed at various levels

Altitude (m)	460	610	765	915	1070	1220
Glen Lyon (24 seasons 46–7 to 69–70)	75	100	125	150	—	—
Ben Nevis (11 seasons 50–1 to 60–1)	66	103	139	107	202	220
Ben Nevis (1883 to 1904)	—	—	—	—	—	230
Cairngorm (13 seasons 55–6 to 67–78)	79	116	158*	178*	191*	200

* a few days should be added for June
Source Manley, G. 'The mountain snows of Britain', and 'Scotland's semi-permanent snows', *Weather* 26(1971), 192–200 and 458–71

Snow-lie, however, can be extremely variable, depending on patterns of atmospheric circulation, temperature and precipitation. Also, the high degree of exposure to which the Scottish uplands are subjected contributes further to a very uneven distribution and very considerable variation in depth. Above 610m snow tends to be blown off ridges and exposed mountain summits (except in very calm weather), and becomes packed into sheltered depressions and gullies, and particularly, into north-facing corries, to form snow-beds; in such localities snow-cover persists longer than elsewhere. Ben Nevis and the western Cairngorms have semi-permanent snow-beds which may persist continuously for several years;[31] that on Braeriach (1,295m) has existed for 50 years; and until 1933 it was thought that the snow-bed on the north face of Ben Nevis was permanent.[32] The most extensive and longest lying snow-beds occur in the Cairngorms. Here and elsewhere they are associated with distinctive snow-bed (or *chinophilous*) plant communities.[33] These are composed of species tolerant of a particular

depth and duration of snow-cover. It has been noted that areas
dominated by the moor mat grass (*Nardus stricta*) (Fig 3.14), together
with other species intolerant of competition from more vigorous
moorland plants such as heather and blaeberry, coincided with those
areas which were generally observed to have the longest snow-lie. This
type of vegetation provided one of the most objective indicators of
persistent snow-beds when the potential for the development of skiing
in the Cairngorms was initially being investigated in the early 1960s.

The length of the snow-lie increases progessively from the edge
towards the centre of the snow-bed. Meltwater around the periphery
irrigates the zone adjacent to the receding snow margin. Hence a series
of concentric zones results, each composed of a different plant
assemblage and tolerant of an increasingly wet habitat and a shorter
growing season. A characteristic zonation from the outer edge of a
snow-bed is: *Nardus stricta; N. stricta* with sedges (*Carex* spp); wavy hair
grass (*Deschampsia flexuosa*) and the dwarf willow (*Salix herbacea*); the
previous two species with *Nardus* but accompanied by *Gnapthalium* sp;

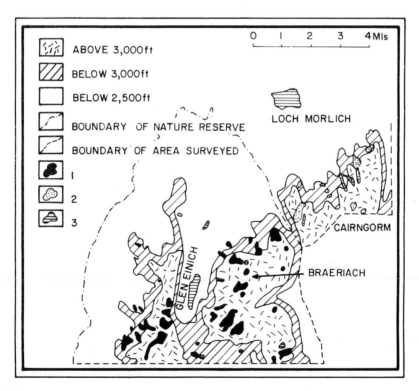

Fig 3.14 *Nardus stricta* (moor mat grass) snow-bed communities in the Cairngorms. 1. Surveyed by
D. N. McVean within Nature Reserve; 2. Areas with *Nardus* conspicuous outside Nature Reserve;
3. Major lochs. From Green, F. H. W. (1968)'Persistent snow-beds in the Western Cairngorms'.
Weather 23 : 206–9 (p.208)

and finally mosses and liverworts in the centre of the bed. The adaptation of animals to snow-cover, shown in the protective colouring of the mountain hare and the ptarmigan for example, is well known, though the onset of the colour change is so constant in the former as to suggest day-length as the dominant trigger factor. On the other hand, snow-cover would seem to have a more direct effect on the behaviour of the red deer in north-eastern Scotland.[34] Snow covers the deer's food supply. Delay in thawing and the commencement of plant growth retards the production of nutrient-rich fresh fodder. As a result, the time when the antlers are shed – the beginning of the rutting season – is delayed.

The Montane Zone

Above the *'potential'* tree-line, bio-climatic conditions become increasingly severe. The Scottish mountains, however, lie wholly within that range of altitude in which atmospheric humidity and precipitation increase. Also summer temperatures, as well as daily and seasonal temperature ranges, are lower, and insolation less intense than in continental alpine areas. Thus the climate of the Scottish mountain tops is more comparable to the humid sub-arctic coastal areas of Iceland and Greenland. It is certainly more rigorous than the high Norwegian plateaux or fjels. In the absence of a continuous snow-cover, considerable ground surfaces are subject to intense freeze/thaw activity and exceptionally high wind force, which can in places prevent the establishment of a vegetation cover.

The transition from the forest-moorland to the sub-arctic montane zone is marked, particularly in the Eastern Highlands, by the replacement of communities dominated by heather (*Calluna vulgaris*) those in which blaeberry (*Vaccinium myrtillus*), sheep's fesue (*Festuca ovina*) and the moor mat grass (*Nardus stricta*) are more abundant. The altitudinal limit of heather is determined by wind force and a more persistent snow-cover (Fig 3.15). With increasing exposure, heather decreases in stature, eventually forming a continuous mat no more than 1–5cm in height. The amount of bare ground increases, as does that of active 'patterned ground' resulting from the alternation of freezing and thawing in the soil and/or underlying rock. Fig 3.15 illustrates the altitudinal zonation of vegetation in the Cairngorms in relation to what are considered the three most important physical factors involved – temperature, wind force and snow-line.[35] The most extensive development of this humid sub-arctic habitat is on the high Cairngorm plateau, much of which lies within the largest single National Nature

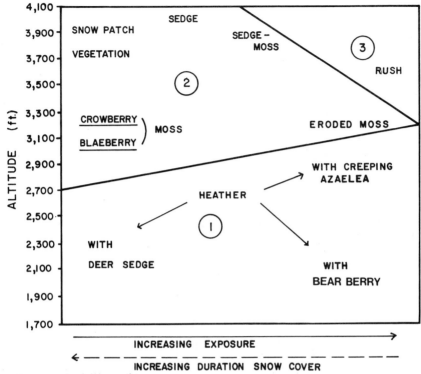

Fig 3.15 Diagrammatic representation of the interaction of altitude, exposure and snow-cover on the distribution of the chief plant communities in the Cairngorms: (1) Heather (*Calluna vulgaris*) zone; (2) Crowberry (*Empetrum*)–Blaeberry (*Vaccinium myrtillus*) zone; (3) Rush (*Juncus*) zone; Sedge (*Carex rigidae*); moss (*Rhacomitrum*); Rush (*J. trifidi*); Deer sedge (*Tricophorum caespitosus*); Creeping azalea (*Loiselenria procumbens*); Bearberry (*Arctostaphylos vva-ursi*). From Watt, Alex. S. and Jones, E. W. (1948). 'The Ecology of the Cairngorms. 1. The environment and the altitudinal zonation of the vegetation'. *J. Ecol.* 36 : 283. p.297

Reserve in Britain (covering approximately 250km²). The ecological significance of the *humid* sub-arctic habitat and the associated upland plant communities has contributed to its designation, at both national and international levels, as a Grade I conservation site.

Climatic Marginality

The most ecologically significant aspect of Scotland's climate is its very high degree of *marginality*. This means that relatively slight variations in either climatic conditions (or in those factors affecting climate such as altitude, aspect, soil etc) can have very considerable effects – indeed effects out of all proportion to the degree or scale of climatic variation. As Miller has expressed it 'Scotland lies so near the edge of the climatic oekumene that quite a small departure towards the unfavourable may often be [ecologically] disastrous and have large

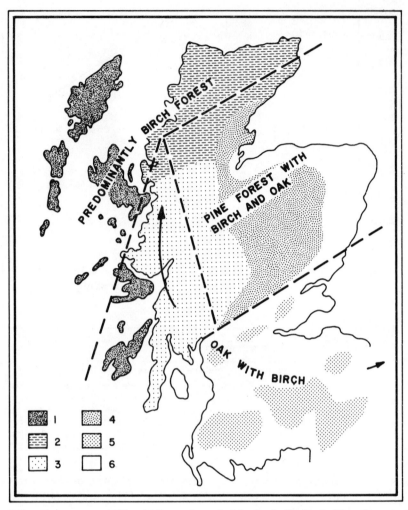

Fig 3.16 Forest zones and vegetation regions: 1. Islands; 2. North; 3. West–Central; 4. East–Central; 5. South; 6. Cultivated land. From McVean, D. N. (1964) Regional patterns of vegetation. Chap. 17 in *The Vegetation of Scotland*. Ed. John H. Burnett. Oliver and Boyd, Edinburgh

repercussions';[36] and the two major factors contributing to this marginality are those of the country's geographical location and altitude.

The combined effect of latitudinal position, range of altitude and, consequently, the high degree of oceanicity has resulted in the convergence westward of the three major climatic vegetational zones in North West Europe (Fig 3.16). In Scotland, the Boreal Coniferous forest zone is all but 'squeezed-out' and there is consequently a particularly rapid transition from the Cool Temperate Deciduous forest to the Tundra zone. The implications of climatic marginality were initially emphasised by Manley,[37] who estimated that the *theoretical* snow-line in Scotland was at about 1,600m, just 300m above the summits of the highest mountains. It would, therefore, require only a slight decrease in summer temperatures to allow the development of glaciers. The presence of the semi-permanent snow-beds, already referred to, in areas with particular local climatic conditions, is indicative of just how close to a glacial environment the periglacial montane zone is.

Long-term Climatic Fluctuations

Studies of post-glacial vegetational chronology, based on macro- and microscopic (large pollen grains) plant remains preserved in peat bogs, reveal alternating periods of more and less marked continental and oceanic conditions in Scotland (Table 3.3).[38] At the climatic optimum (about 5,000–7,000 years ago), when it is estimated that average summer temperatures were perhaps, on average, about 2°C higher than at present, the Cool Temperate Deciduous forest attained its maximum development and extent, and the Coniferous (Boreal) tree-line, particularly in the Eastern Highlands, extended to maximum altitudes of about 914m (3,000ft). Alternating periods of more humid oceanic climate were associated with widespread development of blanket bog. It has also been suggested that the first real impact of man – the deforestation and vegetation burning he wrought – coincided with, and hence greatly aggravated, the effects of the latest climatic deterioration beginning about 2,500 years ago.

Substantial long-term climatic fluctuations have occurred within the last 1,000 years and have continued to be important ecological factors. The climatic limits of cultivation may have fallen some 140m in 300 years in the Lammermuir Hills in south-east Scotland as a result of a deterioration in growing conditions from the middle of the thirteenth century onwards, and by the seventeenth century an upland/lowland fringe, once cultivated, had become climatically sub-marginal.[39] Since then the altitudinal limits of improved land have continued to fluctuate, and the present limit generally lies below the head-dyke which marked its upper boundary from the mid-eighteenth to the mid-nineteenth century. This, however, also reflects a response to a changing economic climate which made the cultivation of areas with severe physical limitations uneconomic.

Table 3.3
Chronology of the main climatic, vegetational and pedological events in late and post-glacial times in Scotland

Years before present	Pollen zone	Period	Climate	Lowland vegetation	Probable soil conditions
13000	I		Very cold		
12000					
	II	Late Glacial	Temporarily warmer	Grasses sedges and open	Early stages of soil and basin peat formation
11000			Very cold	vegetation	High water tables and much flooded ground
	III				Many early soils destroyed by erosion and solifluction
10000	IV	Pre-Boreal	Fluctuating less cold	Birch forest	Early development of brown forest soils and podzols
9000					
	V		Warm		
8000	VI	Boreal	dry summers	Birch, pine and hazel	Brown forest soils and podzols well developed
7000					
	VIIa	Atlantic	Warm and wet	Alder, oak and elm	Extension of brown forest soils to higher altitudes
6000					Gley formation probably more widespread, due to wetter conditions
5000				Decline of elm	
4000	VIIb	Sub-Boreal	Less warm		
3000			Dry	Alder, oak and birch	Podzol formation at the expense of brown forest soils, due to cooler climate and recession of deciduous woodland
2000					
	VIII	Sub-Atlantic	Cool and wet	Clearing of forest by man	
1000					
0					

Source Durno, S. E. 'Vegetational Chronology'. In Tivy, *op. cit.*

Conclusion

Marginality of climate is an expression of the variability of weather conditions which is so characteristic a feature of the Scottish bio-climatic environment. Variability increases with altitude and is ecologically significant particularly in the spring and autumn months, at the beginning and the end of the growing season. At these times temperatures can oscillate rapidly across critical thresholds such as the freezing point and the minimum daily temperatures required for cereal germination or the commencement of vegetative growth of improved grassland. Oscillations in the first case are particularly critical on the margin between the forest and montane zones. Deforestation and a long period of sheep-grazing and moor-burning have, in many areas, led to a gradual deterioration of the vegetation and soil conditions. In many areas, this has led to the eventual removal of the protective insulating cover of organic matter (vegetation and soil). Consequently, frost has been able to penetrate more deeply below the surface than before. More active freeze/thaw has given rise to unstable soil conditions which make recolonisation of vegetation difficult. On steep slopes it may 'trigger-off' accelerated soil erosion which leaves bare scree-covered slopes in its wake. As a result of vegetation and soil disruption, the margin between the periglacial montane and forest zones may have been significantly lowered. Also, the effects of the ensuing freeze/thaw processes may extend down-slope well beyond the areas directly affected, to the detriment of actual or potential land uses in the forest zone. In the short term, variability in upland areas constitutes a major agricultural hazard. It contributes to the economic marginality of those farms whose size and altitudinal range do not allow sufficient flexibility of products and management to minimise the limitations of a marginal climate. Hence more information about the nature, as well as the variations in scale, of this agriculturally marginal zone would be a major contribution to a greater understanding of the bio-climatic geography, as well as to land-use planning and management in Scotland as a whole.

Notes to this chapter are on pages 304–5.

4

Prehistoric Scotland:
The Regional Dimension

William Kirk

For the sea and the earth in which we dwell furnish theatres for action: limited for limited action; vast for grander deeds.

Strabo

As every schoolboy knows, Scotland – like ancient Gaul – is divided into three parts: the Highlands; the Southern Uplands; and the fault-bounded Central Lowlands or Midland Valley. Successive regional geographic texts have entrenched this perception, based on the geology of the country outlined by Geikie[1] in his classic work of 1865, and of course in terms of the modern economic development of the country this tripartite division has considerable significance. However, in the same way that such a stark geological division tends to mask other equally significant physiographical distinctions,[2] so also in the historical geography of the country it is possible to recognise other regional entities that have played important roles in the processes of human occupation and settlement of those terrains that now comprise the political unit of Scotland. Indeed, prior to the emergence of the Kingdom of Scotland in early medieval times the essential history of the lands of North Britain was provincial rather than national, and this chapter seeks to explore the prehistoric foundations of such cultural regionalism. Rather than analysing successive phases of occupation,[3] it attempts to establish the large-scale provincial pattern apparent at the close of the prehistoric period and use this as a frame of reference for comparison with patterns of a remoter past.

Place-names and Regions in the Dark Ages

At the time when written records begin to appear alongside archaeological evidence, some indication of regional–cultural identities can be derived from linguistic groupings, particularly as recorded in place-names; and although a complete place-name survey of Scotland

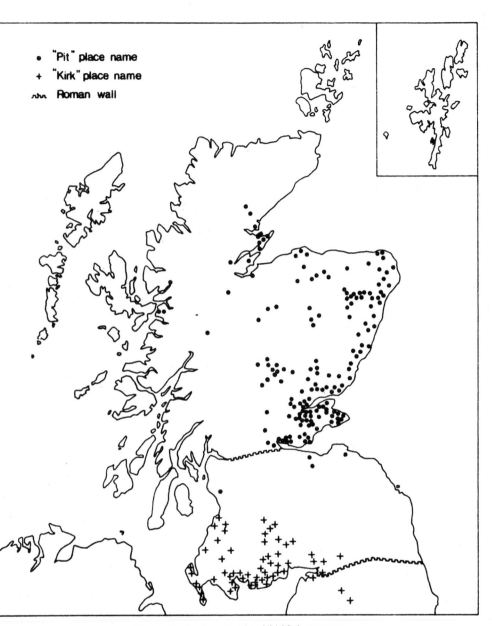

Fig 4.1 Distribution of 'pit' and 'kirk' place names

has yet to be carried out, sufficient work has been done to indicate the broad regional contrasts.[4] Fig 4.1, for example, shows the regional exclusiveness of two such place-name elements – the prefixes *Pit-* and *Kirk-*, the former almost entirely confined to north-east Scotland, the latter to the south-west. It is now generally accepted that the *pit-* element represents an early stratum of place-naming arising from a P-Celtic, Gallo-Britannic branch of the Celtic language to which the shorthand title of 'Pictish' can now be given with some confidence. It certainly predates the introduction of the Irish Ogam script in which many of the Pictish inscriptions of the early Dark Ages are written, and the introduction of Irish Gaelic (Goidelic: 'Q' Celtic) in the later Dark Ages as the dominant place-naming language of north-east Scotland. Its roots could indeed be very ancient with some features dating back to Bronze Age, non-Indo-European languages or to the first arrival of the Iron Age Celts in North Britain. At what stage in such linguistic development it became customary to use the prefix *pit-* to describe a place, or piece of land, is not known, but it appears to have been a popular Dark Ages form. Its survival as a place-name element north of the Antonine Wall and the Forth is significant, as are the clusters to be observed in its distribution focusing on the Abernethy–Scone–Perth district of the Tay, the middle reaches of the Don valley in Aberdeenshire, the inner reaches of the Moray Firth, as well as a coastal zone extending from Fife northward to Buchan.

The *kirk-* element, on the other hand, belongs to a group of inversion compounds first discussed in detail in 1918 for north-west England,[5] but extended more recently into Scotland.[6,7] They represent a compound in which the first element is Norse (*kirkia*, church) but in which the construction of the name follows Gaelic usage (thus *Kirkbryde* rather than *Brydekirk*, St Brigid's church; *Kirkoswald* rather than *Oswaldkirk*, St Oswald's Church). Their distribution is essentially confined to south-west Scotland, with an extension into Cumberland, and the main concentration is coincident with the ancient province of Galloway – now represented by the counties of Wigtownshire and Kirkcudbright. The name Galloway is derived from the Gaelic *Gall-Ghaidhil*, foreign Gael. It is argued that the term refers to 'Norse Gael' and that the *kirk-* place-names provide evidence for the settlement of Norse stock from Ulster early in the tenth century, in an area that had witnessed the early introduction of Christianity and had cultural connections with Ireland, the Isle of Man, and Northumbria. The *kirk-* element indeed cannot be separated from a Gaelic background and there was no similar development in the Hebrides where the Norse were more dominant.

Diametrically opposite to these distributions are those shown in Fig 4.2.[8] The place-name element *-dalr*, valley, is confined to north-west Scotland and, as Nicholaisen points out, it is an indicator of a Norse sphere of influence rather than evidence of permanent settlements. Most uses of the suffix refer to natural features rather than settlements, although at a later date the name of the valley could be transferred to a settlement located within it. The *dalr*, dale, area embraces the more

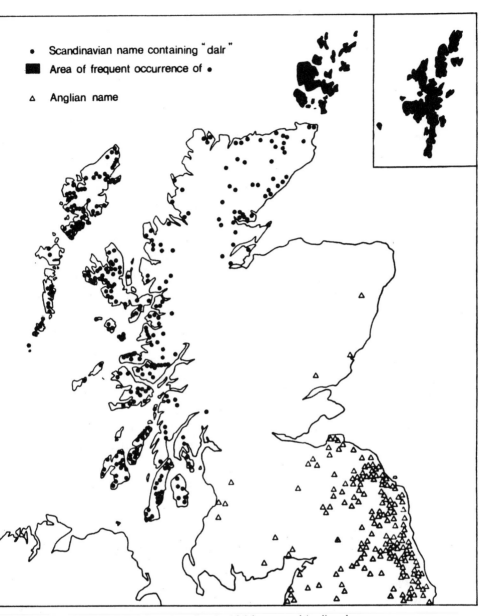

Fig 4.2 Distribution of Scandinavian 'dalr' names and Anglian place names

restricted areas of permanent Norse settlement indicated by such elements as *stadir* (up to mid-ninth century) and *setr/saetr* (up to *c*900AD) and is spatially almost coincident with the longer-lasting and more widely distributed *bolstadr* element. Absence of these associated settlement names south of the Forth–Clyde line allows one to treat the -*dale* names found there as of cognate English origin. The *dalr* area shown in Fig 4.2 then represents in a striking manner a Norse 'theatre of action', of hunting, fishing, summer grazing, raids and visits to Gaelic-speaking neighbours. Apart from a small area of overlap in the inner reaches of the Moray Firth, the *dalr* and *pit* distributions are mutually exclusive and indeed the remarkable absence of Scandinavian place names as a whole in north-east Scotland is highly significant for reconstructions of the cultural history of that province. In north-east Scotland Pictish (*pits*) gives way to Gaelic (*bals*) without the intercession of Scandinavian.

The Anglian names shown in Fig 4.2 also have a clear regional context. Apart from a few instances in north-east and south-east Scotland, the majority of the names occur south of the Forth, in the Tweed basin, the Tyne Valley and the Northumbrian seaboard. The place-name elements included in the distributions shown are -*ingham*, -*ingtun*, *ham*, *worth*, *bothl*, *bothl-run*, *botl*, and *wic*.[8] All are early and indicate the areas of Anglian settlement in the late seventh, eighth and early ninth centuries AD. The Anglian bridgehead was Bamburgh, first occupied in 547, and by *c*640 the Angles had captured the rock fortress of Edinburgh (*Eidyn*), facilitating the settlement of Anglian communities in the Lothians – the former territories of the Votadini tribe of Roman Britain. By the middle of the seventh century the Anglian frontier lay on the Firth of Forth, as the Roman frontier had done previously, and in spite of abortive campaigns in Pictish country to the north it was to remain on this alignment for some two centuries as the Anglian folk consolidated their occupation of the land south of the frontier. Although the place-name distribution does not record the earliest colonies, it does reflect this period of swarming and consolidation. It also reflects the links between Northumbria and the early Christian church in South-west Scotland, particularly Whithorn (the *Candida Casa* of St Ninian reported by Bede of Jarrow *c*730) and the conquest of Kyle in Ayrshire in 750. West of the Clyde–Tweed watershed, however, the Anglians appear to have made little permanent headway into the territories of the British kingdom of Strathclyde.

The regional indications derived from the four place-name distributions discussed above can be subsumed into a composite map of Dark Age Scotland (Fig 4.3), based on documentary, place-name and archaeological evidence ranging from the late Roman period to the coming of the Norse seafarers. The political geography it displays can be interpreted as a core north-eastern province, east of the Druim Alban watershed and extending from the Moray Firth to the Forth, beset from almost every side: by Northumbria in the south-east; Strathclyde in the south-west with its central citadel at Dumbarton; the

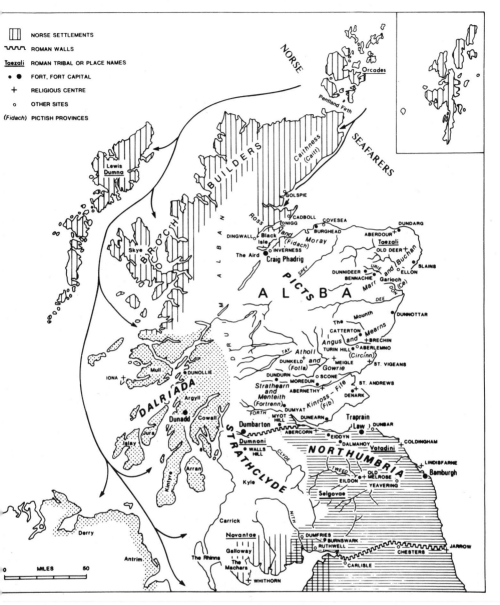

Fig 4.3 A regional geography of Dark Age Scotland

Dalriadic Scots from north-east Ireland to the west, with their military centre at Dunadd and religious centre at Iona; and Norse invaders from the north into the former territories of the Broch builders and along the western seaways.

The north-eastern province characterised by *pit-* names is seen to coincide with the Dark Age (proto-historic) territories of the Pictish people (known to classical commentators as the *Picti*, painted people, and to the Irish Annals as *Cruithni*).[9] King lists dating from the tenth century and references in a twelfth-century tract *De Situ Albanie* named Cruithne as the first King of the Picts and associated seven Pictish territories with a division of his kingdom among his seven sons in the following manner:

Sons of Cruithne	Pictish Districts	Modern Equivalents
1 Circinn	Enegus cum Moerne	Angus and the Mearns
2 Fotla (Foltlaig)	Athfotla (Adtheodle et Goverin)	Atholl and Gowrie
3 Fortrenn	Fortriu (Stradeern cum Meneted)	Strathearn and Menteith
4 Fib	Fife cum Fothreve	Fife and Kinross
5 Ce	Marr cum Buchan	Marr and Buchan
6 Fidach	Muref et Ros	Moray and Ross
7 Caitt	Cathanesia	Caithness

The survival of such district names in spite of later county organisation is noteworthy and may be compared to a similar survival of local territorial names in south-west Scotland, such as The Rhinns, The Machars, and indeed Galloway itself. Quite apart from their eponymous attachment to the legendary sons of Cruithne, the *pays*-like character of these territories ensures a geographical continuity however they are named and grouped for political or administrative purposes. Indeed, from a geographical point of view they have a reality, born of human communities making a living from a recognisable tract of land, that is almost independent of historical change as perceived by historians. To the historical geographer they constitute those durable, small 'theatres of action' for limited, repetitive, everyday deeds that may never excite the attention of the historian or pre-historian but which over countless generations build the landscape. That they achieved names within the Pictish Kingdom is really incidental. They survived that kingdom and undoubtedly pre-dated it.

During the Dark Ages it would appear that the communities occupying such districts were brought under some kind of political confederacy, with an organising concept of kingship and a kingdom that extended initially from Caithness to the Forth and from the Western Highlands to the North Sea. As the Dark Ages progressed, its frontiers were assaulted by the Norse from the north and north-west, by the Dalriadic (Antrim) Scots from the south-west, and by the English Northumbrians from the south-east. Not until the battle of Nechtan's Mere in 685, in which the Pictish forces defeated the

Page 101 View into the large east-facing corries of Beinn A'Bhuird (3860ft), eastern Cairngorms. Corrie floors are littered with morainic boulders left by small glaciers about 10,300 years ago. Higher summits of Ben Macdui and Cairn Toul in right background

Page 102 *(above)* Tap O Noth, Grampian, the most spectacular hill-fort in north-east Scotland. Prominent main vitrified wall at the top and a large outer line of defence halfway down the hillside. Irregularities on upper hillside are platforms constructed or cut for timber houses indicating a high population on the north face of the hill at an altitude of 1,600ft; *(below)* recumbent stone circle and enclosed crematorium, from about 2000BC, at Loanhead of Daviot, near Old Meldrum, Grampian

Northumbrians and killed Ecgfrith the Northumbrian king, did the southern frontier stabilise on the Forth, but the threat from that direction required constant military vigilance. After 800 the northern frontier became active, with Norse settlements in the Northern Isles and Caithness and Viking raids on the Pictish coasts. Ultimately this frontier was stabilised also, with Dingwall and the Cromarty Firth representing the limits of Norse penetration – and place-names – but from Inverness eastward along the Moray Firth coastland defences (eg Burghead) had to be maintained by frontier overlords or *mormaers*, of whom Macbeth is the most publicised.

On the Dalriadic frontier, however, it proved to be very difficult to achieve stability. The first Scottish settlements in the post-Roman period were small and confined to the seaboard, but as they increased in strength the Picts attempted to contain their military and cultural expansion. From the sixth century, according to Irish sources, there was constant frontier skirmishing, with the Picts attempting to hold the watershed zone of Druim Alban and the defile of the Great Glen. Indeed, the first accounts are of the military activities of Brude (Bridei), King of the Picts, operating in the sixth century from a royal fortress near Inverness (probably Craign Phadrig) against the Scots and of his conversion by St Columba. Later the accounts switch to the southern flanks of Druim Alban in the debatable territory of the tri-junction between the British Kingdom of Strathclyde, Scottish Dalriada, and the Pictish terrains of the Upper Forth and Tay. Bede records a Northumbrian victory at Degsastan in 603 against a combined force of Scots and Strathclyde Britons, and other references indicate Scottish raids along the Highland edge into Pictish territory. The Irish annalists give prominence to the military exploits of Onuist (Oengus), who between 730 and 760 not only repulsed Scottish advances into the Perth area but invaded Dalriada and attempted to conquer Strathclyde by reducing the great British fortress on the rock of Dumbarton. Onuist's base appears to have been in the Dunkeld (Atholl) area, and it is significant that it is in this area that in the mid-ninth century the union of Picts and Scots took place in the kingship of Kenneth (macAlpin) of Dalriada, and at the royal centre of Scone. Thenceforth Scots – hard pressed by the Norse on the western seaboard – began to migrate eastward into the Pictish terrains, and Pictland (or more probably Alba) gave way to an emergent Scotland, virtually invested by Scandinavians.

During the period from *c*500 to *c*900 the Pictish forces appear to have been constantly engaged in military operations of one kind or another, and behind the military story it is possible to discern changes in the political geography of Pictland. In addition to the districts referred to above, regions of a higher order can be recognised. Thus it is possible to distinguish between the Pictish communities of the North and those of the South, with an internal frontier on the line of the Mounth – the Highland edge in Angus and Kincardine, backed by the forested and rather infertile valley of the Aberdeenshire Dee. Initially the political core of the Northern Picts appears to have been located in the Inner Moray Firth, with extensions northward through Caithness, westward through the Great Glen, and eastward to the geographically separate territory of Aberdeen, while the core of the Southern Picts appears to have been located in the middle Tay Valley, with extensions north-eastward along Strathmore to Brechin and the Howe of the Mearns area, eastward and southward from Abernethy into Kinross and the Neuk of Fife, and southwestward into Strathearn and the ill-drained lowlands of the Forth Valley. Under strong kings, dominance was achieved over the whole kingdom from either the northern or southern core, with the latter tending to dominate in the later stages; but when the succession was not clear political fragmentation and internecine war appears to have occurred during certain periods – particularly between North and South.

This regional distinction is in part supported by the direction of the initial missionary activities of the Irish Christian Church, and by the distribution and nature of the well-known Pictish symbol stones.[10] From an archaeological point of view the latter are the soundest confirmation of the spatial reach of Pictland as indicated by place-names and documentary records. The Class I stones, characterised by the incision of abstract or animal symbols on roughly dressed boulders, are thought to date from $c500$ to $c750$ with some of the later (eighth-century) examples also bearing Ogam inscriptions (eg at Brandsbutt on the northern outskirts of Aberdeen). They predominate in the territories of the Northern Picts, with clusters in the middle Don-Urie (Garioch-Bennachie) area of Aberdeenshire, the Spey Valley, the Inverness area, and the Golspie-Brora area north of the Dornoch Firth. The Class II stones, on the other hand, consist of dressed stone slabs with an interlace Christian cross on one face and symbols on the opposite face, all sculptured in relief. They are thought to date from $c700$ to the end of the independent Pictish Kingdom $c850$, when they give way to Class III stones, lacking the symbols. The Class II stones are more numerous in the territory of the Southern Picts, with Meigle an important focus, and in the forms of the interlaced cross and the associated iconography they display both Northumbrian and Irish influences. They also depict animals in naturalistic rather than symbolic form and fill spaces with pictorial scenes of hunting parties and battles. Certainly the most powerful impression they give is of a people surrounded by animals, in which pride of place is given to the horse. From the art alone it would be possible to infer a farming population, with pastoralism as the basis of their economy, ruled over by a horse-riding warrior aristocracy newly converted to Christianity but with traditional naturalistic and animistic beliefs still surviving.

Iron Age Foundations for Dark Age Regionalism

The inference made above is supported if the Late Bronze Age and Early Iron Age cultural foundations of the Pictish terrains are examined. The Roman incursions of Agricola and Severus do not appear to have had lasting cultural effects in the land of Ptolemy's *Caledonii, Vacomagi, Venicones, Taezali* and *Decantae*.[11] Of much deeper significance appears to have been the cultural impact and possible settlement of European folk in the pre-Roman period. There are elements in the Pictish language of a pre-Celtic, Old European, form which appear to indicate the presence of settlers from the Continent early in the first millennium BC. From *c*800BC metal-work styles in North Britain also appear to reflect European traditions and, in the centuries that followed, mutual traditions of fort-building were developed. Certainly by the fifth century BC considerable numbers of Celtic-speaking people from Europe, with a Late Hallstatt culture, had settled in South Britain, to be followed by smaller bands of La Tène warriors in the third century BC; but the weight of the evidence suggests that the main inroads of Celtic folk into Scotland took place in the last two centuries BC. The form of the migration appears to have been that of refugee, aristocratic warrior groups, with bands of retainers, who superimposed themselves on a native, basically Bronze Age population of considerable antiquity. They brought with them long experience of frontier warfare and military organisation; European skills in the building of large, timber-laced hill forts; a new tradition in metal-work; chariots and a great love of the horse (cf the chariot graves of East Yorkshire); and above all a military eye for country and terrain utilisation. The great forts they built are sited in locations of strategic and commercial potential for exploiting the regional resources of the land and the main avenues of communication.

Their regional impact again demonstrates the contrasting theatres of action in Scotland. Two indices of the pattern of their superimposition on the native population are the distributions of vitrified forts and brochs.[12] Even with the reservation that the former may have been constructed over a much longer span of time than once surmised, and leaving to one side the debate on the manner of their vitrification, the distribution of the vitrified forts bears all the marks of successive military occupations of strategic locations. Clusters pick out those nuclear areas already mentioned in relation to the Picts – namely the Perth–Abernethy area, the Don-Urie area and the Inverness area – with alignments along Strathmore, in Galloway, in Ayr, in the Lothians, and along the Great Glen, and at strategic points commanding the west-coast inlets, particularly the approaches to the Clyde.

In contrast, the brochs[13] are almost exclusively found in the North-west beyond the Great Glen, with remarkable concentrations in Caithness, where the Caithness flagstone afforded excellent building material, and in Skye and other western seaboard areas. Originating in the first century BC, possibly as a structural development from earlier small circular forts or small promontory forts in Skye and the Northern Isles, the building tradition continued until the fourth century AD when it was superseded by wheel-house construction. The tradition had certainly disappeared well before Norse settlers occupied the same terrains and possibly before the Caithness area was drawn into the Pictish Kingdom, but at its height reflects both the available material and the stone craftmanship of the people of the far North and West. That the brochs were family defensive structures capable of withstanding raids rather than long sieges is indicated by their size and in some areas their proximity to each other, but the political circumstances that stimulated their construction remain in doubt. The siting of many of them suggests that they were a defensive reaction to sea-raiders – possibly slave raiders – and indeed the economy and outlook of the broch-dwellers as reflected in the material culture associated with the structures is clearly sea-orientated. They were peasant-fishermen, a maritime folk with basically a Bronze Age culture, containing antique elements born of the harshness of their environment, with a top-dressing of Celtic aristocracy. Their relationships with the fort builders to the south-east have been variously interpreted on the assumption that they were contemporary. Hamilton,[14] excavator of the well-known broch and wheel-house complex at Jarlshof in the Shetlands, suggests that there was considerable hostility between the two communities, with raids in both directions and the establishment of a military frontier zone between the two territories. Many of the forts sited in this area may be regarded as strong points in such a system built along the edge of the broch province. Such a military interpretation is indeed reasonable in view of

the later military history of the area under the Norse, but it is clear that
the mutual exclusiveness of the two distributions is also indicative of a
deep-seated cultural and environmental divide in this area between
maritime and land-based communities. The Broch men, the wheel-
house men, the Dalriadic Scots, the Norse, the Norse–Gaels of
Galloway, all participate in a western 'Atlantic' cultural evolutionary
pattern, distinct in many ways from the eastern 'North Sea' terrains
with which we have chiefly been concerned. Druim Alban then appears
to have constituted not only a physical divide but an important cultural
divide throughout much of the later prehistoric period. From time to
time it was breached, only to reassert its influence in later periods. Its
significance is recognised in various regional models (Fig 4.4).

For example, a scheme that includes four provinces (Fig. 4.4B) – A
(Atlantic), SC (Solway–Clyde), TF (Tyne–Forth) and NE (North-
east) – divided into subsidiary 'regions' (31–52) in continuation of a
regional scheme (1–30) suggested by C. F. C. Hawkes for Southern
Britain,[15] was put forward by Feachem.[16] The regions of the *Atlantic
Province* comprise: 45, Shetland; 46, Orkney; 47, Caithness; 48,
Strathnaver; 49, Cape Wrath/Wester Ross; 50, Skye/West Inverness-
shire; 51, Argyll–Bute; 52, Outer Hebrides. The regions of the
Solway–Clyde Province comprise: 35, Strathclyde; 36, Galloway; 37,
Dumfries. The regions of the *Tyne–Forth Province* comprise: 31,
Northumberland; 32, Lower Tweeddale; 33, Lothian; 34, Upper
Tweeddale/Upper Clydesdale. The regions of he *North-Eastern
Province* comprise: 38, Strathearn; 39, Strathtay; 40, Strathmore; 41,
Strathdon/Strathdee; 42, Strathspey; 43, Buchan; 44, Cromarty/
Moray. The criteria used to suggest regional distinctiveness are the
structural variations and distributions of hill forts, settlements, brochs
and duns, along with associated cultural material and indications of
tribal terrains. Thus Region 33 (Lothian) is seen as part of the territory
of the Votadini people, centering on the great oppidum on Traprain
Law, but with other impressive forts such as that on Salisbury Crags,
Edinburgh, and numerous homestead settlements forming part of the
regional complex. Similarly Region 34 is regarded as the territory of the
Selgovae tribe, with its ultimate centre at the oppidum of Eildon Hill
North, a 40-acre site with at least 300 huts. Region 36 is prehistoric
Galloway, the territory of the Novantae tribe, with the hill fort of Moyle
and numerous small promontory forts. Within the later Pictish
terrains, for example, Region 41 is characterised by almost circular,
multiple stone-walled structures of a distinctive local type (eg Barmkyn
of North Keig, and the interior of Barmekin of Echt) and the great
'vitrified' fort of Dunideer, but it will be noticed that Buchan (43) is

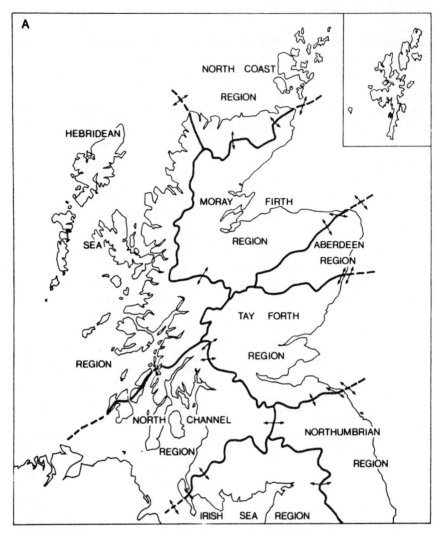

Fig 4.4 Alternative schemes of prehistoric provinces and regions

regarded as a separate region traversed by the Ythan–Deveron corridor.

Although it may be doubted whether structural features alone can be regarded as the definitive criterion for regional differentiation, there is little doubt that in their linkages with other cultural and environmental characteristics they do provide an archaeological insight into those geographical 'theatres of action' mentioned above. The reality of an Atlantic province is clearly established for the Iron Age, and the importance of the Great Divide of Druim Alban is confirmed – although it should be noticed that Feachem turns the northern terminus of the main boundary eastward from the watershed to the Dornoch Firth,

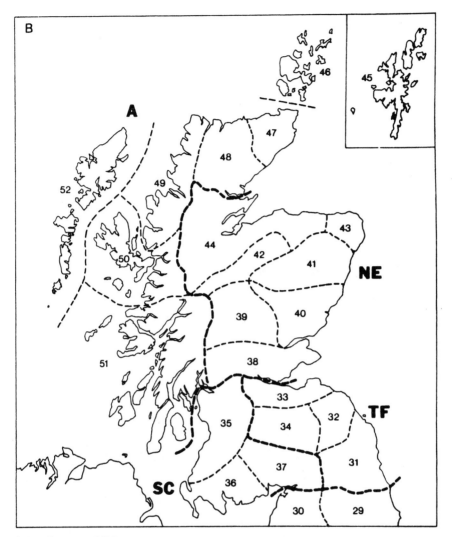

(after Feachem 1961)

presumably to take account of the broch distributions, and in the South regards the Clyde boundary as sufficiently discriminatory to create a Clyde–Solway province. The Dornoch boundary also accords with the later penetration of the Norse, and as MacKie[17] indicates in his discussion on the brochs and the Hebridean Iron Age, the northern areas do show distinctive sub-cultural features many of which can be associated with the pre-Broch period. The boundary tri-junction near Loch Lomond is also noteworthy in view of the discussion above of the Dalriadic–Strathclyde–Pictish convergence, as is the distinctive relationship of Regions 36 and 37, though one would question the alignment of a major boundary between Regions 37 and 30, in view of the role of the Solway in relation to the Irish sea–cultural region.

It is instructive to compare Feachem's system with that proposed by Kirk[18] in 1957 (Fig 4.4A) with reference to the spatial behaviour of the first agricultural colonists of Scotland. The regional framework suggested took into account cultural differentiations but was also an attempt to delineate environmental theatres of action within which changing techniques of land-use introduced by farming populations or diffusion of agricultural ideas appeared to have occurred. Emphasis was placed on the regional contexts of evolving man-land relationships in different natural settings; corridors of cultural contact; and on the major settlement episodes of agricultural colonisation.

Neolithic Agricultural Colonisation

Until recently it has been generally accepted that the major peopling of the eastern terrains of Scotland took place in the period c1900–1700BC, with the main archaeological indicator of this colonisation being the single inhumation burial in a stone cist usually accompanied by one or more pottery Beakers. As a result of recent excavations and pollen analysis of vegetational remains, however, this view may have to be revised in favour of a more gradual peopling of these terrains following the arrival of the first Neolithic, pioneer farming groups c4000BC. Nevertheless, there is little doubt that the skeletal remains of the short stone cists represent a substantial population of farmers with links across the North Sea to Holland and adjacent areas of the European mainland. On present evidence it was they who first occupied in any substantial way the prime agricultural tracts of the eastern lowlands, and provided henceforth the basic population of those terrains. The distribution of Beakers (Fig 4.5), with coastal clusters in the Inner Moray Firth, Aberdeen, the Tay and North Berwick areas, and diffusion patterns into the interior, suggests the operation of four theatres of action – namely the *Moray Firth Region*, the *Aberdeen Region* (whose identity appears to be further confirmed by the distribution of carved stone balls), the *Tay–Forth Region* and the *Northumbrian Region* – together comprising what may be called 'Continental' Scotland, but which could alternatively be regarded as North Sea Scotland.[19]

In contrast, the western seaboard areas were characterised during the period of primary agricultural colonisation by the presence of collective tombs[20] in a variety of architectural styles within a broad Megalithic tradition (Fig 4.5), originating in the fourth millennium BC but still current when the Beaker folk occupied the eastern coastlands.

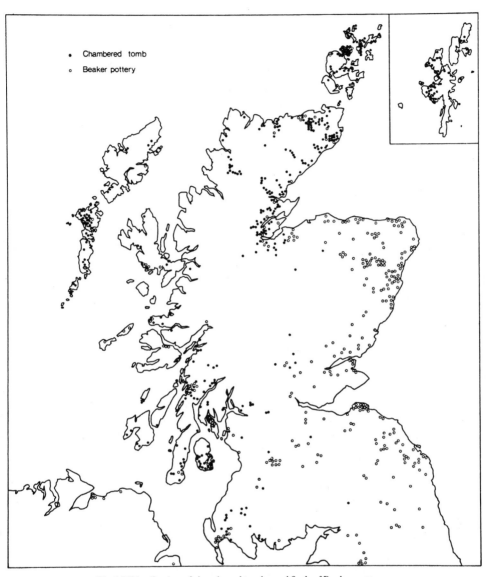

Fig 4.5 Distribution of chambered tombs and finds of Beaker pottery

In population origins, climate, vegetation, sea conditions and the limited extent of agricultural land this was another world – an Atlantic world, in which the diffusion of ideas and men depended on sea communication. It would appear, therefore, that the most satisfactory regionalism to express the cultural/behavioural systems of this world, and the distinctive traditions that can be recognised in its several areas, is one based on the recognition of the following sea regions: a *North Coast Region*, including the Orkneys and Shetlands with their distinctive series of megalithic tombs and stone artifacts of a treeless environment, in which elements of a circum-polar stone age lived on in the presence of Neolithic settlements such as Skara Brae; a *Hebridean Sea Region*, centering on the Minch and the Isle of Skye, with its hybrid series of passage graves; a *North Channel Region* embracing Ulster, Kintyre and the approaches to the Clyde, characterised by the Clyde series of chambered tombs and Lyles Hill ware; and an *Irish Sea Region*, through which some of the architectural ideas were diffused from the Severn–Cotswold area of chambered, long barrows, and in which the Galloway seaboard again reflects the convergence of Irish and Northumbrian and sea-borne traditions.

As in later periods, Atlantic and North Sea Scotland remained culturally separate for long intervals and the zones of contact were few. It should be noted, however, that from the earliest periods the Great Glen appears to have operated as an important corridor of communication between west and east. The presence of Lyles Hill ware in Moray and Aberdeen and the occurrence there of porcellanite stone axes from the axe factories of Tievebulliagh and Rathlin Island in Antrim are evidence of Ulster and west coast connections, as may be also the remarkable series of Clava cairns and Recumbent stone circles. The function of the Great Glen later as a trade route for Irish bronzes, including halberds and daggers, to north-east Scotland and the European mainland also testifies to this important link between the Atlantic and the North Sea. The Caledonian Canal of modern times is merely a recent expression of an ancient form of spatial behaviour.

Overview of Prehistoric Regional Development

This ranging backward in time from the firmer regionalism of the proto-historic period into the more dimly perceived regionalism of the prehistoric millennia suggests a remarkable continuity in the regional framework of human behaviour in Scotland. Technological change, the development of new tools in stone, bronze or iron, the infusion of new ideas, or the coming of new people, may alter behavioural patterns from time to time and transform social structures, language, architecture and settlement forms, the quality of life, and the range and quantity of material possessions; but at certain scales of human adaptation to the environment, regional constraints and potentialities appear to exert themselves repetitively.

In part this may be a reflection of the limited mobility of prehistoric communities in Scotland. Faced with the obstacles of the great forests that then covered the land, and the swamps and bogs and extensive mountain barriers, movement by water would appear to have been preferred. Even if the evidence for a definitive account of the evolution of water transport in prehistoric Scotland is never discovered, the dominantly coastward orientation of much early settlement, particularly on the Atlantic seaboard and along the great firths of the east coast, indicates coastal mobility and maritime knowledge from the earliest times. From the first strandloopers of mesolithic times, who left their shell-middens and flint assemblages on raised beaches and river terraces,[21] to the boat people of the Western and Northern Isles, to the fishers and fowlers of the lowland estuaries, to the Roman and Norse raiders and traders, to the rise of ports on the east coast to service North Sea and Baltic trade, and ultimately the growth of Glasgow as gateway to the Atlantic, the sea has played a powerful, continuous role in the life of Scotland. The peninsularity of the country can never be ignored as a factor in its history, and for much of its early history the land regions may be regarded as landward expressions of wider sea regions.

Within each of the land regions it is possible to recognise a primary zone of coastal settlement with at first little impact on the local ecology and landscape, but as population pressure built up in the primary terrains successive colonisation movements proceeded inland into the forests.[22] From about 3000BC early forest clearance by farming communities coincided with a climatic change toward more continental conditions, characterised by long, warm summers and hard winters. The better soil areas, usually in the hill-foot zones, were cleared for cultivation, and in a predominantly mixed economy livestock, ranging in the uplands in the summer and lowlands in the winter, were powerful agents of vegetational modification. Undoubtedly seasonal transhumance, from lower to upper river valleys, from lowland to upland pastures, and from island to island in the west, played an important part in opening up the country and extending the pioneer fringe by a series of leap-frogging movements whereby the temporary summer settlements of one century became the permanent settlements of the next.

But for much of the prehistoric period the population was small,[23] even with the possibility of immigrant surges in the centuries after c2500BC, and, apart from fire and the browsing of livestock, the tools for forest clearance were limited. Iron axes, for example, were not widely available until the arrival of substantial groups of iron-using Celtic colonists in the last centuries BC. So for some three thousand years progress was slow and inroads into the great forests were spatially discrete. Where human impact was concentrated by the limited availability of habitable terrains, such as along the north-west seaboard, within narrow straths and glens, or around the rims of confined basins on the margin of the Grampian Highlands in Aberdeenshire, palynological evidence suggests that forest clearance was early and resultant ecological change profound. Elsewhere effort was more dispersed and intermittent, with large tracts of forest constituting frontier zones between settled areas. With the accelerated growth of peat in the uplands, in part possibly man-induced but associated with a climatic deterioration towards more maritime, Atlantic conditions from early in the first millennium BC, the dividing effect of these highland areas became more pronounced. In such conditions ill-drained lowland areas reverted to swamp and peat bogs, sometimes at the expense of earlier farmland, (eg Achnacree), and also constituted barrier zones. Considerable areas of the Hebridean region, denuded of its earlier pine and birch forest, became virtually uninhabitable. It is thus not surprising that when the Roman armies invaded Scotland in the early centuries AD they located their northernmost frontier in the Clyde–Forth lowlands and that refugees fleeing in front of their advance sought refuge in the brochs of the North-west, beyond the rain-sodden peat bogs of the Highlands. The land between the Roman walls was given an economic stimulus by the markets of the Roman garrisons – particularly for livestock, timber and probably corn – and forest clearance accelerated, but the line of the Antonine Wall[24] would never have been chosen as an outer boundary, notwithstanding the shortness of the line, if the central lowlands of Scotland had been the economic and political core it was to become centuries later. At that time it clearly had barrier characteristics.

Indeed, each of the suggested land regions appears to have experienced individual sequences of events, within regional frontiers whose efficacy varied from time to time, but whose presence provided outer peripheries to the activities of central cores or nuclei of settlement. By placing too much emphasis on the establishment of overall 'Scottish' chronologies of ecological and cultural change, regional diversities are frequently overlooked. In palaeoecological studies, for example, there has been a tendency to apply a stratigraphic sequence of eco-climatic zones, based on pollen analysis of a few, widely separate sites, to the entire country, despite the knowledge that local and regional climates and bio-potentials of various parts of the country today differ markedly. General climatic changes of temperature, precipitation, wind speed and direction, cloud cover and sunshine incidence, snow-cover and frost frequency, length of growing season and other such factors can find very different regional expressions between west and east, between south and north (where the day-length in the growing season becomes an important factor), between highland and lowland, and between coast and interior. In some areas even small climatic changes will result in the transgression of crucial ecological thresholds, whereas in other situations major climatic changes will produce only minor ecological results. The use of absolute methods of dating, such as C^{14}, is beginning to allow the establishment of isochronous zones on a regional basis against which ecological changes can be measured, rather than assuming that ecological sequences based on traditional pollen zones are universally synchronous. Similarly one cannot assume that forest clearance sequences brought about by human agencies are synchronous throughout Scotland – indeed it would be surprising if they were. It is now necessary to use a combination of dating techniques to establish the sequences within the specific geographical contexts of each region before comparative regional analysis can indicate more general synchronisations.

Conclusion

Much of the history of Scotland has been the history of those several provinces which were ultimately brought together to provide the territorial basis for a modern state. This chapter has attempted to demonstrate the antiquity of those provinces, insofar as they can be construed as regions or theatres of action for human communities from the earliest phases of human colonisation. Although participating in general processes of cultural and ecological change, each region generated its own problems and processes as a consequence of differing environmental opportunities and constraints and differing rates of cultural development and adaptation. In each region it is possible to identify core areas, often established in the process of primary agricultural settlement, and peripheral areas, which constituted zones of secondary colonisation and frontier buffer zones with other communities. The regional framework established in this manner proved to be remarkably durable, in spite of external pressures and influences. Individual cultural traits might change, and the power of specific cores wax and wane, but the whole structure has considerable geographical momentum. Indeed almost a thousand years of statehood, increased mobility and economic development, demographic changes, and the transformation of the Central Lowlands from frontier zone to economic and political core have not entirely obliterated the ancient regional structure, either in reality or perception.

Notes to this chapter are on pages 305–7.

5

Patterns of Rural Settlement from Medieval Times to 1700

James R. Coull

FROM medieval times to the seventeenth century, Scotland had its own characteristic rural settlement patterns, and there is evidence of considerable change during the period, and of regional variety. Any detailed description and analysis is, however, precluded by the fragmentary and uneven nature of the evidence, though recent research allows at least the sketching of major characteristics and trends with more certainty than was previously possible.

The sources on which any account is based must be primarily documentary; and while such sources as charters of land grant and rent rolls are very useful, they can only be a partial mirror of the society which produced them. They can be supplemented by the maps produced from the time of Timothy Pont (*c*1600) onwards, although it is very rare for lay-outs to be shown with any detail before the eighteenth century. While systematic study of place-names could help elucidate a developing settlement pattern, very little has been done for the post-medieval pattern in Scotland. Similarly, archaeology has proved its great value for all periods from remote pre-history to the Industrial Revolution, but there have been very few excavations in rural Scotland for this period. Hence reconstruction has to be based primarily on a careful use of surviving documents, allied to a knowledge of the land itself. Settlement in Scotland was predominantly rural throughout the period, and was determined by the fact that the lives of the great majority were dominated by the need to provide their own subsistence. In effect, this meant that most people lived in the group settlements called ferm-touns, and farmed the land to raise both crops and stock. While ferm-touns could vary in size, it has generally been claimed that they seldom had more than about a dozen households, in contrast to the bigger villages frequent in much of England and in many parts of Europe. In Scotland, the settlement pattern was varied too by occasional kirktons (the main community foci), the miltons (where the essential work of grinding grain was done), and more rarely (before the Reformation) by monasteries and granges. We can assume that individual farms belonging to more substantial men were never lacking in the Scottish feudal system, and the best surviving marks of these are the many 'mains' farms throughout Lowland Scotland. These were generally the home farms of estates. Associated with estates is another distinctive element of the settlement pattern – the castles and mansions of the lairds who, before the modern age, were very much the leaders of society and the people who made the decisions about land use and the deployment of resources.

The above summary of the pattern of rural settlement is not intended to imply that the period was static. Short-cycle changes included the relatively frequent rebuilding of houses; this was necessary because much of the building material was turf and wattle, materials which might well not survive more than a single generation. On a longer time perspective, there was a general (if fluctuating) increase in population numbers, and in Scotland this was characteristically accompanied by a splitting and multiplication of ferm-touns, rather than a continued build-up in size of existing ones. There is also some indication that land use intensified as a result of the increasing population and, later, commercial incentives. While the dominant general trend must have been an increase of settlement over time, one also finds evidence of retreat or desertion connected with famine, disease and war, as well as examples of retreat from the upper margins of cultivation in response to climatic fluctuations. It is now increasingly clear that in the seventeeth century life was becoming more secure and that commercial production was playing an expanding role; associated with this were changes in the character, lay-out and function of settlements which presaged the industrial age. Recent work has shown that, at least in south-east Scotland, by the late seventeenth century there was a considerable range in the size of rural settlements, with substantial villages in existence.[1]

Increase and Spread of Settlement from the Medieval Period

The evolution and spread of settlement in Scotland from the medieval period must have continued a process which we can trace to the Dark Ages by means of place-names; and at least in Lowland Scotland, the pace is likely to have accelerated during the more stable early medieval period. While the allocation of many place-names to particular periods is hazardous in Scotland, there can be no doubt that some examples of the basic elements – such as 'ton' in Lowland

Scotland and the Gaelic 'baile' in the Highlands (both usually indicating group farms) – indicate new settlements of the medieval period or even later. We should note here that the number of settlements and the size of population in medieval times (and indeed for centuries thereafter) have previously been under-estimated, due to the incompleteness of the record. This is particularly the case for Highland Scotland.

Some regional differences in settlement characteristics existed as early as the medieval period. Barrow[2] has shown that in south-east Scotland, where the emphasis was on arable farming, villages were a main category of settlement. (North of the Forth, where at this time there was probably more emphasis on pastoralism, there is little evidence of nucleated settlement.) The South-east in fact showed an Anglian influence, the village often having parish status, with the church frequently in the village, near the lord's hall. The linking of such villages with outlying settlements suggests something of the structure of the multiple estate found in Southern Britain in the Dark Ages and after. While the landholding pattern of the peasantry is unrecorded, we know that that of each of the lesser gentry was characteristically in scattered blocks, and the occurrence of the word 'rig' in a Latin form 'reia' reveals the technique of ridge ploughing, which was necessary for land drainage before the time of improved farming. The situation north of the Forth is less clear, but the prevalence of 'davoch' (as opposed to the 'oxgang'), as the main unit of land mensuration, shows elements of an older Celtic structure. If there was less grouping around a village, and the church tended to stand separate, there was almost certainly some other kind of linking of settlements into functioning farming communities.

While it would be unrealistic to attempt any complete account of rural settlement for medieval times, it is possible to show that there was a considerable proliferation of settlements from the medieval period onwards. Dodgshon[3] has demonstrated the occurrence of the splitting of townships from as early as the twelfth century, and the signs are that this was a common expedient as population grew. The modern map of Scotland has frequent indications of this, with numerous cases of multiple settlements, designated by such terms as 'Upper' and 'Nether', 'Easter' and 'Wester' etc appended to the same root name. Scotland here contrasts with much of England and continental Europe, where the main trend was for the growth of one settlement, despite increasing complexity in landholding and increasing distances between scattered parcels of land. (Land parcels tended to become more sub-divided with increasing population.) In much of the Continent, the

Page 119 (*above*) Broch of Gurness in Orkney; example of the only type of architecture invented in Scotland; built around the years BC/AD. Impressive use of sandstone slabs for internal support, compartmentation and furniture; (*below*) Site of Balbridie, near Banchory in the Dee Valley, north-east Scotland. It is the site of a Neolithic timber hall (*c*5500BC), the first substantial timber building of the European style to be found in Scotland. Represents the home of the first colonies of European settlers in this part of Scotland

Page 120 *(above)* Urquhart Castle on a sandstone promontory in Loch Ness, a Norman motte-and-bailey structure added to in later centuries; constantly pillaged by clan warfare during the fifteenth and sixteenth centuries. A common place to sight the famous monster! *(below)* Crathes Castle and gardens, Dee valley, north-east Scotland; an example of a sixteenth-century tower-house now owned by the National Trust for Scotland. Built by Burnett of Leys, one of the earliest landowners in Deeside, granted lands by Robert the Bruce in 1323. The castle was continuously in use by the Burnett family until recently taken over by the National Trust

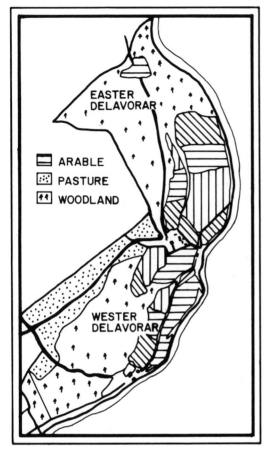

Fig 5.1 Example of a township splitting with expansion: Easter and Wester Delavorarar (Banffshire), 1773. Source: Dodgshon, R. A. 'Medieval Settlement and Colonisation', in Parry, M. L. and Slater, T. R. (Eds.): *The Making of the Scottish Countryside* (1980) Croom Helm, London

additional security of bigger settlements appears often to have countered any tendency to split; but although Scotland's history was certainly not trouble-free, the organisational advantage of smaller settlements appears to have been a prevailing factor.

It appears that township splitting in Scotland could occur both when a toun was shared between different proprietors and when it belonged to a single estate. Whittington[4] has formulated a complete sequence of development within the land of a township for several Perthshire examples. This has been derived by what might be called an imaginative 'back-projection' method rather than from definite estate evidence, but as well as showing the likely sequence of events, it also shows how different classes were catered for, including those with little or no land.

While the dominant trend from medieval times is clearly that of multiplication and spread of settlement, famine, disease and war, as has been mentioned, could mean that settlements had their populations reduced or indeed became deserted. The not infrequent occurrence of this in the seventeenth century, when food supplies were tending to become more secure, suggests that it can only have been more common earlier. The maps of Timothy Pont from *c*1600 show, in all parts of the country, settlements that can no longer be identified,[5] and later maps often illustrate the same thing. While the issue is complicated by the occasional re-naming of settlements, there are also those which have not survived.

A particular case of the retreat of settlement has been studied by Parry in the area around the Lammermuir Hills in the South-east.[6] Here there is evidence that cultivation and settlement retreated downslope during the 'Little Ice Age', after the secondary climatic optimum of the early medieval period. Thousands of acres of previously tilled land were abandoned; fifteen settlements are on record as having been deserted by 1600, and a further twelve subsequently. This is no doubt a specially prominent example, but regression at the hill edge during this period almost certainly occurred in other parts of the country. Another example of an area of former cultivation beyond the boundary of later cultivation is a large area of land above Strathardle in Perthshire.

Field Systems

While a considerable amount has been written on the traditional field-systems of Scotland, till recently these accounts have been based largely on the somewhat biased views of eighteenth and nineteenth century improvers who wished to remove the old systems. However, recent work on sources of the seventeenth century and earlier has given important new perspectives.

In a society living on the land, field systems were intimately related to the settlement pattern.[7] It is apparent that the prevalent infield-outfield system, even if it represented a low intensity of land use by modern comparison, did represent a balanced (and to some extent, flexible) use of land resources by communities at or near subsistence level. (The term 'run-rig' has also been used to denote the old infield-outfield Scottish field-system, but this term has been variously understood and is in fact less clear.)

The essentials of the infield-outfield system may be summarised as follows. The infield was an area close to the settlement and under more or less permanent cultivation. It received most of the available manure. Land in the outfield was cultivated for periods only. On both infield and outfield crops were raised to feed the people, but the system also catered for livestock by grazing them on the surrounding common land or muir, and (while crops were not in the ground) on the outfield and infield as well. The actual workings of the system are best recorded at a late stage, in the accounts of the eighteenth century, at which point the infield usually had little respite from alternate crops of barley and oats, and the outfield was cultivated in sections by folding the stock on them prior to ploughing. The land in both infield and outfield was characteristically divided into strips between the cultivators. Not a few cases have been found of a 'sunwise' division of strips, similar to the Scandinavian 'solskifte':[8] in these cases the strips were allocated to the different members of the ferm-toun in turn, following the path of the sun around the sky.

Earlier attempts to explain the Scottish system on cultural grounds as 'Celtic' can now be rejected. The system has also been plausibly explained as representing an intensification in land use with increasing population. The earlier basis for this theory was generally the idea that these had been a development from shifting to fixed cultivation; in effect, from a situation where only the outfield was cultivated to a point when cultivation on the area nearest the settlement became permanent – hence the infield. While there can be little doubt that intensification of land use occurred, more recent investigations strongly suggest that it took a different form.

The terms 'infield' and 'outfield' are not recorded at all before the fifteenth century, and it is well into the sixteenth before they are at all frequent. The early records, such as they are, could indicate an actively evolving system from the fifteenth century. Careful scrutiny of the evidence has suggested that the infield in fact came *first*. Although intensification was presumably possible to an extent on the infield, it also took place by the extension of cultivation into the common muir, and it was these extensions which were to become the outfield.[9] It has

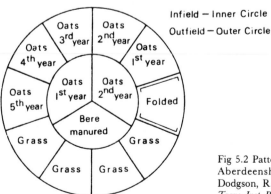

Infield – Inner Circle

Outfield – Outer Circle

Fig 5.2 Pattern of infield-outfield cropping in Aberdeenshire (after J. Wilson). From Dodgson, R. A. 'Infield-outfield in Scotland': *Trans. Inst. Brit. Geog.*, 59 (1973), p.19

also been postulated that intensification was enhanced by folding part of the stock during the summer on areas of infield designated for subsequent cultivation, thus concentrating the manure that would otherwise have gone to the common muir.

The increasing commercial opportunities of the seventeenth century led to intensification within the infield-outfield system, especially in locations where there were market opportunities. Thus on the Dundas estate near Edinburgh it proved possible, by liming the land and introducing legumes into the rotation, both to increase the proportion of infield land and to raise yields.[10] Related changes included the decrease in the joint and multiple tenancies,[11] in favour of single tenancies, often with written leases,[12] and an increase in landless labour. Also there was the decrease in rents in service and kind, in favour of money rents.

Pastoral Farming and Settlement

While there can have been very few settlements devoted entirely to pastoral farming at any time in Scotland, livestock husbandry was always important in a country with so much hill and muir. The relative importance of livestock in the mixed farming systems of Scotland naturally varied and was at its greatest in the hills, but it was also important on the better land on low ground. There is also the probability that the relative importance of cropping rose with the intensification of land use.

In most settlements, draught oxen and sheep must have been the most important livestock, and it is well known that the traditional wealth of the Highland clans was measured in head of cattle rather than extent of land. Horses, pigs, goats and poultry also played a part in stock farming. It was possible for some members towards the lower end of the scale in the ferm-touns to have stock (usually one or two cattle) but no arable land: the term 'grassmen' usually denoted these. In contrast to mainland and Hebridean practice, the grazings in Orkney and Shetland were untaxed; this stemmed from their Norse-derived udal land tenure.[13]

Catering for the needs of the livestock in summer was usually little of a problem, as there was generally adequate grazing available, although from the more closely settled areas on low ground it might be necessary to move some of the stock to areas of muir or hill. Providing for the stock in winter was, however, a problem. By the spring stock were usually in very poor condition, and many beasts died in the winter. Very little hay was made for the stock, even in the Highlands. Cultivated land produced food for the people, but for nearly half the year there was very little growth in the land to provide for the stock. Hence stocking levels were usually set by winter conditions, and there was generally an attempt in ferm-touns to adjust stocking levels to the availability of grazing by a stinting system – the soumings. A 'soum' was, in principle, a cow's grass and members of a toun had a souming allocation for their stock. The arrangement usually had some flexibility, including varied and sometimes intricate systems of equivalence between cattle and other animals;[14] ie one cow was equivalent to around five sheep.

It was also general, at this period before enclosure and improved farming, to keep the stock on the common and on uncultivated sections of the outfield while crops were in the ground, and this must often have involved herding. It was also possible for some privileged stock, like milk cows, to be tethered on small patches of grazing near the homestead. A mark of increasing commercialism in livestock farming is the fact that principal rents in the pastoral areas of the Lowlands had been almost entirely converted to money by the end of the seventeenth century.[15]

Shielings

Shielings played a part in stock husbandry in many hill areas. The essence of the shieling system was the seasonal movement to grazings at a distance from the main settlement, for a period of around two months in summer. The people lived in 'shiels' or huts, and these huts with the surrounding grazings were the shielings. The movement might be made in more than one phase, and generally involved a partial split in the ferm-toun community, as some members and most of the stock moved to the shielings. This allowed the use of seasonally available grazings away from the ferm-toun, and also lessened the danger of stock eating growing crops. The system is often associated with dairying, but could also cater for beef cattle and other stock. At the time when they are best recorded, in the seventeenth and early eighteenth centuries, shielings generally, though not always, involved movement to higher pastures in the hills. In Assynt, for example, much of the movement was to shielings at relatively short distances from the main settlement and at no great difference in altitude.[16]

Patterns of movement could become somewhat complex, owing to various changes and developments in landholding. At the simplest, the members of a toun in the hills would simply use shielings farther up the main valley, or in a side valley; but movements to sites 20 miles away across watersheds were known, for example, in upland Banffshire.[17]

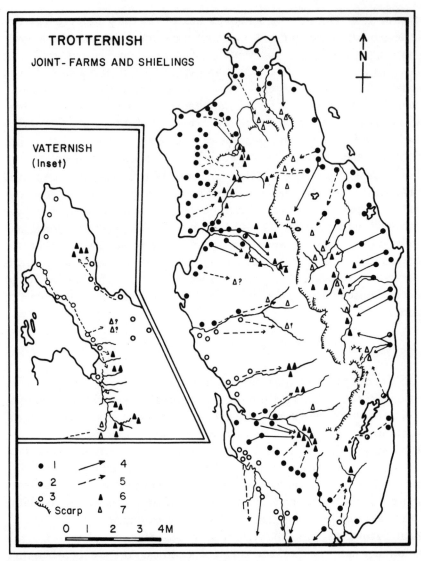

Fig 5.3 Relationships of shielings to parent townships: Trotternish and Vaternish, in MacSween, M. D. 'Transhumance in North Skye', *Scot. Geog. Mag., 75* (1959), p.77

The use of shielings represents an adaptation to environmental conditions. Its origins are lost in prehistory, but it has documentary record from the medieval period onwards. The term 'simmerin', along with place-names with the element 'shiel', indicate its occurrence in southern Scotland, and in the Highland area the Gaelic terms 'airdh' in the west and 'ruidh' (or 'ruigh') in the east show the presence of shielings. Later on, shieling grazings were also used in the commercial raising of beef cattle.[18]

Housing

In the ferm-touns of Scotland throughout this period the houses and other buildings must have been simple and constructed of local materials. In the absence of archaeological evidence, very little is known about peasant housing of the medieval period. In the seventeenth century,[19] estate data show that the typical house was still the cruck-framed long house, and the most valuable part of it was the timbers of the cruck frame. The walls were generally at least partly of turf, the roof thatched, and the fire in the centre of the floor. Although by the seventeenth century cattle were sometimes housed in detached byres, it was still known for them to have one end of the main building; and depending mainly on the prosperity of the householder, the building could be up to 20m long or more. The long-house style did of course survive longer in the islands, the best known example being the Hebridean 'black house', and here the availability of stone was partly responsible for a transition to stone building up to roof level.

The leaders of rural society were housed in a grander and more permanent fashion, as is shown by the many castles scattered throughout the Lowlands, but more rarely found in the more sparsely populated and poorer Highlands. The earliest and simplest castles consisted of square stone towers, but these were frequently elaborated into the L- and Z-plan types by the addition of projecting wings. By the seventeenth century the lessening need for defence, together with accelerating economic development, led to the construction of more comfortable and commodious housing for the gentry. This was particularly the case after 1660, with such examples as Drumlanrig Castle (Dumfries-shire) built for the Duke of Queensberry and Kinross House built for Sir William Bruce.[20]

Conclusion

In all, the settlement patterns in Scotland between the medieval period and the seventeenth century show a slow evolution and expansion, and this was accelerating by the end of the period, as feudal organisation retreated before the rise of capitalism and as subsistence gave way to commercial production. Variations in the settlement pattern were associated with class differences, and also with regional environmental contrasts – especially that between lowland and highland.

Notes to this chapter are on pages 307–8.

6

Patterns of Rural Settlement, 1700–1850

J. B. Caird

THE rural landscape of Scotland today bears little relationship to the landscape and patterns of rural settlement of 1700, although a small number of existing mansion houses and policies or estate grounds can be traced back to the seventeenth century. Before 1700 the granting of written leases, payment of rents in money, and the application of lime had begun, but only on selected estates. The 'Seven Ill Years' of the 1690s, the political and economic uncertainties of the Union of Parliaments before and after 1707, and the 1715 and 1719 Risings all delayed further advances being built on the basis for development laid in the late seventeenth century. Progress was slow until the 1745 Rebellion ended, but Adams[1] identifies two signs of change in the 1720s – the foundation of the Honourable Society of Improvers in the Knowledge of Agriculture in 1723, and the establishment of the Board of Trustees for Fisheries and Manufactures in Scotland in 1727. From the 1720s to the middle of the nineteenth century the foundations of the present rural landscape and settlement patterns were laid. During this period massive changes in the numbers, distribution and balance of population within Scotland started to occur. They continued up to the middle of the present century.

In 1707 Scotland's population was about 1,048,000 but its regional distribution is unknown. Table 6.1, however, shows that in 1755 just over half of the population was in Northern Scotland; a century later more than half was in the Mid-Lowlands and only a third in Northern Scotland. Some 65 per cent of the population in the 1790s was rural, living in settlements with a population of less than one thousand; by 1861, only 42 per cent were located in rural areas.

By 1850 the basic contemporary division of the country into a predominantly urban south and east and a predominantly rural north and west had evolved. This radical redistribution of population had taken place as a result of comprehensive estate reorganisation, the

Table 6.1

The changing distribution of population in Scotland 1755–1851

	Northern Scotland		Central Scotland		Southern Scotland		Scotland	
	'000	%	'000	%	'000	%	'000	%
1755	647	51	469	38	149	11	1,265	100
1801	741	46	682	42	185	12	1,608	100
1851	1,022	35	1,594	55	273	10	2,889	100

Note Central Scotland is defined as the Counties of Ayr, Clackmannan, Dumbarton, Fife, Lanark, East, Mid and West Lothian, Renfrew, Stirling and the City of Dundee. Counties to the north and west, and to the south and east respectively, are included in the Northern and Southern groupings

Source 1755, Webster's Enumeration; 1801–1851, Census of Scotland

implementation of new techniques in agriculture, and a new, power-based technology. The latter, first, harnessed water-power for manufacturing purposes, drawing a population displaced by the changes in agriculture to the rural water sides, and second, in the nineteenth century, adopted steam power, so that the population concentrated on the coalfields and in the towns and cities of the Mid-Lowlands.

Agricultural Improvements and Estate Reorganisation in Lowland Scotland

Despite the scattered improvements achieved before 1700, the rural landscape was dominated by unenclosed patches of infield and outfield with hamlet clusters of fermtoun, cottartoun, milltoun and kirktoun. The Military Survey of mainland Scotland – better known as Roy's map – constructed between 1747 and 1754 by William Roy, gives a clear impression of the landscape in the middle of the eighteenth century.[2] Roy described it as rather 'a magnificent military sketch than a very accurate map of the country' but the major elements of the landscape are clearly depicted. The map shows the bulk of the cultivated land in rigs but does not distinguish infield and outfield. Meadowland and rough grazing, from which fuel in the form of scrub woodland and peats were procured, are also shown and the settlement clusters, mainly of thatched, single-storey cottages are clearly marked. Contemporary estate plans[3] at much larger scales confirm the general lay-out of the landscape. But, in addition to these traditional elements, Roy also depicted enclosed fields and parks, usually round the estate houses but also on farms of substantial tenants where fields had been enclosed and farmhouses and steadings built. Blocks of woodland plantations are also shown. O'Dell's maps of mainland Scotland, derived from the Military Survey, show farmed land, enclosed farmland, woodlands and plantations and make it clear that by 1750 only a small fraction of rural Scotland had been subjected to the improvers' attentions.[4]

The Improvers

The men who changed the landscape and settlement pattern of the countryside were the great landowners, lairds and 'bonnet lairds' (proprietors of small estates) who virtually controlled the economic life of Scotland before the Industrial Revolution. Timperley[5] has shown that the aristocratic landowners controlled just over half of the total agrarian wealth of the country in the 1770s, the lairds some two-fifths, and the bonnet lairds, the most numerous group but with the smallest properties, the remaining 5 per cent. The great landowners were well represented – by dukes, marquises and earls – in the membership of the Society of Improvers. Judges of the Court of Session were also represented and Edinburgh lawyers were another influential group, accounting for 29 per cent of the membership – they not only transacted legal business but also acted as estate commissioners, looking after financial affairs.[6]

The landowning classes could procure information from agricultural treatises, but they also passed it on through personal contacts. They were a relatively small and tightly knit social group and the new ideas of land management were rapidly diffused within their circle. Hall of Dunglass, writing to the Earl of Marchmont in about 1737, stated that he had sent 'three of my most knowing tenants to Ormistoun, where they have learned more of labouring and improving their grounds in two days than they have doon all ther life. I have sent for a plewgh that two horse draws as easile as four ane ordinary plewgh.' Describing Ormistoun village to the Earl, he further commented: 'I have sent for a double of his tacks [leases] and feus.'[7] The Board of Management of the Annexed Estates, which was established in 1752 to administer estates forfeited to the Crown after the end of the rebellion of 1745–6, and on which twenty of the great landlords served as Commissioners, was also significant in fostering change. The terms of Lt-Col David Watson's *Instructions to Surveyors to be employed in Surveying on the Forfeited Estates* were to be used widely in the process of improving estates throughout Scotland.[8]

The actual reshaping of the landscape was carried out by land surveyors who surveyed and measured the existing estates and drew up plans of proposed improvements. They designed the new lay-outs and, acting as agricultural consultants, assessed the value and potential of land, fixed rents, and advised on rotations and the planting of trees and hedges. Some of them were originally schoolmasters, skilled in mathematics, others nurserymen, practising farmers and architects. These land surveyors produced some 50,000 plans in the course of a century of agricultural and landscape improvement. Peter May, who was one of the most successful of the profession and whose career spanned the years 1752–89, was appointed to survey the annexed Lovat Estate in 1755, and continued to undertake similar public and private commissions till he became factor on the Earl of Findlater's Morayshire estates and later factor to the Earl of Bute.[9] May and his fellow land surveyors may be said to have created the detail of the contemporary landscape.

The chamberlains and factors of the estates superintended the execution of the surveyors' plans. An advertisement of 1770 described their work:[10]

His business will be [amongst other things] to buy and sell cattle, to pay and oversee workmen, to receive and pay money in general and to keep regular Accounts, Books and Journals; to contrive and line out fences, Plantations and Pleasure grounds; to agree for the excavation thereof, and to calculate and measure the contents and value of most kinds of work. In short, he must be able to superintend the works of one who has a great farm, is a great grazier, incloser, planter and builder.

The first generation of improvers in the period from the 1720s to the 1740s were landowners and lairds who possessed sufficient capital to carry out the development of their estates. They took a detailed interest in all aspects of development, and though many of them held offices of State and were not permanent residents on their lands, their letters to factors and other employees reveal their deep involvement. John Cockburn of Ormistoun in East Lothian, a Lord of the Admiralty, wrote regularly to Charles Bell, his gardener, giving information and instructions:[11]

I gave J Dods [his overseer] orders about the Cattle and the management of the grass for them so as upon no account any kind shall go into the Pigeon Field or the two east of it till I order it . . . Inclosed I send a list of trees for the Wood this year. Mr Hepburn said he knew of Oaks: let 1200 of them be got.

Cockburn also founded an agricultural discussion group at Ormistoun in 1736 to diffuse the new agricultural methods. These early improvers were often 'book farmers' rather than practical men and their enthusiasm sometimes outran their purses; financial difficulties forced Cockburn and others to sell their estates. The second phase from the 1750s to 1770 saw more business-like dealings between estate owners, land surveyors, factors and tenants. By 1760, the large capitalist tenant had emerged and the tenantry did most of the improving.

The Improvement Process

The structural basis of the improvements was the abolition of run-rig. Some estates had lands intermixed with other estates in proprietory run-rig as on the Haugh of Aberfeldy (Fig 6.1), where Sir Robert Menzies was the principal landowner but the Laird of Moness owned eleven very scattered plots within the Haugh. Fig 6.1 also shows that Sir Robert Menzies' land was divided among six farms in scattered plots, the farm of Middle Straid consisting of eight plots, although such a complex division of land is not at all typical. Consolidation of intermixed properties was usually by agreement but some disputed cases went to the Courts. Commonties – areas of grazings shared by several proprietors – were also divided.[12] Abolition of tenant run-rig presented no difficulty: farm leases on an estate about to be improved were renewed on a year-to-year basis till all the longer leases ended and the estate could be reorganised in a series of consolidated farms.

Enclosures

After the land surveyor had mapped out the new commercial farm units, enclosure took place. The earlier enclosures were round the mansion houses and on the 'Mains' or home farms, with stone dykes or hedge and ditch surrounding the farm and providing internal field boundaries. The size of the fields varied according to the type of husbandry envisaged: they were arranged to suit the planned rotations and pasturing of stock. Fields on clay soils tended to be smaller than on lighter soils, and rectangular fields were generally favoured for convenience of ploughing and because they could be subdivided by temporary fences to facilitate the folding of livestock on turnips. If a six-course rotation was envisaged, six (or multiples of six) fields were created.

Fig 6.1 (*opposite*) Proprietary runrig on the Haugh of Aberfeldy in 1763 showing a fragmented part of two estates belonging to Sir Robert Menzies and the Laird of Moness. The farms are also fragmented. Plan by A. Winter, by courtesy of the former Town Clerk of Aberfeldy, redrawn by Carolyn Bain

A Plan of the Haugh of Aberfeldie etc. as Kavel'd in Property
Between
Sir Robert Menzies and the Laird of Moness

A. Winter fecit 1763

D .782

1.90
GRASS Dundaie

DUNDAIE

Moor

Middle Straid 4.885

Middle Straid

Wester Straid .520

Moness (2)

GRASS D .902

Dundaie 1.127

Dundaie 2.515

2.066

Dundaie

Dundaie .925

W.S. 426

Middle Straid 2.207

Wester Straid 2.830

W.S.

MIDDLE STRAID

WEST. STRAID

Moness (3)

Moness (4)

Dundaie 2.025

Park Dyke of Moness

Wester Straid 2.150

W.S. 1.178

SIR ROBERT MENZIES

MONESS ESTATE

Waddes Road

GRASS W.S. 2.150

Middle Straid 1.042

W.S. .668

Dundaie 2.50

Moness (5)

Middle Straid 3 1.569

W.S. 0.375

GRASS D .450

Moness (6)

W. Straid 1.75

Moness (7)

Croft-dow 1.329

Wester Straid 1.180

Dundaie 1.0

Borlig 1.078

W.S. 0.081

.330 Borlig

Mr. Spalding 1.120

Moness

W.S. .480

Mr. S. 459

B.

B. .500

Dundaie .430

Moness (8)

Croft-dow .900

Moness (9)

Middle Straid

Borlig .75

Middle Straid 2.10

MIDDLE STRAID

MONESS

Dundaie 1.735

Moness 1.735

Moness (12)

Dundaie

Borlig

Middle Straid .637

2.538

3.034

Mr. Spalding

Mr. S.

Middle Straid 1.315

Mr. S. .981

Wester Straid 2.145

TAY RIVER

Moness (10)

Aberfeldie Town lyes here

Mr. Spalding .988

Mr. S. .422

Contents

Mr. Spalding 4.55 yard included

Middle Straid 2.690

Moness (11)

Burn of Aberfeldie

Contents	Corn-land	Grass	Sums of each farm
Dundaie	15.175	3.300	18.475
Wester Straid	13.911	4.629	18.540
Middle Straid	16.763	.950	17.713
Croft-dow	2.229	—	2.229
Borlig	5.752	—	5.752
Mr. Spalding	11.058	—	11.058
Totals	64.888	8.879	73.767

0   100
English Yards

Redrawn from a plan by courtesy
of the former Town Clerk of Aberfeldy.

In the Carse of Gowrie, the reorganisation of estates and reshaping of the landscape started in the earlier period of improvements. Before 1735, when reorganisation started, the farmed land consisted of irregular plots of infield and outfield shared by groups of tenants living in hamlet clusters of 'rudely constructed, straw thatched houses of mud and clay'. According to James Donaldson, factor on the Panmure estate, the land 'was astonishingly unproductive . . . in many places over-run with rushes, disfigured by pools of water, at that time the usual haunt of lapwings'. Yet the agricultural system was advanced – at least on the infield which was manured and cropped in 'four divisions' of wheat, barley, oats, and pease and beans. The outfield was cultivated as long as it produced 3 to 4 bolls per acre, then left in pasture till it recovered its fertility.

Crop Rotation

In 1735, Hays of Leys (east of Errol Village) began to improve his estate and introduced summer fallowing, the sowing of grass seed, and open drains. He also rebuilt the farm houses and steadings. Crauford at Monorgan, near Longforgan, followed his example. By 1794, on the flat lands of the Carse, the six-course rotation consisted of: (i) summer fallow with the land dunged; (ii) wheat; (iii) pease or pease and beans; (iv) barley undersown with a mixture of red clover and rye grass; (v) clover (or hay); (vi) oats. On the lower hill slopes above the Carse (the 'Braes of the Carse'), a five-course rotation was followed and on the higher areas, where the land was enclosed, a longer eight-course rotation included three years of pasture. Other crops grown were potatoes and small quantities of flax, which was spun and woven in the villages. There were also over twenty extensive and valuable orchards producing apples and pears. Nineteen-year leases, continued for the life of the tenant, were usual. Three farmers were renting 500 acres of arable, and one third of the farms were between 100 and 300 acres. The rest were 30–40 acres, but there were also small lots let to villagers.

Other Elements of Improvement

In 1764 the old Scots plough was still in use, drawn by two horses and four oxen or four horses and two oxen. The threshing machine was first introduced in Castle Huntly in 1787, and by 1794 there were sixty-one, driven by horses or by water power. Two-storeyed stone or brick farmhouses roofed with slates were built after 1775 on the Kinnaird estate by the proprietor so that the villages, 'in place of being a deformity, have now become an ornament to the country'.

Wages were rising and many of the improvements in areas such as the Carse of Gowrie – turnpike roads, planting, enclosing and the construction of open drains – were carried out by 'strangers', many of them from Inverness-shire. This was because young people of the Carse were being attracted by high wages in the manufacturing towns of Perth and Dundee – clearly there was competition for labour. Grain was being exported from the Carse ports, cattle were being reared and fed on the farms or brought in as flying stock, and Northumberland sheep (Cheviots) had been introduced to Mylnefield, west of Invergowrie. Drainage was incomplete in 1794 and a loch of 30 acres, the Qua near Glendoick, evident on Ainslie's map of Forfarshire, 1794, was not drained till the nineteenth century. Agriculture on the Carse and the adjacent Braes had become commercial.[13]

Systems of Improving

The reorganisation of estates and enclosures was carried out in different ways and at different paces according to the policy of the owners. On the Eglinton estates in Ayrshire, when leases were terminated, the factor took farms 'in hand', enclosed them, left the land in grass, limed them at a rate of one hundred bolls to the acre, built a farmhouse and steading, and then the farm was let.[14] More usually the tenant was bound to an improving lease to carry out enclosure and sometimes the necessary capital was advanced.

In the upland areas and the South-eastern Highlands, enclosure generally took place later than in the Lowlands, and in upland Perthshire it was achieved by a gradual reduction of tenants until a single tenant remained.[15]

The reorganisation of the estates, ending multiple tenancies and abolishing sub-tenancies, displaced many people, including cottars who also had a stake in the land. Some became farm workers on the new commercial farms, others went to the new planned villages (see below), but on a few estates provision was made for some of the 'displaced persons' by creating small individual lots, some of which were let to estate workers such as gamekeepers or tradesmen (blacksmiths for example). It also appeared necessary to create smallholdings to keep a reservoir of population in the countryside to provide seasonal labour during the harvest, and poor land on the upper edges of the improved farmland, on the interfluves and unreclaimed moss-land became the refuges for those dispossessed. Such settlements are most obvious in north-east Scotland and on Blairdrummond Moss, west of Stirling, but many proved ephemeral as they were added to larger farms at the end of a lease.[16]

Estate Reorganisation in the Highlands and Islands

In the Highlands and Islands, apart from the areas of soil derived from Old Red Sandstone rocks round the inner Moray Firth, arable land was restricted, and in 1700 the economy was based on subsistence crops of oats and bere and the rearing of black cattle. The crops and methods of cultivation within the framework of the run-rig system and the settlement clusters were probably not different in the Highlands and Islands from those in the Lowlands, except that there was greater dependence on the grazings, but innovations took longer to penetrate the isolated west and north. The essential difference lay in social organisation: apart from Orkney and Shetland, the clan system prevailed and hereditary chiefs parcelled out their lands in *tacks* – groups of farms leased to tacksmen who rented farms to groups of small tenants or worked the farms with labour provided by sub-tenants. This system was not unproductive in good years. The 4,000 cattle swum across the narrows between Kylerea and Glenelg in 1772 had increased to 20,000 by 1810. Four-year-old beasts bred on the arable land and slowly matured on the shieling grounds were much sought after by Lowland farmers, as they increased by one third to one quarter of their original weight after six months on lusher grazings.[17] The agricultural structure was thus different from the Lowlands where the 'gudeman' or substantial tenant was already making progress towards commercial farming, stimulated by market demand from the burghs.

After the 1745–6 rebellion, the Disarming Acts and the abolition of heritable jurisdictions removed much of the distinctive character of Highland society and many of the clan chiefs became absorbed into Lowland society. The more discerning attempted to emulate the achievements of the Lowland landowners and tried to reorganise their estates. The Annexed Estates Commissioners also contributed significantly to the improvement of estates in their charge. The improving movement spread first to areas bordering the Lowlands, and the second Duke of Argyll, whose estate stretched from Kintyre in the south to Morven and Tiree in the north, had adopted the new ideas before 1740. As influential participators in the government of Scotland, the Argyll family had close contacts with the improvers. The second Duke's successors embarked on a comprehensive reorganisation of his estate. The tacksmen were removed, single tenancy farms established, villages created and iron smelting and carpet-weaving developed. A new mansion house, Inveraray Castle, was built and new policies laid out from 1744 to 1758. The old unsightly burgh of Inveraray was removed to the present site in a new, planned development. Campbeltown and Tobermory were developed as fishing ports and attempts were made to develop mineral resources.

The Development of Crofting

In the North-west Highlands and in the Inner and Outer Hebrides the population rose by one third between 1750 and 1800. This accentuated the problems of reorganising the estates, with increasing population pressure on restricted areas of arable land. The sea provided alternative resources for development – seaweed and fish. Seaweed had long been cut or gathered and used as fertiliser, but in Orkney after c1720 it was also manufactured into kelp. Ash derived from the burning of cast and cut weed contained alkalis used in soap and glass-making; its production required no capital but a large labour force. In 1799 the Duke instructed his factor: 'As you inform me that small tenants can afford to pay more rent for farms in Tiree than gentleman farmers owing to the manufacture of kelp, this determines me to let the farms to small tenants.'[18]

The opportunity to develop Tiree by promoting kelp manufacture, instead of creating commercial farms, led to the farms being divided into consolidated smallholdings or crofts of 1.6–4 ha, with the pasture land attached to the farms becoming common grazing for the crofting townships. The crofting system probably originated on the Argyll estates, with the crofts essentially designed as part-time farming units with a seasonal occupation – kelp manufacture or fishing. This form of reorganisation of farms into crofting townships spread rapidly in the north and west in the first two decades of the nineteenth century. In Caithness and Shetland the development of fishing also required a new labour force and crofts were created for fishermen. At Ullapool in Wester Ross the British Fisheries Society had taken over the farm of Ullapool in the course of developing a fishing settlement, and the Board of Governors was anxious not to provide too much land in case the fishermen neglected to fish.[19] With the rising population new land was often taken in from moorland in the process of creating crofting townships. In Benbecula, between 1805 and 1829, the arable land increased from about 1,200ha to about 1,850ha at the expense of pasture land, as a result of the creation of crofts.[20]

Most of the crofts were not enclosed, nor were the agricultural innovations applied in the Lowlands adopted in the crofting area.

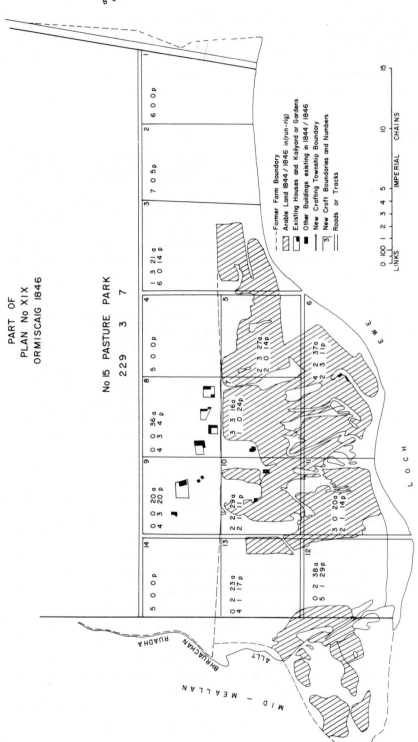

Fig 6.2 Part of Plan No. XIX Ormiscaig (Gairloch), 1846. Surveyor – G. Campbell Smith of Banff. The survey of the estate was begun in 1844 but the plan is dated 1846. Redrawn by Carolyn Bain from the *Atlas of the Townships of Gairloch*, Sir Kenneth S. Mackenzie, Baronet, 1848, by courtesy of Brigadier Mackenzie of Gairloch

Enclosure of crofts by fencing did not become widespread until the 1950s. One rather late example of the lotting (dividing into lots) of an existing farm with several tenants into crofts is Ormiscaig (Gairloch Parish), north west of Aultbea (Fig 6.2). The arable in run rig in 1846 is shown with one loose semi-linear cluster of houses and kail yards inland from the arable, and five other scattered buildings on the arable area. The boundary of the existing farm is also shown. The land surveyor superimposed a very regular lay-out of fourteen almost square or rectangular crofts on part of the existing farmland and the two acreages (in acres, roods and poles) give the 'old' arable (a) and the pasture (b) for the new crofts. The boundaries of the new crofting township were also straightened and the result was the highly regular lay-out which still exists. Three further 'square' crofts were carved out of the moorland inland from numbers 1 and 2 at a later date.

The Highland Clearances

The manufacture of kelp and the creation of crofts which retained large numbers on the estates virtually ceased in the late 1820s when prices fell after the Napoleonic Wars. Cattle prices had also fallen in 1815. Many Highland and Island estates became bankrupt and were sold – all the estates of the Outer Hebrides changed hands, and their new owners, mainly from the improved areas, removed the remaining tacksmen and their sub-tenants and cleared a relatively small number of crofting townships, installing in their place mainland farmers paying much higher and more secure rents. Clearance of sub-tenants and some crofters, followed by the potato famine of 1847–50, led to large-scale emigration.

Inland, north of the Great Glen, the estates were reorganised. The emphasis was on sheep farming in the straths and on the development of crofting townships on the western and northern coastal fringes, on the poorer soils at the inner edges of the Old Red Sandstone rocks and on the raised beaches of the eastern seaboard. In 1750, the numbers of cattle and sheep had been almost equal, but the northward advance of improved breeds of sheep changed the balance in the southern and eastern Highlands and by 1800 sheep were dominant. After 1815, with the fall in cattle prices, wool and mutton increased in value and farmers from the Scottish Borders and northern England leased the extensive grazings on the shieling grounds but also required the arable ground on the river terraces and the haughland for wintering. The influx of sheep led to the clearance of the small tenants whose farms were unenclosed – Glen Strathfarrar was cleared between 1801 and 1810 and the first

Sutherland clearance took place in 1806. In 1810, Atkinson and Marshall from Alnwick in Northumberland started sheep farming around Lairg and soon leased over 40,000ha. The number of sheep in Sutherland increased from 15,000 in 1811 to 130,000 by 1820.[21] Almost all the interior straths were cleared (as numerous ruins of former settlement clusters eloquently testify) and poverty was the lot of the small tenants still farming in the traditional ways. At Rosal in Strathnaver thirteen families depended on 20ha of arable land.[22] The creation of small crofts without ancillary employment would have produced neither an acceptable income nor rental.

The population displaced from the straths were resettled in crofting townships along the coasts (almost always on poorer land), at the inner edge of higher quality land where commercial farms had been created (as along the east Sutherland coast), on patches of moorland, or in new planned villages such as Brora or Helmsdale. Not all accepted resettlement and many emigrated. After 1874, when wool prices fell, some of the sheep farms both north and south of the Great Glen were converted to deer forests, which were sporting estates purchased or leased by the affluent aristocracy or successful industrialists. By 1912 the deer forests with their castellated shooting lodges and isolated gamekeepers' cottages reached a maximum area of some 1,500,000ha (reduced to less than 1,250,000ha by 1955). Some 40 per cent of this land lay above an altitude of 450m, however, and was thus marginal even for extensive sheep farming.[23] Estate reorganisation of such a radical nature explains the very sparsely populated interior straths and glens, and why the population of the Highlands north of the Great Glen is largely confined to the coastal areas. Nowhere else in Scotland is the authority of the landowner in deciding how estate reorganisation and development should take place more manifest.

The Elements of the New Settlement and Land Use Patterns
Mansion Houses and Policies

One of the first signs of change in the settlement pattern was the rebuilding of some of the tower houses, which took place from the late sixteenth and seventeenth centuries, preceding the reorganisation of the estates. Most were either added to, sometimes by building further storeys as at Glamis, or subjected to major reconstructions in which classical mansion houses were built around the old tower houses. The building of new houses increased in the eighteenth century with William Adam and his son Robert among the most prominent architects. A typical example is Mellerstain in Berwickshire which was constructed in two stages – the two wings by William Adam in 1725 and the central block by Robert Adam in 1770.

Around these mansion houses, gardens were laid out, in some cases designed by the architect, as at Arniston, Midlothian (built between 1726 and 1732 for Lord President Dundas).[24] This continued the tradition dating back to the early seventeenth century of embellishing the surroundings of earlier houses with formal gardens. After 1760, large areas of parkland were developed around the mansion houses of the larger estates, with the Mains farm grazing parks often included. This development was seen as an integral part of the general improvement of the estate. Hallyburton, on the edge of the Sidlaws near Coupar Angus in Perthshire, provides an excellent example.

Plantation and Afforestation

Not only did the landowners assiduously improve the agricultural land, but they also planted with trees the poorer soils and steeper slopes. Cockburn brought to Ormistoun a wide range of deciduous and coniferous trees used in planting hedges, shelter belts and plantations, and the Old Statistical Account – written half a century later – describes the countryside as 'enclosed with hedges of Whitethorn, mixed with sweet briar and honeysuckle and hedgerow trees'. The native Scots pine was much used on the Tyninghame estate and indigenous oaks were planted at Darnaway in Morayshire. In the policies exotic species such as spruce, larch (introduced to Scotland in 1725) and cedars were planted. The fourth Duke of Atholl was the first to plant larch on a large scale and during his lifetime he planted over 6,000ha with 27 million trees. In the first half of the nineteenth century Douglas fir, sequoia and sitka spruce were introduced from North America while the rhododendron spread over many estate policies.

Crops and Livestock

New crops were introduced. Clover had been introduced in the seventeenth century. Turnips were probably first cultivated in the Lothians and the Merse as a field crop (c1740) and were found especially useful both as a cleansing crop and for stock feeding on the light loams or 'turnip soils'. The potato, which probably came from Oxford to the Physical Garden of Edinburgh before 1683, did not become a field crop until the middle of the eighteenth century – it was little suited to stock feeding but demand came from the growing urban population. Potatoes were introduced from Ireland to South Uist in

1743 after a visit by Clanranald to a kinsman in Ulster, and by 1775 the potato was universal in the Highlands and often used to break-in reclaimed moorland.[25] There were also improvements in cereals as wheat spread northwards from the Lothians and the Merse, barley replaced bere, and new varieties of oats appeared. Almost all the current garden vegetables grown in Scotland are contained in early eighteenth-century lists – at first they were only cultivated in the mansion house gardens, but a market garden was operating in Edinburgh by 1746, and by 1812 there were seventy-six such enterprises producing fruit and vegetables in the area.

Stock breeds were also improved by selective breeding. Among the cattle breeds, the Aberdeen Angus developed in this way and the Shorthorn evolved from the crossing of native Scottish cattle with Midland English breeds. The Ayrshire is descended from the Dunlop cattle – during the second half of the eighteenth century, John Dunlop of Dunlop brought in some cows of a larger size, probably of the Dutch, Teeswater or Lincoln breeds, and crossed them with the native Kylo. The Earl of Marchmont also obtained cattle from the Bishop of Durham and brought them first to Berwickshire and then to his Ayrshire estates. By 1780 the breed was well established in North Ayrshire,[26] and diffusion of dairy farming from that centre resulted in the first large dairy herd in Wigtonshire being established in 1794. Dunlop cheese-making on farms had spread to the northern Rhinns of Galloway by 1830.

The modern breeds of sheep were evolved in the eighteenth century in the Scottish Borders. Enclosure allowed segregation for selective breeding and turnips provided fodder for a larger animal. The Cheviot evolved c1761 from the Scottish Dunface or old Scottish Shortwool; the Border Leicester c1770 by crossing the Cheviot with the English Leicester; the Blackface or Linton breed seems to have come from the north of England.[27]

Farm Implements

In addition to crops and livestock, far-reaching innovations were made in implements and, in this sphere, the landowners were influential early on. The Earl of Stair imported a Dutch plough in 1730 and sent a man to England to learn to make implements. In 1767 James Small, a Berwickshire implement-maker, patented his two-horse swing- or chain-plough, which rapidly replaced the cumbersome old wooden ploughs drawn by four to six oxen or a mixed team of horses and oxen. All the ploughs in use at an Alloa ploughing match in 1784 were Small's. It was a lighter plough and the chain allowed a variable depth of furrow but was probably only suitable on cleared land. Its curved mouldboards were cast at the Carron Iron Works but the first all-iron plough was not manufactured until the beginning of the nineteenth century. Iron harrows (replacing the primitive wooden implements), seed drills, leather harness, and threshing machines were all in current use by the end of the eighteenth century, but mechanised reapers and the spinner digger for harvesting potatoes did not come into use until after 1850. The rise in agricultural wages which resulted from competition for labour from the textile industry hastened the adoption of farm machinery.[28]

Farm Buildings

Farm houses and outbuildings were also profoundly modified or, more usually, completely rebuilt as an essential element in estate improvement. The earlier farm buildings – mainly elongated byre-dwellings – belonged to the vernacular building tradition that used materials available locally such as turf, wattle, clay and some stonework. The roofs were thatched with heather, reeds or marram grass. From plates in Slezer's *Theatrum Scotiae* of 1693 it is evident that some improved farmhouses had been built before 1700. The new farmhouses and steadings followed after mansion houses and manses, and the prototypes were usually the Mains farmhouses and outbuildings, with the farmhouse sometimes incorporated in a range of buildings, but more normally separated from the steading. Using architects' pattern books, factors or builders erected the farmhouse, then the steading, and – by the end of the eighteenth century – the single-storey farm servants' cottages. The plan often formed a rectangle or square with the byre, stable, cart and implement sheds arranged in a 'U' shape around a central open court. Farm servants' cottages were often set in a row parallel to the lines of the steadings.[29]

The Impact of Reorganisation and Improvement

Parry has calculated that, as a result of the reorganisation of the estates and the introduction of new agricultural structures, techniques, crops and implements, between 1750 and 1866 the cultivated area of Scotland was increased from 1,200,000ha to 1,700,000ha. Reclamation on the lower upland areas accounted for 200,000ha, which more than balanced areas lost by a retreat from formerly cultivated areas above 300m, some of which would have been lost by the creation of sheep farms in the early nineteenth century in the upper glens and the straths. In addition, the introduction of Small's swing plough reduced the space lost in the older furrows by the construction of long, straight, low cultivated ridges. Cultivation on the farm land which replaced the infield and outfield system meant an increase of 50 per cent in annually cultivated land and improved varieties of crops also increased yields. As a result, between 1750 and 1825, there was probably a net gain in farmed land of 40 per cent, and agricultural productivity probably increased by 100 per cent.[30]

The Planned Villages

One further element, added to the settlement pattern of rural Scotland as part of the reorganisation of the estates, was the planned village. In 1700 and on the Military Survey some fifty years later the only substantial rural settlements were the burghs of barony, villages promoted by landowners from the fifteenth to the early seventeenth centuries with a view to increasing trade by establishing weekly markets. The other rural settlement forms in the first half of the eighteenth century were hamlet clusters comprising fermtouns, milltouns and sometimes cottartouns and kirktouns. The last acted as parish centres which, with the demise of the fermtouns, expanded to become rural service centres with the church and manse, smithy, inn and, later, shops.

In the overall plan of estate reorganisation the planned villages became a significant element. They would absorb the people displaced by the commercialisation of farming, keep the population in the countryside, and become the focus of rural manufacturing. In founding villages, the landowner displayed both concern for the displaced persons on his estate and self-interest in collecting an income from feu duties. Village foundation was yet another example of developing the total resources of the estate.

One of the earliest planned villages was laid out by Cockburn of Ormistoun on his East Lothian estate in the 1730s, but the beginnings of deliberately planned villages can be ascribed to the Commissioners of the Annexed Estates who founded settlements for soldiers and sailors discharged after the Seven Years' War. The farm of Whiteley, near Burrelton in Perthshire, was chosen because 'it contained a good deal of Improveable Muir'. Strelitz, as this settlement was called, was designed in 1763 on a grid plan of square 6-acre fields, each divided in half to give sixty-three 3-acre plots for the settlers, and a linear village was laid out (Fig 6.3). These soldiers' settlements proved to be

Page 145 Fort George, built on raised beach promontory of Ardersier in the Moray Firth, was built as a military garrison to help subjugate the Highlands after the 1745 uprising. First government contract in the Highlands (won by William Adam); the fort was built by John Adam to one of the most advanced defensive designs in Europe. Incorporates barracks, bakehouse, brewery and chapel to maintain a garrison of soldiers. Never used in anger

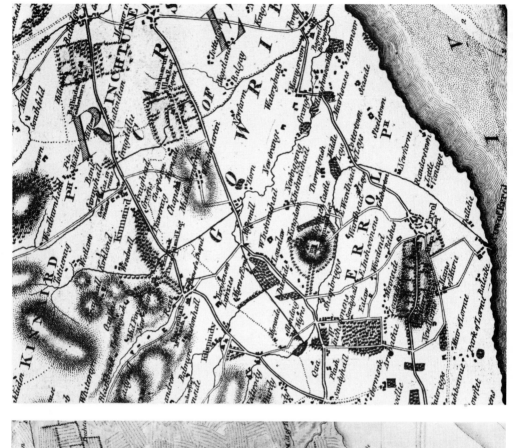

Pages 146–7 *(opposite left)* Part of the Carse of Gowrie round Errol, *c*1750. The mansion house and policies at Errol are shown with the village, a burgh of barony with a charter dated 1641; a considerable number of farms have been enclosed but some unenclosed fermtouns with lands in runrig remain; *(opposite right)* the same part of the Carse at the end of the eighteenth century: most of the fermtouns have disappeared and improvement has spread to the hill edge; some drainage and straightening of streams has been carried out although the Qua, a loch of 12.5ha NNW of Errol, remains. Plantations and roads have increased since 1750; *(above)* by 1866, improvements have been completed, particularly in drainage: the Qua has disappeared. Farm roads and the railway have been added

Page 148 *(above)* Stanley village and mill, Perthshire. The planned village of Stanley was built to house workers in the cotton mill on the right bank of the Tay, some 9km upstream from Perth. The village was laid out in 1786 on a grid-iron plan which is still evident in the part of the village nearest the mill. Remnants of the policies of Stanley House (now demolished) can be seen upstream from the mill and the townscape beyond the expanded village was also replanned and enclosed in the late eighteenth century;

(below) Errol and the Carse of Gowrie, Perthshire. The village of Errol owes its origin to a burgh of barony charter granted to Butter of Ardgaith in 1644. In the late eighteenth and early nineteenth centuries, Errol was predominantly a linen textile village. In the bottom left of the photograph is part of the policies of Errol Park: beyond the village, the nearest farm is East Leys and Hay of Leys began the agricultural improvement of his estate in 1735, probably the earliest attempt at agricultural improvement in the Carse of Gowrie

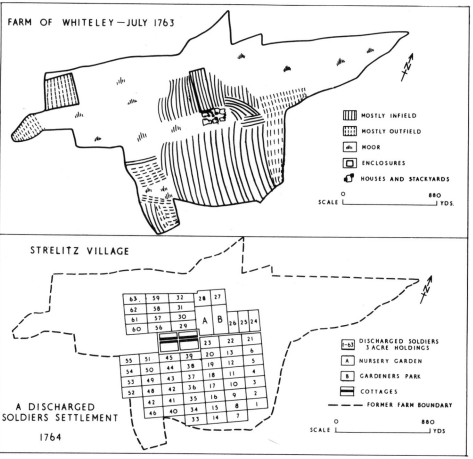

Fig 6.3 The farm of Whiteleys, mainly unenclosed in 1763, was converted by the Commissioners of the Annexed Estates into a Soldiers' Settlement in 1764. The conception of a planned village, with plots for the settlers, was followed later in other planned villages. Based on J. Lesslie, Plan of the Farm of Whiteley, 1763 (R.H.P. 3410) and G. Roy, A Plan of Whiteley Farm, 1764 (R.H.P. 3411), Scottish Record Office

ephemeral, however, for 3 acres was insufficient to attract long-term settlers. One village built by the Commissioners, Kinloch Rannoch, has survived as a service centre. Their influence in fostering the development of Crieff and Callander (founded c1740, before the annexure), their planning of the soldiers' settlements, and the founding of villages by individual members were other significant contributions by the Commissioners of the Annexed Estates to the improving movement in Scotland.

Between 1770 and 1850 some 130 planned villages were founded, mostly by enterprising landowners. They can be broadly classified as estate, textile and fishing villages. Estate villages, on the one hand, provided houses for tradesmen, foresters and other estate workers. Kenmore (Perthshire), built c1763, at the principal exit from the policies of Taymouth Castle, also included the parish church and an inn. Tomintoul (Banffshire), where feu duties were first paid in 1774, developed as a general service centre rather than as a textile settlement, as had been the original conception.[31]

Textile villages are the most numerous and widespread category, and factory villages were founded on water-power sites, many in the 1780s. At Balfron (Stirlingshire) the landowner built houses and a large spinning mill. At Deanston (Perthshire) a company village was laid out along the banks of the Teith, and at Stanley (Perthshire) the Duke of Atholl feued 12.5ha for the building of a village and invested £2,000 in building houses for a Company which had as participants Dempster of Dunnichen, a notable improver, Richard Arkwright and several Perth merchants. The building of a six-storey cotton spinning mill started in 1786 and was followed later by a flax mill. Other textile villages, for handloom weavers, were founded later nearer the urban textile centres – Dempster of Dunnichen founded Letham in Angus, and Luthermuir was established on barren moorland in Kincardineshire. Many of these textile villages included small arable plots and grazing, as the following excerpt from an advertisement for weavers for a textile company at New Byth, Aberdeenshire, shows:[32]

> . . . married men who have families, and any others that may incline it, can be accommodated with a croft of land, and a cow's grass and fire (peats) at a very easy rate.

Landowners were keen to settle weavers on their estates as they would engage in harvest work and were good payers of rent.

The development of fishery resources was another reason for village building, and not only the British Fisheries Society, which was responsible for the development of Ullapool in 1786, but also estate-owners engaged in such projects. Along the Caithness coast several fishing villages were developed during the herring boom of the early nineteenth century, and Lybster was founded after a wooden pier had been built at the mouth of the Riesgill burn, c1815. It has been claimed that Lybster was the third most successful fishing port in Scotland in 1833; in that year there were 248 boats, 1,006 fishermen, 723 gutters and 47 curers, who produced 34,712 barrels of herring.[33] On the Sutherland estate, Helmsdale was built between 1817 and 1830 as a refuge for those evicted from the inland straths but also to develop fishing. Brora, founded in approximately the same period and for the

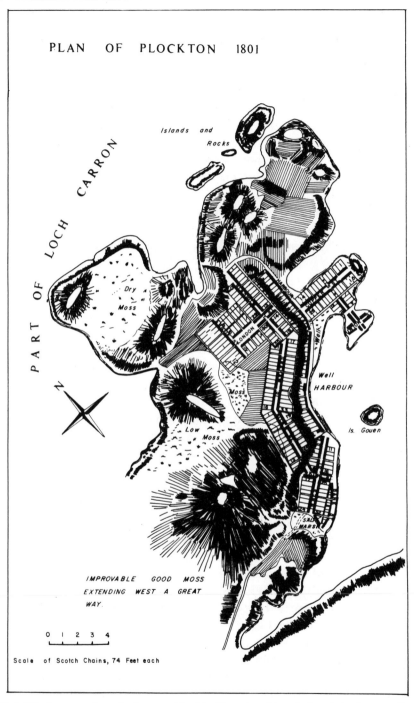

PLAN OF PLOCKTON 1801

PART OF LOCH CARRON

Islands and Rocks

Dry Moss

Moss

Low Moss

Well HARBOUR

Is. Gouen

SALT MARSH

LONDON

IMPROVABLE GOOD MOSS
EXTENDING WEST A GREAT
WAY.

0 1 2 3 4

Scale of Scotch Chains, 74 Feet each

Fig 6.4 Plockton was planned to be a considerable village also with agricultural plots but a smaller village materialised; the drying out of the harbour area at low tide would not facilitate fishery development. Plan of Plockton, 1801, by courtesy of National Trust for Scotland, redrawn by Carolyn Bain.

same reason, had a smaller harbour, and coal-mining and salt pans also formed part of the industrial base. Plockton (Wester Ross) was intended to develop as a fishing village, but much of the intended village was never built. More successful in the long run were the Aberdeenshire and Moray Coast villages, also landlord development.

An integral part of the reorganisation and improvement of many estates, especially where no burgh of barony existed, the planned villages are one of the most striking permanent memorials to the activities of the Scottish landowners between c1735 and 1850. The original function of the villages was often ephemeral, but their settlements – mostly with their characteristic rectangular street patterns and often incorporating squares – have survived as rural service centres and some have become tourist resorts.

Conclusion

If agricultural improvement had begun on a few estates before 1700, between 1700 and 1850 the landscape and pattern of settlement of rural Scotland was moulded into its present shape. The sequence of the changes is clear. The landowners were the refashioners and the original innovators. They first improved their immediate surroundings, building mansions and laying out policies. Then, once their lands had been consolidated out of the fragmentation of proprietary and tenant run rig and their land surveyors had laid out the modern system of farms and fields, they diffused the new agricultural techniques through clauses in leases and Agricultural Societies, creating a nucleus of good practical tenant-farmers. The ordinary farmers followed, carrying out improvements and adopting the new husbandry as ordered in the leases. Shelter belts and plantations were added, as adornments with a practical value. The improvement of the estates was accompanied by social change: the rural population no longer had access to land but now consisted of commercial farmers and farm servants earning a wage. But agriculture, albeit the main enterprise, was not the sole one: planned villages were laid out and industries developed, some related to the production of the estate (as at Ormistoun), others providing alternatives to agriculture (as in the case of the textile and fishing villages) and creating employment for the people displaced by the reorganisation and improvement of the estates. The estate was the unit of improvement, and improvement took place at a time and a pace and in a style determined by its owners.

Regional differentiation evolved during this period. The soils and climate of the Lowlands were suited to arable farming and stock-fattening in the drier east, and very large farms with hamlet-sized populations were created. In the western Lowlands and the South-west, dairying grew in response to the market opportunities and smaller, often family farms, with smaller fields, evolved.

In the Highlands change was slower. In the south and east, consolidation from run rig occurred before 1800 and, with the coming of sheep, extensive sheep farms were created on the upland areas. Nonetheless, many multiple-tenancy farms, still with hamlet clusters, survived till later in the nineteenth century, eventually becoming single-tenancy, but still small, farms. Fewer villages were laid out in the Highlands than in the Lowlands.

In the north and west, change was even slower still. Attempts were made to improve estates and retain the massive population by developing fishing and the manufacture of kelp, but few villages developed. Crofting townships or farms replaced the tacksmen and their sub-tenants and multiple-tenancy farms. In the early nineteenth century, sheep and mixed stock farms were created which displaced large numbers of people. Some of the sheep farms became deer forests after 1870. Between the Crofters' Act of 1886 and the eve of World War II, much of the land cleared to create farms was resettled by crofters.

Over rural Scotland, the population declined. At first there was internal redistribution to the industrial villages on the watersides. Later the adoption of steam power drew the population to the coalfields and the towns. In the Highlands, the tide of emigration, which had started before 1800 with the departure of the tacksmen, accelerated in the first half of the nineteenth century (with the clearances and the failure of the potato), both to the Lowlands and overseas. It cannot be denied that opportunities in the Lowlands have always been greater, soils more fruitful, and mineral resources more plentiful, so that Lowland ideas and values prevailed in Scotland. By 1850, the population distribution and balance had largely adapted to the intrinsic resources and their modern commercial utilisation and the basic pattern of Scotland's rural landscape and population distribution had been laid.

Notes to this chapter are on pages 308–9.

7

The Urban Scene, 1760–1980

Ian H. Adams

SCOTLAND'S urban scene has been in constant change for over two hundred years. Above all, the changes have been technological, each change having a profound impact on urban geography. Power resources have been transformed from water to steam and then to electricity. Horse power in transport has given way to canal, railway and the internal combustion engine. Industrial innovation has shifted from cotton textiles, wool and linen into coal mining, iron and steel, and heavy industry, before falling into a void of de-industrialisation in the twentieth century. Towns have sprung up on coastal sites, on coalfields or where planners thought they should be. Other towns have sunk into a lethargy that makes them look as though time is passing them by. Glasgow's rise to and fall from international status has been faster than that of any other city in western Europe.

Within the city man has been changing his use of space. Medieval cores were left to the poor as new residential suburbs for the well-to-do were built in adjacent fields. In turn, these were surrounded by belts of tenements intermingled with industry and railways. The well-to-do abandoned their gracious urban living, leapfrogging to the ever-expanding suburbs. These new suburbs, thanks to the railway, could often be miles away from the central city – the age of the commuter had begun. The cable cars and electric tram cars also opened up new opportunities for suburban living. The year 1919 marked the turning point of Scotland's residential patterns with the passing of the Housing and Town Planning (Scotland) Act. It marked the recognition that the inherited housing problem was beyond individual, commercial or charitable solution, and only the State could marshall the resources to house the working population. The people of Scotland were on their way to becoming Europe's leading state-housed population. For the remainder of the twentieth century Scotland's urban landscape was the outcome of legislative action. The clear-cut boundary between town and country, the residential ghettos based on land-use allocations for different tenurial systems, the driving out and isolation of industry by segregating land uses – all have their origins in late nineteenth-century ideals transformed into today's human landscape.[1]

The Medieval Inheritance

In the middle of the eighteenth century approximately one tenth of Scotland's population lived in burghs, many of which were little more than villages. At the same time, the first stirrings of what was to become a great upheaval were taking place in the countryside. Changes in rural management were to release a huge proportion of countryfolk. They had really but two destinations: if they wanted to remain in Scotland they had to find work in the towns, or they would emigrate and find land in the New World.

Yet, the pre-industrial city offered little work for the countryman. The few trades open to him were lowly and unskilled. For example, he could work on the docksides of Greenock or Leith, become a sedan-chair man in Edinburgh, a nail-maker at Cramond or an urban cow-keeper in Glasgow. There were no factories to offer him semi-skilled work. But new trades were beginning to proliferate, one of the most important being that of the mason. Bridges had to be built for the new turnpikes; country mansions by Robert Adam were springing up all over the land; new water mills were being established for the linen trade; and the first residential squares began to make their appearance in Edinburgh.

The form of these pre-industrial cities retained its medieval splendour. The great high streets with their flanking tenements and lands formed the core of these essentially market towns. Booths lined the streets and spilled over much of the open space. A few of the more prosperous burghs (Edinburgh, St Andrews, Crail etc) had more than one high street. The tenement buildings still retained their mixture of social classes: the better-off lived at the lower levels and the social scale was then descended – up to the poor in the garret. It was a world of barely tolerable congestion that was on the verge of exceeding social acceptability to those who could afford to choose.

The Georgian Suburbs

The professional class, Scotland's proto-middle class, chose to move out of the crowded medieval high streets. These people desired the universally acclaimed norms of amenity: the gracious square, the large communal gardens, and homes with numerous spacious rooms. Their model was London, which had set the pace for over a hundred years.

Edinburgh led the way in planning George Square and later the New Town, which was to become the prototype for the rest of Scotland's cities. Ironically, from as early as the 1730s, but more prolifically in the 1760s, proto-urban planning schemes had been tried by Scotland's landowners with the planned village movement.[2] Nearly 300 villages were planned, most employing the same norms as were later developed in Edinburgh's New Town. Although it has been suggested that the model for Edinburgh was the Ville de Stanislas in Nancy, France, in fact there were vigorous indigenous models in such places as New Keith.[3] Only a handful of these villages developed into full-blown towns but Huntly, Fochabers, Cullen and Grantown-on-Spey deserve recognition. The fact that the vast bulk of the foundations came to naught was the result of the coming Industrial Revolution, which was to make more exacting locational demands than did a landowner developing his estate.

Industrial Settlement

The development of textile machinery and its demand for power laid the foundation for the next phase of urban development. From small beginnings at Penicuik and Rothesay in 1778 the Scottish cotton industry grew rapidly, and by 1838 there were 192 cotton mills in the country. Flowing water was the main source for power in these early stages of industrialisation. That fact alone dictated that the factories had to be located near ample and reliable sources. Surprisingly these are not as abundant as might be thought. When Arkwright came to Scotland in the early 1780s he identified three sites of outstanding opportunity: New Lanark on the River Clyde; Stanley on the River Tay; and Persley on the River Don. In time each was to see the establishment of a major textile works, launching Scotland into the age of the factory.[4] Yet little major urban development is associated with these foundations, for they were limited by the amount of power that could be taken out of the river. This can be seen in the basin of the River Tweed where the same water was used time and again by various mills along the rivers' banks, giving a pattern of towns of comparable size – Hawick, Galashiels, Peebles, Selkirk, Innerleithen etc. Similarly, in Perthshire and Angus a concentration on linen production stimulated the growth of such towns as Arbroath and Blairgowrie.

Growing population and increasing levels of division of labour gave plenty of opportunity for the development of specialised trades, the emergence of the retail sector, and the proliferation of service occupations. Nearly every industry was affected by the application of water power during this period. A revitalised agriculture benefitted from the introduction of grain-threshing mills and from the building of flour and pot-barley mills which supplied the burgeoning urban markets. Water-powered machinery in distilleries began to put whisky production on to a factory basis. Ironworks and iron foundries used water power to provide blast, to drill cylinders and to forge iron.[5] The paper industry, which saw such a rapid growth in these early years of the Industrial Revolution, was largely water-powered.[6] Even in 1838, on the eve of the railway, water power still provided more than one third of the power used in textile mills.

The Industrial City

As demand for power began to exceed the capacity of Scottish rivers to produce sufficient levels, the steam engine – which had been waiting in the wings for two decades – began to penetrate many more operations. Either the work had to migrate to the coalfields or ways to bring the coal to existing markets more cheaply had to be found. Thus the attraction of putting coal cheaply on the domestic markets of Glasgow and Edinburgh was one factor that led to the building of canals – first the Forth & Clyde, which was completed with the aid of a government grant in 1790, then the Monkland (1793) and the Union Canal (1822).[7]

The rise of industrial Glasgow began in 1792 with the installation at Springfield on the south bank of the Clyde of its first steam engine used for spinning cotton. Progress was still slow, for only just over 200 power looms had been installed by 1801. Steam power then began to be applied.[8]

> The extension of power loom factories, and of the cotton trade generally, became so rapid as almost to exceed belief . . . The factories are a prominent architectural feature of the city – or at least of its suburbs and outskirts; and, not only by their number, but by their great size and their prevailing symmetry and neatness, they often strike strangers from agricultural districts with amazement.

By the middle of the century about one-eighth of the population of Glasgow between the ages of ten and forty was employed in textile factories and vast numbers were engaged in ancillary trades.

Although the cotton industry began to decline rapidly from 1857, little unemployment was caused because the rise of a new iron industry was sufficiently vigorous to take up the slack. Glasgow benefited from the development of James Beaumont Neilson's hot-blast furnace which led to an increasing number of city suburban foundries, one of the most notable being Dixon's Blazies. For thirty years, including the decade of the railway mania, iron production flourished, but the industry started to decline in the 1870s in the face of cheaper production from the Cleveland field near Middlesbrough.

Once again this setback was amply compensated for, this time by the growth of shipbuilding. From 1860 to 1914 marine engineering became the greatest source of employment, bringing together coal, iron and steelworks, and heavy engineering in the Glasgow area. In the peak years just before World War I, one-third of all the world's steamships were launched on the River Clyde.[9] The inter-war period marked the beginnings of the decline of Glasgow which has gone on remorselessly down to the present day.[10]

Coalfield Towns

Whilst textiles provided the economic base for the first industrial towns, iron and steel gave rise to fewer but more substantial towns linked to local mineral resources. The lighting of the first coal-burning furnace at Carron in 1760 heralded a revolution in iron-making, both in techniques and size.[11] Carron was soon the largest foundry in Europe, employing 1,200 men who transformed the agricultural hamlets of Stenhousemuir and Larbert into industrial towns. Thereafter the location of ironworks was severely limited by the inadequacies of the transport system, and new settlements had to be developed in out-of-the-way sites close to pockets of coal and iron ore. Settlements such as Shotts, Wilsontown, Muirkirk and Glenbuck had much in common with early cotton towns and mining villages: largely unplanned, with poor houses and minimum services, they were dominated by a single industry and often by one proprietor. By the 1820s the Scottish iron industry was in poor shape, relying on poor quality clay-band ores and coking coals.[12] Dramatic change came in 1828 with Neilson's patent hot-blast process, which allowed the use of the much more abundant blackband ores. By 1835, sixty-five of the eighty-eight Scottish blast furnaces were situated in or about the Monklands. The speed and size of these developments left little scope for good town planning. One result was Coatbridge and Airdrie, a miniature conurbation straggling between foundries, railways and canal.

Motherwell grew up around the bustling railway junction from which lines penetrated the surrounding coal and iron ore reserves. No town in Scotland grew as fast, for Motherwell was the centre where ironmasters invested heavily in open-hearth steelworks after 1871. By the late 1880s it was the leading open-hearth steel district making ship plate in Britain. The plate was shipped to Clydebank, which was a small village of 816 people in 1871 and a town of 30,000 by 1901. In the rush to house so many people, standards were poor: in 1911 four-fifths of the houses had two rooms or less. Falkirk was another burgh which saw rapid growth in the years after 1871 when shipbuilding was the chief growth point of the Scottish economy. From a population of 9,547 in 1871 it grew rapidly to 17,282 in 1891, during which time nineteen foundries had been established in or near the burgh and much of the output was shipped to Clydebank.

Urban Reform

During the nineteenth century Scotland experienced what has been called the 'urban transition' – the change from an overwhelmingly rural society to a predominantly urban one. The transformation was unprecedented anywhere in the world and it caught people unprepared as they entered the new industrial age. Cities which were expected to be places of civilisation were increasingly found to be full of the most loathsome problems. After the first phase of exhilarating industrial innovation and thus of urban opportunity, the emerging middle classes increasingly rejected the earlier views of urban civilisation. From the 1820s the question of mass poverty was central to the argument about cities: in particular the industrial towns' vulnerability to the trade cycle produced widespread distress of a kind hard to ignore.

Disease, too, raised its head, as the inadequacy of water supplies and the abundance of sewage gave plenty of opportunities for bacteria to flourish. But it was the appearance of cholera that brought matters to a head in 1832. This was the first of four pandemics which spread from Asia in the early and mid-nineteenth century. It entered Britain through the collier port of Sunderland in October 1831[13] and made its first appearance in Scotland on 17 December in Haddington, a major stopping place on the Great North Road. Haddington was also a market centre and in the next few weeks the disease spread around East Lothian and especially into the industrial villages along the shores of the Firth of Forth. By early February 1832 cases were appearing in the filthy insanitary closes of the Old Town of Edinburgh where it spread like wildfire. Outbreaks were to recur in 1848–9, 1853–4 and 1866.

The old governing bodies of the royal burghs had almost broken down in the early years of the nineteenth century under the stress of earlier maladministration and under the new problems of growth and congestion. The Burgh Reform Acts of 1833 and 1834 introduced new principles and established effective authority in the growing towns. Commissioners were authorised to levy rates for the purposes of watching, lighting, paving and cleansing the streets, for the improvement of water and gas supplies, and for the prevention of infectious diseases. Furthermore, they were to regulate slaughter-houses, apprehend vagrants and name and number streets and houses. Legislation extended these powers to all parliamentary burghs in 1847, and to places with populations over 1,200 in 1850 and over 700 in 1862. Many industrial towns, such as Motherwell, Coatbridge and Airdrie, first achieved independence in this way and became known as police burghs.

The 1840s saw the rise of the public health movement, and a beginning to sanitary improvement which, although it scarcely amounted to a transformation of urban society, at least suggested that the insanitary condition of towns could be controlled and improved.[14] The Royal College of Physicians in Edinburgh had recognised the need for the appointment of medical officers of health, and during the cholera epidemic of 1848 measures were proposed for creating a board of health. After the collapse of a house in the High Street, Edinburgh, in 1847 involving the deaths of thirty-five people, a medical officer of health was appointed by the town council, and in the same year a special sanitary department was set up in Glasgow. The towns were indescribably filthy at this time: few streets were drained, there was no main sewer system, and cesspools served such houses as had piped water supplies.[15] But reform was at hand: Edinburgh started to build sewers after obtaining its Police Act in 1848 and within thirty years the whole city was served by them.[16]

Adequate water supplies, however, remained almost non-existent until the second half of the nineteenth century. People were beginning to realise that there might be some connection between disease and bad housing, but it was not yet understood that foul water led to infectious diseases. By the middle of the century Edinburgh had improved its water supply, but the citizens of Glasgow were still supplied by inefficient water companies. Glasgow Corporation commissioned Robert Stephenson and I. K. Brunel to report on their plan to tap the pure waters of Loch Katrine. An Act was passed in 1855 and water began to flow to the city in the extraordinarily short time of four years. Glasgow's provision of ample water for all its citizens set an example for others to follow.

Mature Urban Society

Scotland achieved its peak of industrial pre-eminence between 1870 and 1900. The railway network bound the whole country together, bringing in the produce of the countryside to fill the great urban markets with grain, cattle, potatoes and milk. The great mass of people in the cities led to the concentration there of food-processing industries – meat-curing, baking, confectionery, dairying and preserve-making – that satisfied the Scottish sweet tooth. Large-scale brewing took over from a universal domestic industry and Edinburgh became the main centre, with Alloa and Glasgow important producers. With economies of scale and the railway network, manufacturers were able to send these agriculturally based goods back to small towns and villages throughout Scotland. Industrial scale increased enormously during this period. Large factories dominated cities like Glasgow and Dundee, and towns like Clydebank, Greenock, Falkirk and Kirkcaldy were fiefdoms of industrialists. Imperial trade was the basis of the trade of Scotland, for the scale of these industries had little to do with the national market.

In the early 1880s, however, the prevailing mood of optimism changed to one of despondency. Cities now seemed not just to contain problems, but they themselves were a problem: the problem of mass poverty, with its components of unemployment, physical degeneracy, overcrowded, inadequate housing, and economic exploitation, and with concomitants like immorality, vice, crime, and religious and political disaffection. Increasingly a larger role was proposed for government. The scale of government also increased, and the establishment of the office of Secretary for Scotland in 1885 (it remained in London until 1939 when it was transferred to Edinburgh and renamed the Scottish Office) was the recognition of the increasing complexities of modern industrial urban society.

The Tenemental Townscape

Housing became a prominent political problem in the last quarter of the nineteenth century.[17] The boom of the 1870s gave rise to a great deal of jerry-building. A jaundiced professional eye observed:[18]

> The character of the carpentry or joiners' work of these four or five storey flats needs no description. It might have been executed by an amateur casual. The mason and the plasterer do the principal work, and when the sashes are hung, the doors hinged, the flats are ready for their victims.

The types and quality of buildings provided cannot be separated from the financial system that backed them. Lenders of money to builders and small-time investors demanded structural strength but showed little concern for the internal lay-out of houses. The more families a proprietor could squeeze in, the better was the chance that his bonds would be honoured.

High land prices necessitated building to very high densities. The dwellings were approached by a narrow passageway or close leading from the street to a stone stair at the back of the building and this gave access to the upper floor flats. Common water closets, which were added later, were usually at either side of the stairs and were entered from the half-landing. With the introduction of legislation specifying minimum standards of light, space, structural design and sanitation, many of the late Victorian working-class tenements adopted a simple two-room, kitchen and toilet lay-out with four flats per floor in four-storey tenements. One could say that the cumulative forces of the various Acts of Parliament – dealing with housing, public health and police – were beginning to make an impact on standards of living as well as creating a more ordered landscape.

Stagnant Towns

On the whole, Scotland avoided the worst of the great depression which accompanied the collapse of the foreign trade boom in 1873. But depression did catch Scotland up in the 1890s and in many ways has never really left the country. Before 1890, 75 per cent of the Borders' woollen trade was directed to the American market, but the McKinley Tariff of 1890 effectively placed a 90 per cent duty on woollens sent from Scotland. After the Dingley legislation in 1897 this duty rose to 100 per cent, and the Payne-Aldrich schedules which replaced it ranged from 95 to 145 per cent. By the early 1900s the trade to America had slumped to 5 per cent. The impact on Border towns was catastrophic: between 1891 and 1901, the population of Hawick fell from 19,204 to 17,303 and that of Galashiels by about one quarter. An observer wrote in 1899 that the Scottish tweed trade was 'withering and decaying and casting a blight over a once bright and busy part of the country'.[19] He spoke of rows of empty houses, a dwindling population and a steady flow of emigrants to Canada and the United States.

Planned Society

The pessimism about the cities and the depopulation of the countryside combined, in the 1890s, to produce a perceptible nostalgia for rural life. A back-to-the-land impulse was central in Ebenezer

Howard's *Tomorrow* published in 1898 (retitled *Garden Cities of Tomorrow* in 1902). His ideas found fertile ground in the minds of such groups as the Fabian Society, which organised a conference in 1900 and issued a number of pamphlets, including Raymond Unwin's *Cottage Plans and Common Sense*. Scotland's inheritance from this movement has been profound and includes: the whole of the philosophy of the planning profession, including its garden-city concepts and its conventions regarding the segregation of land uses; the cottage-type house; the green belt; land-use legislation; the prevalence of council houses; and urban renewal policies that are completely at odds with Scottish urban tradition, which was based on the congested tenement but with ample services in close proximity.

Dunfermline was to play a significant part in the evolution of town planning into an accepted discipline. Patrick Geddes was commissioned in 1903 by the Carnegie Trust to prepare a 'civic survey' of the burgh. Another planning opportunity arose in 1910 when a new naval dockyard was proposed on the mudflats beside the Firth of Forth in the barony of Rosyth. About 1,200 houses were required to house the dockyard workers and Dunfermline produced a plan whose scope amazed early planning circles. For the first time a municipality was trying to plan on a massive scale and the council wanted to make sure that no part of the area should become the 'happy hunting ground of the jerrybuilder'. Before any progress had been made, however, Britain was at war, and a hurried Act of Parliament had to be obtained to start the new town. The result was far more radical than anyone expected, for the normal Scottish building acts and bylaws which favoured tenement construction were suspended, enabling dwellings of the 'garden-city cottage type' to be erected.

Rosyth remained the main example of the pioneer planners' experiments with garden cities, and it was left to the post-World War II Labour Government to implement Howard's ideas in the New Town movement. Experience of the one-class dormitory suburb of the inter-war years left a feeling of revulsion in planners' minds. Baillie Jean Mann of Glasgow, who had been instrumental in setting up the Scottish branch of the Town and Country Planning Association, dismissed the results of inter-war house building as being largely unplanned, 'resulting in a nation of bus-catchers and strap-hangers'. She suggested in 1941 that at least four new towns would be necessary for Scotland after the war. Indeed, by 1945 it was felt that up to eight new towns would be required in central Scotland.

The Clyde Valley Regional Plan proposed the establishment of four new towns at Cumbernauld, East Kilbride, Bishopton and Houston, to cater for approximately 250,000 people who would come mainly from the Glasgow area. The new era started with the designation of East Kilbride in 1948. In the meantime, a new town was proposed in Fife to serve new mining developments near the burghs of Leslie and Markinch. A green-field site was selected at Glenrothes, but construction of the town had barely started when the National Coal Board began to revise downwards its manpower needs. The turning-point came in 1962 when the ill-fated Rothes Colliery was abandoned and the town had to start the long process of attracting new industry.

The lack of building land in Glasgow brought the necessity for overspill to crisis proportions and to relieve the city, Cumbernauld was designated a new town in 1956. The decision to build Cumbernauld's town centre on the top of a hill, with the whole of the residential area grouped closely around it, gave an opportunity to build a unique town. From the beginning pedestrians were segregated from the roads and the town was designed for universal car ownership. Livingston new town was the outcome of continuing pressure to house Glasgow's overspill, for by 1960 it was evident that a new town was needed outside the Clyde Valley. Furthermore, Livingston was given a strategic role in revitalising the declining regional economy of West Lothian.

The designation of Irvine new town in 1966 marked a complete break from the garden-city concept and green-field location. The new town incorporated the two old burghs of Irving and Kilwinning, together with a number of surrounding villages and smaller communities. The designation and cancellation of Stonehouse new town brought this phase of urban development to an end in 1976. The decision was deliberately associated by the government with Glasgow's East End Project, and the impression was given that only by cancellation of the new town would funds become available to rehabilitate the East End of Glasgow.

By any standards the post-war new town movement was one of the most adventurous national housing policies ever put forward. Although each town has had different circumstances in which to develop, each has reached a level of self-sustaining maturity. East Kilbride has been an outstanding success, reaching maturity in record time. Cumbernauld gained international recognition in the field of town planning, when in 1967 it won a prize for community architecture awarded by Reynolds Metals Company of America in a competition whose entries ranged from Tapiola in Finland to Brazilia. Yet the standard work on Britain's new towns criticised it severely:[20]

It is questionable whether this is a good site for a new town, and whether a more protected one should have been chosen. Hill towns in southern Italy enjoy a warm sunny climate, but a town in an exposed and windy part of Scotland is very different.

The Landscape of Council Housing

One of the most notable features of the Scottish urban landscape is the dominance of the council house. No less than 57.6 per cent of the population live in state housing, compared with 29 per cent in England. The Scottish city became socialised not from any specific political ideology but through the need to rectify urban injustices created in the nineteenth century. From that time, the official contention has been that by relieving people of environmental problems, the many and complex social problems would also be relieved. Housing was by far the worst problem: according to the 1861 census, 34 per cent of families in Scotland lived in one room and 37 per cent in two rooms. As noted earlier, the boom in tenement building in the 1870s gave rise to a great deal of jerry-building, but the volume of building rarely caught up with need.

Relevant parliamentary legislation began in 1855 and a number of acts were passed thereafter, mainly concerned with public health issues and housing. Indeed, overcrowding was so great in Glasgow that the Corporation attempted to limit the problem by licensing the capacity of houses of three rooms or less. Few attempts to house the working class (such as the city improvement acts) were really successful until the passing of the Housing and Town Planning (Scotland) Act of 1919. Based on the Royal Commission on Housing in Scotland, central government took on the responsibility of finding the capital, while delegating the building and management of housing to local authorities.

At first the schemes were modest, though of high quality. Then in the 1930s steps were taken to build larger schemes to replace slum housing in the worst areas of Scottish inner cities. The outcome was some of the most notorious council schemes – Blackhills in Glasgow and Craigmiller in Edinburgh. Post-war Scotland saw the rapid extension of state housing by local authorities and the Scottish Special Housing Association (SSHA), whilst private building came close to a standstill. Massive schemes for 20,000 to 50,000 people were tacked on to the edges of the cities – Easterhouses, Drumchapels, Wester Hailes and Whitfields.

The tower block became the hallmark of council building in the

1960s, and made Glasgow the foremost exponent of high-rise living in Europe. Approximately 65,000 people, almost the population of Greenock, live in some 200 blocks, including the 31-storey Red Road development. Of the four cities, Dundee has the highest proportion of public housing – 55.6 per cent compared with 25 per cent in 1945. In 1970 Dundee had 204 houses in the public sector per 1,000 population, compared with 170 in Glasgow, 149 in Aberdeen and 102 in Edinburgh.

Urban Scotland Today

Today urban Scotland is an unhappy compromise between the Scottish burghal traditions of the compact tenemental town and the low-rise, low-density English urban form which has been imposed through various pieces of legislation from Westminster. Space standards were always low and congestion high – the halfway house of suburban living was not a traditional Scottish way. For some time Scottish local government has suffered from the fact that much urban and housing legislation has been promulgated in English terms – and often in purely London terms. The result is that increasingly solutions offered do not even address themselves to Scottish urban problems, far less solve them. The policy of selling council houses shows this all too clearly, for places like Dundee, Coatbridge, Paisley and Motherwell are council house towns with some 60 to 80 per cent of the inhabitants housed in this form of tenure. The provision of council houses in Scotland outstrips that of any other country in Europe, and there are clear indications that there will be negligible additions to the national stock of this form of housing in the future. Indeed, cities like Glasgow have such a surplus that the district council is selling off its unwanted property for 'urban homesteading'.

The trends of suburbanisation, which had been furthered by increasingly widespread car ownership, began to be reversed in the 1970s as people began to renovate, restore and conserve older tenemental property in the inner cities. Buildings that once were thought fit for demolition are now being looked on as valuable assets. Even the argument of inadequate space standards no longer applies, with the lowering of the birth rate and the increasing number of single-person and aged households. The vast number of gap sites in and near Scotland's city centres will probably attract neo-tenemental building such as can already be seen in Edinburgh's Southside.

The decline of traditional industries which has been going on for most of the twentieth century has reached its zenith in the 1980s, and many of the industries introduced since World War II are also vanishing. With the exception of north-east Scotland, which benefits from developments associated with North Sea Oil, there is little industrial employment outside government. Forestry is declining; so is agriculture; fishing has been severely reduced; and the paper industry has virtually gone, including the great pulp mill at Corpach, near Fort William. The steel industry survives around Motherwell but the future of even this industry is uncertain. Shipbuilding is barely surviving, and has vanished forever in Dundee. Car manufacture at Linwood is no more, and at Bathgate the future is uncertain. The much vaunted electronics industry is withering. The urban impact of all this is profound: although people are better housed they see little economic growth which will lead to the regeneration of a modern industrial society. Today unemployment is not standing on street corners, but staring at the TV set.

Scotland has inherited an urban society that is at odds with its national geography. Because the period of its most dynamic growth occurred in the nineteenth century during the Imperial era, it developed on urban and industrial scales that are no longer appropriate. Furthermore, much of the social overhead capital created in that age of boom, especially for the working classes, proved of little benefit to successive generations. The ill-built one- and two-roomed tenements in which two-thirds of Scotland's population resided at the turn of the century, together with the beginnings of Scotland's economic stagnation, created vast problems which consumed an inordinate amount of local energy just to mitigate them. Glasgow, the Second City of the Empire, is rapidly declining to a population of a mere 690,000 from its once proud million. Most other towns in Scotland are stagnant and the nation's population is shrinking. None can tell the future of urban Scotland, but it is not difficult to forecast that the social and physical fabric of the Scottish town will provide consistent concern for the generations to come.

Notes to this chapter are on pages 309–10.

8

The Development of Transport Systems

J. H. Farrington

THE aim in this chapter is to review the evolution of transport infrastructure and services in Scotland. The story is complex. Private investment and state capital, competition and co-operation involving private companies, local authorities, governments and individuals are all set in a physical environment that is often difficult for the development of transport systems. Our main concern is with the evolution of Scottish transport from the eighteenth century onwards, since it is the developments of this time that have produced the transport systems in use today. Changes since the late nineteenth century are discussed in greater detail, because they have most immediate relevance to the present transport scene.

Trade and communication before the eighteenth century were confined mainly to unmade tracks (used by packhorses, livestock and pedestrians rather than by wheeled vehicles), though – where possible – the sea, lochs and rivers were used for navigation and floating timber. In the early seventeenth century the Justices of the Peace were given the duty of supervising the repair of roads leading to market towns and churches, though they had no practical way of carrying this out. In 1669 the Statute Labour system was enacted, requiring tenants and cottars to provide labour, horses and carts for road repair, but – as in England – this system was resented and ineffective. During the early eighteenth century the labour duty was increasingly replaced by inadequate money payments and road maintenance was little improved.[1]

Travel problems during this period have been summarised as follows:[2]

> Travellers who recorded their impressions tended to range from the patronising to the abusive. Scotland was not in fact a very convenient country to travel in if you were a stranger. The easiest way to move was often by water. As each of the many royal burghs monopolised the import-export

trade in a finite landward area, merchants did not normally traverse the realm. Gentry moved from one castle to another. Humble folk who had to travel . . . tended to camp out. Inns were therefore few and poor . . . Spring and Summer were the travelling seasons and the only sensible time to move goods in any bulk by land.

Nevertheless, by the early eighteenth century, domestic and foreign trade had developed in commodities such as herring, woollen cloth, linen yarn, salt, and iron ore, and regular horse-post services between the main cities had been introduced. Water transport was preferred for bulky goods, but navigable water – even in this time of small vessels – did not penetrate large areas.

Significantly, one of the long-distance trades most important until as late as the early nineteenth century was the movement of livestock, a commodity which could transport itself without made roads. Surplus livestock from the Highlands and Islands was driven annually to the richer English pastures – particularly in East Anglia – to be fattened for sale in southern markets, principally London. This arduous trade has been well documented by Haldane, who estimated that 150,000 sheep in the mid-eighteenth century, and 100,000 cattle by the end of the century, were crossing the border annually.[3] The droving trade declined after the 1820s, when steamships and then railways offered a more expensive but better quality service. Scottish agricultural practices also improved, and drovers' routes became more restricted. Although a significant trade, livestock droving did not bring lasting physical improvements in the form of established made roads.

Mid-eighteenth to Mid-nineteenth Centuries
Roads

The development of roads which were in large measure the forerunners of the present (non-motorway) road network took place in two distinct ways. First, roads were built under the turnpike system – this occurred mainly in north-east, central and southern Scotland. Second, roads were built with government aid or financed directly by government – these were mainly in the Highlands.

Under the turnpike system, trustees were sanctioned by Act of Parliament to build or improve a stretch of road to a standard suitable for wheeled vehicles, and to levy tolls on traffic. This introduction of private enterprise into road-building and maintenance, replacing statute labour by money payments, overcame some of the problems of the Statute Labour system. It encouraged men of means and initiative to improve communications in their locality, thereby also benefitting themselves by increasing the value and yield of their estates and businesses. The system was successful in those areas of Scotland where trustees had a reasonable assurance of satisfactory traffic volumes, and it was therefore inevitable that turnpike developments would occur mainly in the areas of greatest economic activity.

The main period of turnpike building was from 1750, with construction increasing after 1780 and lasting until the mid-nineteenth century. Faster, more reliable and more frequent stagecoach services were introduced on the new roads. By 1764, for example, a daily stage coach completed the Glasgow–Edinburgh route in nine hours, and by the early nineteenth century people and goods could be moved by road throughout the lowlands with regularity and reasonable reliability. But bulky goods were still difficult and expensive to transport overland, and canals were being built as early as the 1760s to meet this need.

The turnpike system had little impact on north and west Scotland, where low population densities and a relatively unproductive and difficult environment combined to make turnpike roads an unattractive proposition, even for the most philanthropic invester. The Highland landowners probably saw little need for made roads when livestock droving stood to lose, rather than gain, by road construction, and fears for the continuation of the clan system in the face of improved communications also discouraged local support for turnpike-type roads.

The state became involved in Highland road construction between the 1720s and 1760s, initially for military reasons. In 1724 General Wade was sent to Scotland to disarm the rebel clans and subdue the Highlands, for which purpose he was authorised to improve roads linking the main garrisons at Fort William, Fort Augustus and Inverness. Wade's roads deteriorated quickly as a result of the climate and insufficient provision for maintenance, but his achievement stands, for he was 'the first to recognise in practical fashion that the problem of the Scottish Highlands was then, as it remains today, largely one of communications'.[4] This statement is something of an over-simplification, but Wade certainly pushed road-building, for the first time, into the forefront of Highland affairs.

The extension of the military road system continued until the 1790s with about 600 miles still in fair repair by 1799 (Fig 8.1). At least £300,000 was spent between 1725 and 1800; despite disappointing physical results, the achievement in helping to shape ensuing policies in the Highlands was significant. In particular, the precedent for state involvement in improving Highland communication was established by 1800.

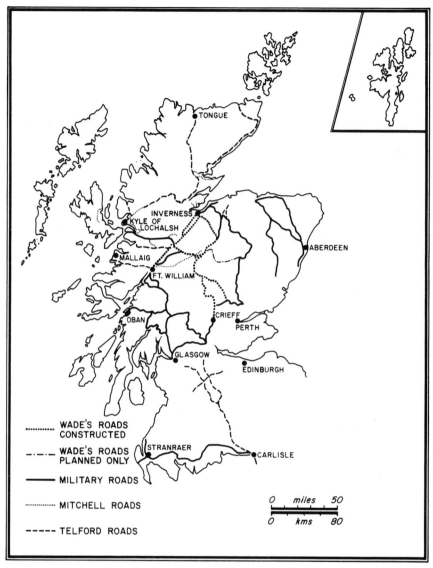

Fig 8.1 State Road Construction in Scotland in 1821. Based on A. O'Dell and K. Walton *The Highlands of Scotland* (1962) Fig 36

Between 1801 and 1803 Thomas Telford reported to the Treasury on his surveys for the improvement of road and canal communications and for improving the region's economy. The aims of providing jobs, stimulating the economy and removing the need for emigration were the basis of government policy, which – through Acts of Parliament in 1803 – established two Commissions charged with Highland road and bridge building and with constructing the Caledonian Canal. The system for financing road-building was simple and fair. Requests for specific roads were made to the Commission for Roads and Bridges, whose surveyor Telford (or later his assistants) made an estimate of the cost; half of this would be put up by the government. When the applicants had deposited their half of the cost, detailed surveys were made and the contract put out to tender. A significant innovation resulting from the Commission's work was the levying of a property rate by Inverness-shire in 1803–4 to finance proposed roads, and Ross, Sutherland and Caithness counties followed suit.[5]

By 1821, work on the Highland roads was almost finished. Over £450,000 had been spent, about £200,000 of it from local contributions, and 875 miles of road and 11 large bridges had been built. The average workforce was 2,700, with over 3,500 in one year.

Canals

The distinction between road-building in the Highlands and in the Lowlands had an approximate parallel in canal construction. The lowland canals – almost entirely concentrated in the Central Belt – were financed by private capital joint-stock companies under Act of Parliament, though public money was loaned to complete the Forth & Clyde Canal. In the Highlands the road-building Commission was complemented by the Commissioners for the Caledonian Canal, and the other Highland canal – the Crinan – began as a private company but passed into the Commissioners' control.

Two of the central belt canals – the Monkland and the Edinburgh & Glasgow Union (Fig 8.2) – were built for the classic purpose of supplying cities (Glasgow and Edinburgh respectively) with coal. The other two – the Glasgow, Paisley & Johnstone and the Forth & Clyde – began as proposed ship canals, though only the latter performed this function. Bulk movements of commodities such as coal, iron, wood, stone, grain, lime and cotton were the staple traffics, and related industries were attracted to the canals' banks. In addition to these traditional canal traffics, however, a considerable passenger traffic was developed on Scottish canals, with onward links by connecting stage coaches. The canals brought relatively cheap, comfortable and speedy transport for large sections of society. For example in 1834–5, the Glasgow, Paisley & Johnstone carried 373,290 passengers,[6] and in 1836 the Forth & Clyde carried 197,710 passengers.[7] Other lowland canals included the Aberdeenshire, built to link Inverurie and a rural hinterland with Aberdeen harbour.

Traffic on all the canals was adversely affected by railway

Page 173 *(above)* Typical 1930s (slum clearance/overcrowding alleviation) council estate; now heavily stigmatised despite quality of building material. Sandilands, Aberdeen; *(below)* typical flatted council property of the 1950s; Mastrick, Aberdeen

Page 174 *(left)* The lower-middle-class tenements in the Warrender area of Edinburgh, built in the 1890s

(below) The upper-middle-class Grange district in the Southside of Edinburgh showing the substantial stone detached villas

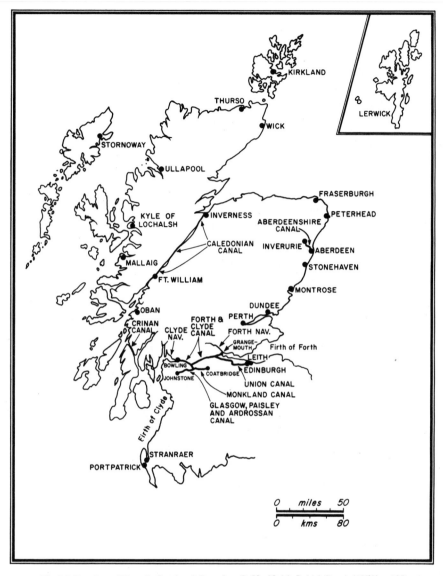

Fig 8.2 Canals and Ports in Scotland. Based on C. Hadfield, *British Canals* (1979) p.125

competition from the 1840s, and by 1869 they had passed into railway ownership. The Aberdeenshire's route was used in part for the construction of the Aberdeen–Huntly railway between 1848 and 1854, and the Glasgow, Paisley & Johnstone Canal was replaced by a railway in 1881. The others remained in existence much longer, though they deteriorated. The Monkland was formally closed for navigation in 1950, the Forth & Clyde in 1963, and the Edinburgh & Glasgow Union in 1965.

The Crinan Canal was built to improve communications between north and west Scotland and the Hebrides, on the one hand, and the Clyde and west central Scotland, on the other. Problems encountered during construction continued long after the opening in 1801, and eventually the canal was vested in the Caledonian Canal Commissioners in 1848, thus passing into public ownership after having begun as a private venture. The Caledonian Canal was always firmly a public conern, with the aims of avoiding the dangers of the Pentland Firth passage, providing a strategic link between the North Sea and the Atlantic Ocean for the Royal Navy, and – perhaps most significantly – giving employment and reducing emigration from the Highlands. The Great Glen route proved to have appeared deceptively simple, and great problems were encountered in construction and maintenance. It was incomplete when it opened in 1822, and by the 1840s it had cost over £1 million.[8] The Caledonian and Crinan canals never justified themselves in strict economic terms, but from an early date their operation has been accepted as a state obligation, ensuring their retention for use by the leisure-conscious mid-twentieth century society.

Ports and Harbours

Ports and harbours shared in the trend towards improved transport facilities during this period. The impetus for improvement (deeper channels, more and larger berths, and landward links) came from town authorities, fishing and merchant interests, canal, railway and shipping companies, and government interest in emigration problems and communications in general (including particularly England–Scotland and Ireland–Scotland trade). Pressure on ports increased as ship size increased, and as a result of the increased trade marking the development of an industrial economy. Ports became:[9]

> ... a bottle neck which had to be broken if the industrial development of Scotland was not to be checked ... The facts that most parts of the Lowlands were relatively close to navigable water; that ships, especially coasting ships, were quite small; and that elaborate harbour works were not necessary to cope with the bulk of shipping using Scottish ports, all contributed to the dynamism of the 18th century economy. By 1800, however, the improvement of at least the major Scottish harbours had become a necessity.

The Clyde had long been a difficult navigation, but Glasgow's trading position was safeguarded by the use of jetties to increase scour, together with steam dredgers, from the 1830s. Also outports – mainly

Port Glasgow and Greenock – allowed larger ships to trade with central Scotland. The Forth & Clyde Canal's terminus on the Clyde at Bowling remained small in comparison with established Clyde ports, but its terminus at Grangemouth (begun in 1784) – with land for expansion and good inland links successively by canal, rail and road – developed into one of the two principal Forth ports. By 1816 it rivalled Leith – Edinburgh's own port (established as early as 1329) – and the element of competition brought benefits to shippers in the form of port improvements. Other east-coast ports competed for overlapping hinterlands, and bodies of Harbour Commissioners were usually set up to carry out improvements. A combination of factors – including inland links, the physical nature of the site, and the facility of navigation through harbour approaches – tended to eliminate those ports unable to keep up with the increased size of shipping. Dundee and Aberdeen emerged as dominant ports. Railway expansion after the mid-nineteenth century, and the adoption of steam propulsion in the fishing industry, further tended to concentrate activity on fewer ports. Railway expansion particularly affected coastal shipping.

Traffic at several east-coast ports, notably Leith, Dundee and Aberdeen, included in this period coastal passenger services to England and other parts of Scotland including Orkney and Shetland. This role of mainland terminal for island settlements was also the main *raison d'être* of several northern and western ports, such as Wick, Thurso, Oban, Mallaig and Kyle of Lochalsh. All were enhanced in this function later in the nineteenth or early twentieth century by railway links. Portpatrick in Galloway afforded access to the short sea crossing to Ireland in the days of sail, but it was '. . . a terrible place for both trains and ships to get into'.[10] Attempts were made to improve it with public money, but in 1874 it was abandoned as a packet station and replaced by Stranraer. After the 1830s, railway companies' competition and expansion strategies led to their acquisition of some ports, notably Grangemouth, and they took a close interest in other port developments.

Railways to the Early Twentieth Century

As long as the motive power of land transport remained the horse, speed and capacity were inevitably restricted; and Scottish canals were restricted by too many topographical features to spread the effects of their better load-carrying capabilities, and (in some cases) shorter journey times, over a wide area. The railways were thus an important development.

The infant railway system was present in some areas during the very period when most attention was paid to canals and roads. The earliest railway was probably a wooden waggonway on Tranent estate near Prestonpans, and was in existence in 1722 to carry coal to the port of Cockenzie. During the period up to the 1830s many other waggonways were built, usually for the same purpose of moving coal to ports, canals or factories, but generally using cable, horse or gravity power. A significant exception was the 1831 Garnkirk & Glasgow Railway, which competed with the Monkland Canal by operating steam and horse-hauled services for passengers as well as goods.

The early Scottish railways were local in origin and function, but between 1837 and 1842 several elements of a trunk system were authorised and built: the Glasgow, Paisley, Kilmarnock & Ayr Railway; the Glasgow, Paisley & Greenock Railway; and the Edinburgh & Glasgow Railway. These had good financial prospects, and their success (the Edinburgh & Glasgow carried over one million passengers annually by the mid 1840s, three times the original expectations) contributed to the Scottish railway mania of 1845–6.

In 1841 a Royal Commission – appointed to consider the need for railways between England and Scotland – reported that one route would suffice, via Crewe, Lancaster and Carlisle. In the event, however, competition between railway companies, fostered by Parliament in the public interest, produced four routes. These were via the Glasgow & South Western Railway, the Caledonian Railway and the North British Railway (which had two routes). By the time these trunk routes were completed, in 1862, railways in central and southern Scotland had spread to serve coalfields and ports, textile towns and agricultural areas, cities, coastal resorts and embryonic suburbs. Intense competition for traffic and territory resulted in many of these traffic sources being served by more than one company. Access to central Glasgow in particular was regarded as an important goal, and the multiplicity of lines and stations that had resulted by the 1890s affords a dramatic example of the results of competition.[11]

From 1848 the rail network spread north of the central belt – to Perth, Dundee and Aberdeen – mainly through the absorption of smaller companies into the rival North British and Caledonian companies. The North British rush to bridge the Firths of Forth and Tay played a part in the hasty and inadequate construction of the first Tay Bridge, which collapsed in 1879 with a passenger train on it. This delayed the construction of a similar structure over the Forth, so that the present Forth Bridge – built to a different design and opened at Queensferry in 1890 – incorporates a large safety margin. In 1888 and

1895, races from London to Aberdeen took place between the rival companies of the east coast and west coast routes, represented on the Scottish sections by the North British and Caledonian respectively. The arrivals in Aberdeen of the racing trains at 5am could have had little appeal for the ordinary traveller, then as now, and the trains were ultimately reduced to a locomotive and three coaches. Nonetheless, the winning time of 512 minutes for the 540 miles from Euston to Aberdeen (16½ miles further than the east coast route) was a great operational achievement, albeit at some risk to safety.[12]

The railways of the North-east and the Highlands were built mainly by the Great North of Scotland Railway and the Highland Railway, originating in Acts of 1854 and 1865 respectively. The main exceptions were the lines to Oban and Mallaig (opened in 1880 and 1901 respectively), which were products of North British and Caledonian competition for Western Isles traffic, and the Invergarry & Fort Augustus Railway at the southern end of the Great Glen (opened in 1903). The lateness of these lines, and the fact that two – the Mallaig and Kyle of Lochalsh lines – received government aid, indicate that the great tide of railway development financed by private capital was virtually spent by the time it reached the north of Scotland.

The construction of the Scottish railway system spanned the nineteenth century and was a most important element in the contemporary processes of agricultural, industrial, social, rural and urban change. It has been assessed[13] as 'the single most dramatic development across the face of virtually all Lowland Scotland, and later and to a lesser extent in the Highlands . . . [The Railways were] . . . crucial determining factors in the growth of the Scottish Victorian economy . . .'

The Changing Scene, Late Nineteenth Century to World War II

Several changes took place during this period which disturbed, in some ways profoundly, the railway's domination. Even during the railway age *par excellence*, up to World War I, other modes of transport of course remained important. The canals still carried bulk traffics, though they declined still further in the face of road competition after 1919. The roads themselves remained the principal mode on routes not served by the railways, especially in the Highlands and Borders. Coastal shipping and ferries remained of basic importance in the north and west, with harbour improvements and the introduction of steam propulsion. The Lowland ports were progressively enlarged – by the railways, by Harbour Trustees or by local authorities – in order to cope with trade expansion.

Railways, Tramways and Roads

This section discusses the growth of competition for the railways, mainly in the form of the internal combustion-engined vehicle, but also, in the main urban areas, in the form of tramways. The latter provided most competition in Glasgow, beginning in 1898 with the electrification by the Corporation of its horse-tram routes to Springburn. Within four years the rival railway service was withdrawn, and the competition soon spread as the tramway system reached out to such distant places as Loch Lomond, Hamilton, Motherwell and Renfrew. At its peak the Glasgow system carried 225 million passengers a year, providing more accessible, cleaner, cheaper and more frequent services than the suburban railways.[14] Glasgow also boasts the only underground railway in Scotland, opened in 1896 and connecting in a circle the central area and west end. The system was cable-hauled, using stationary steam engines, until electrification in 1932–5.

Edinburgh's railways were less severely affected by the trams, which moved by gripping steam-driven cables,[15] but electrification in 1922 made the latter competitive with inner suburban railways, while motor buses began to compete in the outer suburbs. Rail closures followed in the 1920s and 1930s. An intensive suburban rail service in Aberdeen from Culter to Dyce was killed by tram and bus competition, but lasted until 1937.

The railways thus faced significant competition for urban passenger traffic as early as the last years of the nineteenth century. Soon road competition for both passenger and goods traffic began to have serious effects in all areas. Ironically, in 1904 the Great North of Scotland Railway began to run one of the earliest motor bus services in Britain, between Ballater and Braemar. A multitude of bus companies and road-haulage operators subsequently sprang up throughout Britain, particularly after 1919 as trained mechanics from the armed forces made use of surplus army vehicles. By the mid-1920s there were thirty bus operators serving the Glasgow to Paisley route. A service between Annan and Carlisle begun in 1925 carried 54,750 passengers in its first year.[16] Legislation to control these activities – in the interests of the consumer, the railways and the road operators themselves – was introduced, mainly in the Road Traffic Act of 1931 and the Road and Rail Traffic Act of 1933. These restricted freedom of competition within the industry, and it has been argued that this stifled new enterprises and harmed the consumer, while the railways as common carriers continued to suffer.

The main effect of the Road Traffic Act in Scotland was to produce the major bus combine of SMT, an amalgamation of the Scottish Motor Traction Company and the Alexanders' bus groups. In the north of Scotland the Highland Transport Company was formed in 1930, its backers including the London, Midland & Scottish Railway. A large number of independent operators remained in Aberdeenshire, and in the Highlands and Islands, where they also carried Post Office mails under contract (an interesting precedent in view of the later development of Post Office buses – see below). Apart from the city corporation undertakings, the other main Scottish operator was David MacBrayne Ltd, originally a shipping company but also a bus operator from 1906. Subsidy was paid to MacBrayne's steamer operations as early as 1891, and in 1928 the firm exacted higher subsidies by refusing to tender for mail contract renewal.[17]

Despite legislation controlling road vehicle licensing and operation in the 1930s, the railways, with their direct track costs and high labour overheads, felt the effects of competition, and branch lines throughout Scotland began to lose their passenger services, adding to the closures already noted in urban and suburban areas. The reasons are well-known – road vehicles generally offered more frequent (if not always more comfortable), door-to-door services, at lower cost to the consumer (at least for short and middle-distance trips). The railways put a brave face on it as regards some of their prestige services. Five years after the grouping of 1923, which left Scotland divided between the London, Midland & Scottish and London & North Eastern Railways, competing services were introduced on the England–Scotland routes, when the LNER ran the Flying Scotsman non-stop between the two capitals. The LMS retaliated with the Royal Scot to Glasgow, though an agreement on a time of $8\frac{1}{4}$ hours was made between the companies. This was dropped in 1937, when times of 6 and $6\frac{1}{2}$ hours were run. Further improvements were prevented by the outbreak of World War II in September 1939.

Despite these prestigious operations, however, it is true to say that British railways were already undercapitalised by this time – efforts to make savings and meet road competition were resulting in the deterioration of assets such as stations and rolling stock. The railways were therefore not 100 per cent fit when they were called upon in 1939 to make an even greater co-ordinated effort than had been required in World War I, when the routes leading to Cromarty and Scapa Flow in the North of Scotland, in particular, had carried traffic well in excess of their designed capacities.

Air Transport

Air transport began to develop in Scotland in the 1920s, and the first regular air service in Britain was established in 1933 between Glasgow (Renfrew), Kintyre and Islay; it did not continue for long, however. The advantage of air transport in the north and west – with the many islands, peninsulas and mountains – was such that many services were pioneered in the 1930s, including: Aberdeen to Kirkwall and Sumburgh; Glasgow to Campbeltown, Islay, Barra and North Uist; and Inverness to Aberdeen, Perth and Stornoway. Two of the notable pioneers were Fresson and Gander-Dower, respectively with Highland Airways and Aberdeen Airways. The latter bought and developed property at Dyce for Aberdeen Airport, while Fresson is well known for his establishment of Orkney Isles services,[18] but both men pioneered many Scottish routes. They and the other pioneers risked more than their capital in bringing the benefits of air travel to remote areas, putting many of them for the first time within reach of a return day trip to their regional centre, and extending accessibility to medical facilities.

Transport since 1945

Since World War II Scottish transport has continued to operate within a framework incorporating a number of trends and problems, most of them not unique to Scotland. Following the nationalisation of transport services in 1948 (which included the railways and canals, much of the bus and airline industries, and long-distance road haulage), local and national government has played an increasing role in the planning of transport development and investment policies. The same authorities have also increasingly subsidised the operation of public transport, including bus, rail, sea and air services. At the same time as public road and rail transport's share of the passenger market has declined because of growing overall car ownership, the capital and running costs of all transport systems have increased. Without subsidy the position of a great deal of public transport in Scotland would be at best marginal.

Another trend has been an increase in personal mobility for some sections of the population, while the mobility of others without the use of a car has been reduced. The latter have suffered from centralisation in the provision of education, health, retail and entertainment facilities, and declining public transport provision, particularly in rural areas.

Road Transport

Apart from the city transport undertakings, most stage carriage bus services are operated by the Scottish Bus Group (a subsidiary of the Scottish Transport Group), though there do still exist independent operators of stage carriage and school services, particularly in rural areas.

Stage carriage operators may, under the 1968 Transport Act, apply to the local authority for subsidy to make good the deficit on a service. They also qualify for new bus grants (to be phased out by 1984) and fuel tax rebate. This system of subsidies and grants, together with a welcome desire to serve remote communities, has encouraged a large-scale move into public transport by the Post Office Corporation, who now run a total of over 200 services with post buses. Most of the services are in the Highlands and Islands, the Borders and the South-west, and generally connect small settlements with a local centre, also allowing tourists without cars to reach otherwise inaccessible areas. The financial characteristics of these services have allowed fare levels frequently to be lower than those of Scottish Bus Group companies and even independent operators, but there is a recent trend to make subsidies conditional upon standardised post-bus fare structures. Bus services in many areas of Scotland have been recently extensively revised (1980–3) following the Market Analysis Projects (MAP) which seek to reduce costs and increase loadings while maintaining as far as possible the social service element.

The only Passenger Transport Authority in Scotland is the Strath-clyde PTA, established in 1972 as the Greater Glasgow PTA (under the 1968 Transport Act) and responsible for the provision and co-ordination of all public transport within its designated area. But all regional authorities in Scotland are responsible for transport planning under the Transport Policy and Programme (TPP) system, in which an annual transport plan is submitted to central government in the form of a TPP document detailing the proposed allocation of resources over the next year. Each authority is then given a Rate Support Grant to spend as it thinks fit, provided it meets with government approval. In practice, there are considerable variations in the balance struck in the different regions between road and public transport spending. This is inevitable when these powers are devolved to regional authorities with different political complexions and regional problems. The Highlands and Islands Development Board also takes a close interest in transport problems in its area, especially in relation to employment, tourism and general infrastructure provision.

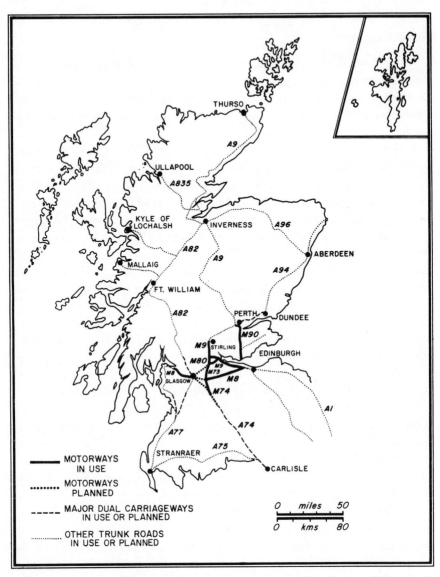

Fig 8.3 Motorways and Trunk Roads in Mainland Scotland, 1980. Based on British Road Federation *op. cit.* 30

The Scottish vehicle ownership rate for 1979, at 262 per 1,000 people, is below the British average of 342 per 1,000 people.[19] This average figure for Scotland, however, is largely meaningless in real terms since it conceals very wide variations. Using enumeration districts as a basis for comparison, different areas of both rural and urban regions may vary from over 1 car per household to less than 1 car per 10 households. The presence of such low car-ownership rates in some rural areas is particularly important, since these areas are at greater risk of losing public transport services when, for example, government spending restrictions oblige local authorities to consider the withdrawal of already reduced bus services.[20]

On the other hand, the total number of vehicles registered in Scotland increased from 1.12 million in 1970 to 1.3 million in 1975, and 1.35 million in 1979.[21] This has led to attempts to alleviate both urban and trunk road congestion by the provision of more parking spaces, ring roads and urban motorways (the latter in Glasgow only), by the bypassing of settlements on main routes, the re-alignment and widening of main routes and the construction of a motorway network based on the Glasgow–Edinburgh–Perth axes (Fig 8.3). This programme has included major bridges across the Firths of Forth and Tay, the River Tay at Perth, and the Clyde at Erskine, as well as the Clyde Tunnel in Glasgow. In the Highlands and Islands, causeways have shortened travel times and replaced ferries; the bridging of the Cromarty and Beauly Firths permits traffic to bypass Dingwall and gives better access to the Cromarty Firth growth area.

Road developments related expressly to North Sea oil exploitation consist mainly of the £200m improvement of the A9 between Perth and Inverness, but also include improvements in the Aberdeen–Peterhead and Dingwall areas. Local authorities incurring oil-related expenditure are aided by special grants introduced in 1979. A government pledge to dual-carriageway the Perth–Aberdeen route was based largely on the grounds of improved access to the oil capital.

Rail Transport

At the end of the war, the Scottish rail system – like the rest of British railways – was in a run-down condition. Major investment eventually came under the 1955 Modernisation Plan – and in the next ten years rolling stock and motive power were renewed, with the progressive reduction of steam haulage in favour of diesel. Competition from road hauliers and the private car became much more widespread in the 1950s, and a formal policy of identifying and closing loss-making services was instituted under Beeching in 1963. This exercise has frequently been criticised, particularly because it underplayed the contribution of branch and subsidiary lines to the main-line network. On the other hand, there was duplication of facilities in some areas, which was unnecessary in view of reduced traffic levels and which Beeching planned to eliminate. In the event, several lines were reprieved on social and political grounds, and remain open. The Inverness–Kyle of Lochalsh line, for example, has become something of

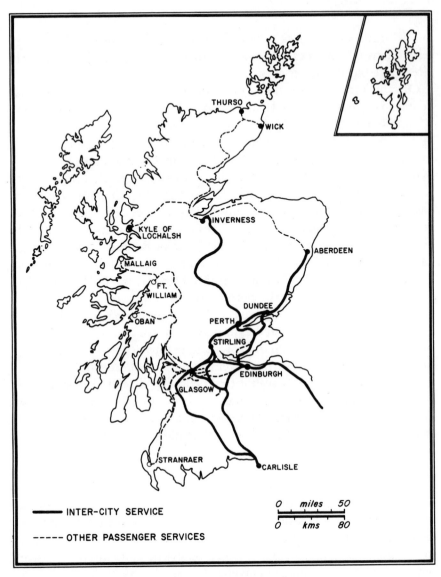

Fig 8.4 Railways in Scotland, 1980

a survivor, having been considered for closure more than once since 1963. In fact, the Highlands have retained more of their railways than most other areas, particularly in comparison with the north-east, the Borders and the south-west of Scotland (Fig 8.4). Stranraer, a railway-owned port, lost its direct line to Carlisle in 1965, and nothing remains of the comprehensive rail net lying between the west coast and east coast main lines, including the 'Waverley Route' through Hawick. The Waverley line closed in 1969.

In 1979 British Rail (Scotland) operated services over 1,855 route miles (of which 232 are electrified), with 290 passenger stations, 95 freight stations and 236 private sidings. The latter represents a disturbing decline from 301 in 1977, despite 50 per cent grants available for private-siding construction in certain cases.

In Glasgow, trunk passenger services have been concentrated on Queen Street and Central Stations, St Enoch and Buchanan Street stations having closed in 1966. A 'new' cross-city line was opened in 1979 – the electrified Argyle Line. (In fact this is largely the re-opened Glasgow Central Railway which closed in 1964.) This links the North Side electric services at Partick (inaugurated, with the Clyde Coast electrification, in 1960–1; the south side electrification took place in 1962) with Central Station, Argyle Street and Rutherglen. It is a joint venture between British Rail and the Strathclyde PTE. The latter have also modernised the underground railway at a cost of at least £43m and it was re-opened in 1980. Thus Glasgow is being re-equipped with urban railways, and will soon have one of the best urban transport systems in Britain, outside London. It must be noted, however, that – with its low car-ownership rates and large peripheral local authority housing estates – its problems of access to the city centre will not easily be solved, even with highly integrated bus and rail systems.

In 1974 electrification of the west coast main line allowed passengers from Glasgow to reach London in 5 hours, while the introduction of the 125mph High Speed Trains (HSTs) on the London–Edinburgh–Aberdeen route in 1978 brought Edinburgh within 4 hours 58 minutes of London, with another $2\frac{1}{2}$ hours to Aberdeen. These trains cannot operate at full speed on the Aberdeen line, though this is being upgraded to take trains at 90 mph where possible. Demonstrating that inter-line rivalry did not end in 1948, the west coast route should see a form of the 150mph electric Advanced Passenger Train (APT) operating by the late 1980s (though it will not then be running at its maximum speed). Rail is now competing with air transport for the London–Edinburgh and London–Glasgow routes. In 1977, rail had 48 per cent and air 52 per cent of the total rail and air traffic (excluding inter-line air traffic), and rail journeys between London and Glasgow totalled 380,000. British Rail are hoping for a $12\frac{1}{2}$ per cent shift to rail with the APT[22] coupled with adroit reduced-fare offers. At the same time, airline fare increases are moderated as a result of this competition plus the competition between airlines, mainly between British Airways and British Caledonian. Oil-related passenger traffic to and from the North-east has encouraged the HST route to Aberdeen, where major station improvements are under way. Inverness passenger services carried 30 per cent more passengers over the early and mid-1970s than in the late 1960s. In contrast to the £200m being spent on the A9 between Perth and Invergordon, £3.7m was allocated in 1976 for rail improvements including the doubling of single-line sections and resignalling between Perth and Inverness. In 1975 the line carried over half a million tons of oil-related materials.[23]

The main rail freight developments in recent years have included concentration on train-load (as opposed to waggon-load) movements between fewer terminals, leased company trains, Speedlink services, containerisation and – in the 'sundries' field – Red Star parcels. The Freightliner system was first established in 1967 to compete with road haulage for general traffic. The principle of rail terminals and road/rail containers is well-known, and it has been successful in retaining a share of the market without producing a large-scale transfer to rail. Scottish terminals are at Aberdeen, Dundee and Edinburgh, with Gushetfaulds and Coatbridge in the Glasgow area. Elgin has a small facility, and Inverness is a probable future terminal location. Road competition increased in the 1970s with the abolition of restrictive licensing on goods carried and routes covered, though the progressive increase in the cost of licensing heavy goods vehicles to cover true costs, and the introduction of tachographs, may bring this competition into a more realistic framework.

Despite periodic 'leaks' to the press, during the 1970s, of proposals from government departments for the closure of all railways north of Glasgow and Edinburgh, BR (Scotland) survives reasonably intact and with many positive achievements to its credits. These include the difficult process of reducing its staff from about 30,000 in 1968 to 18,660 in 1979. But the cycle of investment requirements continues, with much of the stock dating from the 1950s Modernisation Plan requiring replacement. The Scottish rail system will, of course, be affected by government attitudes towards investment. The immediate future may not see policies welcomed by BR, unless oil shortages encourage a recognition of the significance of rail transport, with more electrification on main routes and sufficient capital investment to ensure a continuing railway system.

Sea Transport

The main organisational development in Scottish ports since the war was the establishment of the Clyde Port Authority in 1966 and the Forth Ports Authority in 1968. The former includes Glasgow docks (the main activity is at King George V Dock, Shieldhall and Meadowside) and Greenock (with the Clydeport Container Terminal, opened in 1968 with Freightliner access). The Forth Ports Authority operates the separate ports of Grangemouth (where the first UK container terminal was opened in 1966, and Scotland's only oil refinery opened in 1924), Leith, Granton, Burntisland, Methil and Kirkcaldy. The two authorities control facilities which include the wide range of berthing and storage required by shippers dealing with – apart from containers – conventional and roll-on-roll-off loads, and packaged timber, oil and other bulk cargoes. The trend here, as in other ports, has been towards capital-intensive methods of cargo-handling, and port labour forces have decreased accordingly. The number employed in the Forth ports and Dundee fell from 1,563 in 1965 to 738 in 1977. In Leith and Grangemouth, the number of registered dockers fell from 616 and 575 respectively in 1965 to 213 and 333 in 1978, and the process is likely to continue. Total traffic – including petroleum – through the Forth ports in 1978 was 28.9 million tonnes, and through the Clyde ports, 9.4 million tonnes.

The Firth of Forth is the main exporting centre for North Sea oil, which is piped from the Forties field to Grangemouth refinery. In 1978, 19.3 million tonnes of surplus crude were shipped out from the Hound Point terminal, which can accept 300,000dwt tankers. The Sullom Voe terminal in Shetland took over this function as principal North Sea oil terminal in 1980.

Two other important – and environmentally controversial – terminal developments should be noted. The first is Hunterston iron ore terminal, which makes use of the deep water off the Ayrshire coast and was officially opened in 1979, though its operation was delayed by inter-union disputes. The second is the Liquefied Petroleum Gas loading terminal in Fife. The Clyde and Forth ports are effectively in competition with English ports for Scottish traffic, and some of the decline in traffic is blamed on improved road links. Hunterston should by the 1990s become the main port on the Clyde.

Of the other Scottish ports, Aberdeen emerged in the early 1970s as the main service base for offshore oil activity, with secondary roles for Dundee and Peterhead. The latter port now makes use of the Harbour of Refuge, previously long under-used. Aberdeen was well placed for the earlier phases of oil exploration, and its harbour facilities have been improved accordingly. As activity in the North Sea has moved northwards, servicing activity has developed in the Orkney and Shetland Islands, particularly the latter, but Aberdeen remains the 'oil capital', as well as the roll-on-roll-off ferry terminal for the P&O

Shetland service. Total tonnage handled in 1978 was 1.7 million.

Elsewhere in the north and west of Scotland, one of the main changes has been the move of the Lewis ferry terminal from the railhead at Kyle of Lochalsh to Ullapool, with improved road access. Ferry services in the Western Isles are operated mainly by Caledonian MacBrayne (a Scottish Transport Group constituent) and Western Ferries. Several new vessels have been introduced during the 1960s and 1970s to meet the need for roll-on-roll-off services, though this can lead to reduced flexibility because of the specialised terminal requirements.

Air Transport

Aberdeen, Edinburgh, Glasgow and Prestwick airports are at present operated by the Scottish Airports Division of the British Airports Authority (Fig 8.5). The eight main Highlands and Islands airports, which have an important community function, are operated by the Civil Aviation Authority, and are likely to remain so for the immediate future. However, growth in traffic at Sumburgh (404,000 passengers in 1977), where a £10m terminal for oil traffic is to be built, could make it a candidate for transfer to the BAA. This happened in 1975 to Aberdeen, which has since experienced the fastest growth rate in the United Kingdom, mainly as a result of oil-related traffic. Traffic here, having topped 1 million in 1977–8, is already overloading the terminal building opened in 1977, and in early 1981 the BAA announced expansion plans. Annual growth rates for Aberdeen since 1971–2 have ranged from 14.6 to 64.5 per cent. Scheduled international services are operated, mainly to Holland and Norway.

The main problem in Scottish airport provision concerns the central belt airports. A 1978 White Paper, presenting a review of British airport policy, observed that 'there is probably a greater excess of airport capacity in this region than anywhere else in Great Britain'.[24] Prestwick (386,000 passengers in 1977) mainly handles Scottish transatlantic traffic, and Glasgow and Edinburgh (1,752,500 and 1,021,600 passengers respectively in 1977) domestic and European services. This policy of specialisation is being relaxed, however, with Edinburgh increasing its international services to include international charters, largely at Glasgow's expense. A new central Scottish airport to rationalise this overprovision is financially impracticable (particularly since Edinburgh airport was virtually rebuilt with a new runway and terminal in 1977–8, and investment continues at Glasgow and Prestwick) and was ruled out in the 1978 White Paper.

The roles of airlines in providing Scottish services is constantly

Page 191 *(above)* Council housing typical of the 1970s, Hazelhead, Aberdeen; *(below)* modern high-rise flats typical of the last two decades in Scotland; Tillydrone, Aberdeen

Page 192 *(above)* Bow hauling on the Edinburgh–Glasgow Union canal to the east of Avon aqueduct, 1951; *(below)* the opening in 1975 of the Howard Doris terminal at Strome Ferry on the line to Kyle of Lochalsh, built to serve their construction site at Loch Kishorn, was a welcome boost to freight loadings in a region which no longer generates much rail-borne traffic. The closure of this yard, the aluminium smelter at Invergordon and the decline of traffic to Fearn for the Nigg yard has presented British Rail with a difficult challenge in their efforts to maintain a freight service north of Inverness. These are the cement silos with the specially installed sidings, photographed in October 1975

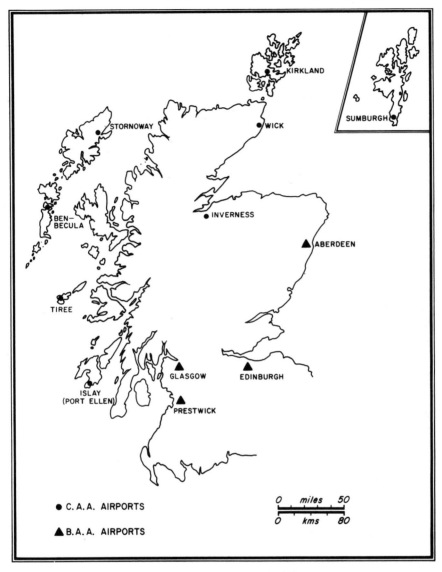

Fig 8.5 Airports in Scotland, 1980

changing, though British Airways (first as BEA) have stood by unprofitable Highlands and Islands routes since taking them over from pioneers such as Fresson under nationalisation in 1947–8. It is possible that smaller operators, such as Loganair or Air Ecosse, with aircraft better suited to these routes than BA Viscounts, could take some of them over with advantage. BA's seven jet services per day between London and Aberdeen now face competition in the shape of Dan Air's services to Gatwick, in line with CAA licensing policy. BA's London shuttle services to and from Glasgow and Edinburgh are successful but also face fares competition from British Caledonian. Other important airlines in the oil-related traffic areas are Air UK (with Aberdeen–Norwich routes plus services to the North of England and the Continent), Air Ecosse (seeking to develop its Scottish routes) and Dan Air (closely involved in Aberdeen–Shetland services for oil personnel, among other routes.

The competitive situation is thus complex, with CAA route licensing policy crucial for the future. With the Authority's stated concern to keep fares at a reasonable level, there are sure to be changes in operating patterns in the near future, brought about by route licence changes and the partial withdrawal of BA's Scottish services.

A major element in Scottish air transport, though not a public service, is the helicopter operation related to North Sea oil exploitation. British Airways Helicopters and Bristow Helicopters are the largest operators, with smaller concerns (such as North Scottish, British Executive Air Services and Ferranti Helicopters) also involved. British Airways Helicopters' headquarters are now at Aberdeen airport, and both the major fleets are divided between there and Sumburgh. The most commonly used type of helicopter is the S-61N (of which British Airways Helicopters have 23), but British Airways Helicopters had taken delivery of six 44-seat Chinook aircraft by 1982. These large helicopters may have a role to play in the provincial scheduled services in the Highlands and Islands, where they would avoid some of the expense involved in the CAA provision of airfields for fixed-wing aircraft. The main services concern the movement of personnel to and from offshore rigs and production platforms, while most materials go by sea. The transition to the production phase of oil activity is not expected to reduce demand for helicopter operations, since production platforms also require regular servicing. At the time of writing, plans are proceeding for a floating airfield off Shetland to provide extra capacity for oil-related traffic using STOL aircraft.

Conclusion

In the evolution of Scottish transport, several themes have been apparent. As in the rest of Britain, there has been a trend from the provision of public transport by private capital towards its provision and direct planning by national and local government using public capital. There were interesting early examples of state involvement in Scotland, and significantly these were almost entirely concentrated in the Highlands and Islands.

Many current issues in Scottish transport are not peculiar to Scotland. Road and rail competition and investment policies, urban congestion, airport noise and development, the debated significance of transport provision in economic development and job creation, the role of national and local government in decision-making, and the role of subsidy in transport provision, are some of the important issues affecting transport throughout the world. In particular, as public money becomes more significant in transport provision, and as a greater understanding develops of the inter-relationships between all socio-economic planning and policy formulation, the aim of gearing transport supply (particularly in passenger terms) to need, measured objectively through socio-economic criteria, is taking on greater priority. This is especially significant in areas where transport provision on the basis of profitability has not proved feasible. It has already been noted that this situation is the norm over much of Scotland, and some form of subsidy in much of Scotland's transport must be accepted at least for the forseeable future. But this should not necessarily be regarded as something to be deplored. Subsidy may be used as a tool to encourage transport operators to provide services on the basis of defined need within practical operating constraints. This approach makes sound economic sense since the correct identification of need and the operation of services to meet that need should ensure the highest loadings possible. However, if sufficient subsidy is not available – and this seems increasingly likely – then the provision of public transport in some mainly rural areas could depend on voluntary efforts.

It is often said with truth that transport is a means to an end. As such, Scottish transport, both privately and publicly financed, planned, and operated, has played a critical role in social and economic development since the eighteenth century. Its success in this role in the future will depend upon the skill with which it can be further integrated into the corporate planning of physical and economic development, while maintaining where feasible the element of competition which has been so important in its evolution in the last 200 years. However, the need for continued subsidy for large parts of the country's transport systems remains, and is likely to do so for the foreseeable future.

Notes to this chapter are on pages 310–11.

9

Rural Land Use

A. S. Mather

ONE of the features of rural land use in Scotland is its great variety. Deer forests and almost unused mountain tops in parts of the Highlands give way in the Lowlands to intensive livestock husbandry and cropping, and in some parts of the country a distance of only a few kilometres separates raspberry field and high-lying grouse moor. The land in much of upland Scotland is used at low intensities, and systems of dual or multiple land use are common. The existence of these systems leads to problems in defining and measuring land uses, and the composition of land use cannot be precisely analysed. Nevertheless, it is clear that Scotland is a much more rural country than many of its neighbours. As much as 98 per cent of the land area is officially designated as countryside.[1] Even if the small towns and villages which lie within the designated countryside are included in the urban area, less than 5 per cent of the land surface is built up, compared with 11 per cent in England and Wales,[2] 12 per cent in Germany[3] and 9 per cent in Denmark.[3]

A basic outline of the structure of rural land use in Scotland is shown in Table 9.1. Agriculture is by far the leading land use in terms of area, but much of its extent consists of rough grazings which are difficult to define and delineate and are probably overestimated in the agricultural census. Farm woodland and scrub are also included in the agricultural area, so that the figure for forestry understates the woodland area. The urban and industrial area is probably overstated, as it contains an element of 'other land', which includes some types of recreational land as well as built-up areas. Long-established land uses relating to field sports are not covered by official statistics, even though they occupy large areas. Official statistics on deer forests were not collected after 1958, when the area ungrazed by domestic stock extended to 465,000ha. Since then, sheep stocks have been cleared from some deer forests, and the ungrazed area is now probably greater. Red deer, however, are not confined to ungrazed deer forests, and they range over an area of about 3 million ha.[4] Statistical returns from grouse moors

Table 9.1

Land use composition c1975

	m. ha		%
Agriculture[a]	6.49		84
Ungrazed deer forest[b]		0.47	6
Grouse moor[b]		1.21	16
Forestry[c]	0.82		11
Urban/Industrial[d]	0.36		5
Total (agricultural, forest and urban land)	8.08		100
Total land area[e]	7.71		100

a Based on the June agricultural census (*Agricultural Statistics (Scotland)*, 1975), plus a further area of 324,000ha reported as existing on statistically insignificant holdings excluded from the annual census (*Agricultural Statistics (Scotland)*, 1976).

b Note that these categories may overlap with each other, and with agriculture. (The census definition of rough grazings does not require that the land be grazed by domestic stock.) The deer-forest area is taken from *Agricultural Statistics (Scotland)*, 1959, and is the last officially available figure. The grouse-moor area is the estimate of J. Tivy (ed) *The Organic Resources of Scotland* (Oliver and Boyd 1973).

c Scotland Development Department, *National Planning Series – Land Use Summary Sheet 2 – Forestry* (1976).

d Select Committee on Scottish Affairs (1972) *Land Resource Use in Scotland, H.C. Paper 51*, Vol 5 (1972), 10.

e Excluding inland water.

have never been officially collected, but such moors are estimated to extend to around 1.2 million ha,[5] part of which is grazed (at least seasonally) by sheep. Compared with these major land uses, the areas used for other forms of rural recreation and for purposes of nature conservation are very small, although they have grown substantially since the end of World War II.

The purpose of this chapter is to outline, within the constraints imposed by the availability of statistics, the characteristics of the major land uses and their prevailing trends. Thereafter, some controversial issues in rural land use are briefly reviewed, including the transfer of agricultural land to forestry and urban purposes, and the alleged under-use of land used for sporting purposes.

Agriculture
Characteristics of Scottish Agriculture

Official statistics based on agricultural censuses indicate that over 80 per cent of the land surface of Scotland is used for agriculture, and that the total agricultural area is around 6.5 million ha. Approximately one quarter of this area consists of crops and grass, and the remainder to rough grazings. The dominant role of rough grazings and the smaller part played by tillage and grass are shown in Table 9.2.

Scotland has around one-third of the UK agricultural area, but it accounts for only 12 per cent of the tillage and 15 per cent of the grass. On the other hand, it accounts for about 70 per cent of the rough grazings. These characteristics are reflected both in the total contribution which it makes to UK agricultural output, and in the composition of its output. Scotland's share of UK output has been fairly stable in recent years at around 11 per cent – a figure which is low in proportion to its share of the agricultural area, but roughly similar to its share of tillage. In Scottish agriculture, the emphasis is even more strongly on the livestock sector than in the rest of the UK. Crops usually account for around 20 per cent of Scottish output (by value), but their contribution has tended to show a slight increase in recent years. More than 50 per cent of the output comes from livestock, principally in the form of fat cattle, and livestock products such as milk, eggs and wool account for a further 20–25 per cent. Thus, together, livestock and livestock products contribute around 75 per cent of Scottish farm output. Horticulture provides around 4 per cent – very much less than in the UK as a whole. Livestock in the form of fat cattle and sheep are relatively more important in Scotland than in the rest of the UK, but the reverse is true of the dairy sector.

Table 9.2
Composition of agricultural land use, Scotland and UK, 1975

	Scotland '000ha	%	UK '000ha	%	Scotland as % of UK
Tillage	582	9	4,819	26	12
Grass	1,081	18	7,199	39	15
Rough grazings	4,499	73	6,555	35	69
Total	6,162	100	18,573	100	33

Note These statistics relate only to holdings included in the agricultural census. Please see note *a* of Table 9.1 about agricultural areas of statistically insignificant holdings excluded from the main census. The area occupied by buildings, roads and woodlands on farms is not included in these figures.

Source: Agricultural Statistics (United Kingdom) 1975

Livestock dominate agriculture much more in some parts of the country than in others. In the South-west and in the Highlands and Islands, for example, livestock and livestock products account for around 90 per cent of output. Output from crops and horticulture exceeds one-third only in east-central Scotland, and even there livestock make the largest contribution.[6]

Regional contrasts in composition of output within Scotland, like the contrasts between Scotland and the rest of the UK, are related to basic environmental controls and to contrasts in demand. Soils and climates suitable for growing cereals and horticultural crops are strongly localised within Scotland, and extend to a relatively smaller area than in England. In the more densely populated parts of the UK, dairying assumes a greater importance in farm output than in Scotland, where the market for liquid milk is relatively small. In Scotland, the area of arable land per person is approximately 0.25ha, whereas the corresponding UK figure is around 0.12ha. With this larger land area per person, Scotland is generally more self-sufficient in food supplies than the UK as a whole (at least as measured by home production as a percentage of total supplies), as Table 9.3 indicates. It is more self-sufficient throughout the livestock sector, but the lesser role of tillage is reflected in lower degrees of self-sufficiency in cereals. The table should be viewed with caution, however, because fluctuations occur from year to year, especially in cereals (where yields and hence production are strongly dependent on weather), and because Scottish agriculture is geared to a British market rather than to national self-sufficiency. If Scottish self-sufficiency were the goal, there would undoubtedly be changes in the composition of agricultural output and land use, with more emphasis on cropping.

Table 9.3
Production as a percentage of total supplies (mid-1970s)

	Scotland	United Kingdom
Beef	100	84
Mutton & lamb	240	58
Pigmeat	70	43
Milk	100	100
Butter	15	9
Cheese	90	61
Wheat	25	45
Barley	80	93
Potatoes	100	91

Sources Scotland: Scottish Development Department *Agriculture in Scotland: its structure and importance to the economy.* Planning Advice Note No 1 (1976).
UK: Central Office of Information *Britain 1977, an official handbook* (HMSO 1978); Ministry of Agriculture: *Annual Reviews of Agriculture.*

Patterns of Agricultural Land Use

The physical environment exerts a strong influence on the pattern of Scottish agriculture, and fundamental contrasts remain between farming based on rough grazings in the Highlands and uplands, on the one hand, and intensive cropping in parts of the eastern Lowlands on the other. The parishes and districts which are the basic units in the agricultural census tend to include both hill land and fertile arable lowland, and so the strong contrasts which exist between hill and arable farming are partly hidden in the official statistics. Nevertheless, it is clear that the main area of arable land, and even more so of tillage, is located around the Firth of Tay and the outer part of the Firth of Forth. Secondary concentrations extend to the Merse district in the lower Tweed valley and around the north-east lowlands to the inner Moray Firth, and thence northwards in attenuated form to Caithness and Orkney.[7] In parts of Angus, Fife and Lothian, tillage accounts for over 50 per cent of the agricultural area, and in parts of East Lothian it rises to over 75 per cent. In the rest of Scotland, the percentage is under 50, and indeed in the greater part of the area under 10.

Crops

Around 80 per cent of the tillage area is under cereals, and in turn barley accounts for over 80 per cent of the area devoted to cereals. Fig 9.1a shows how barley has expanded rapidly over the last twenty years, this being the major change in agricultural land use in the period since World War II. Until the mid-1960s, oats were the leading cereal crop, and indeed in the early post-war period accounted for as much as 80 per cent of the cereal area. Since then barley has become the leading crop because of its higher yield, its suitability for combine harvesting, and its superior feeding value. Part of the barley crop commands high prices for malting and distilling, but most is used for animal feed, and much of it is retained on the farm on which it is grown. The distribution of barley is similar to that of tillage, and the main concentrations are in the lowlands of Tayside, Fife and Lothian. But the drier and sunnier parts of other lowland areas, such as the Garioch district in north-east Scotland and parts of Moray and Easter Ross are also important barley-growing areas. These areas, as well as Angus, Fife and south-east Scotland, have seen an increase in tillage over the last twenty years, while the total Scottish area has remained fairly stable. Much of this regional increase is accounted for by barley, but barley growing has also become more widespread and less concentrated geographically.[8]

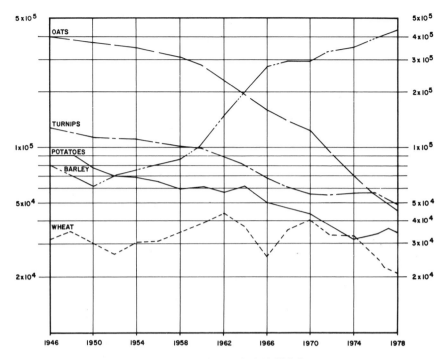

Fig 9.1a Cropping in Scotland, 1946–78, in hectares

Until the early 1960s, it was largely confined to the drier areas of richer soils in the south and east, but it is now the leading cereal over most of the lowlands and also in some upland margins. Barley growing is now closely associated with the feeding of beef cattle, and has spread out from its earlier core area in the east-central part of the country. It has displaced oats as the main cereal crop except in some of the upper parts of the main straths and some upland districts; in the lowlands, oats are now largely confined to areas of poorer soils.

While barley has become more dispersed in recent years, the reverse is true of wheat. The area under wheat rose to a peak around 1970, and has now fallen below its immediate post-war level. As wheat growing has contracted, it has become increasingly concentrated in East Lothian, and at the same time, increasingly concentrated amongst fewer growers, each growing larger areas. Between 1969 and 1975, for example, the number of wheat growers decreased from 2,800 to 1,600, while the average area rose from 13ha to 17ha. During the same period, barley growers increased from 13,700 to 14,700.[9]

A similar process of concentration is evident in potato growing. Until the mid-1960s, potatoes were consistently the leading cash crop, in terms of value.[10] Since then they have been ousted from that position by barley, except in occasional years of very high potato prices, such as

1975. Potatoes accounted for around 10 per cent of the tillage area up to the mid-1960s, but thereafter declined to about 6 per cent. Between 1960 and 1975, the area grown has been halved, but because of higher yields production has fallen by only 20 per cent. Potato growing has become steadily more concentrated in the lowlands between Fife and Kincardine. This area had already emerged as the main focus of potato growing by the end of the last century, but at that time it accounted for less than one third of the total potato area. By 1960, its share was around 50 per cent, and by 1975 it had climbed to over 60 per cent. Potato growers decreased in number from 21,500 to 12,100 between 1969 and 1975,[11] contraction being most evident amongst the small growers. In fact, the real amount of concentration may be greater than these figures suggest, because much of the growing area is let on a seasonal basis to potato merchants, or sold as standing crops.[12]

The other main root crop is turnips, but their area has declined steadily in the post-war period. Turnips at present occupy approximately 9 per cent of the tillage area, but assume a much greater relative importance in the upland margins and straths. The pattern of distribution is quite unlike that of other crops, and relatively little land is devoted to turnip growing in the main areas of tillage. Although turnips are still grown throughout almost the whole of Scotland, their importance is greatest in the stock-rearing areas; but it has declined considerably in recent decades in the main feeding districts. Here, silage making has increased rapidly, and in the main cattle feeding districts of the North-east and South-west, quadrupled between 1960 and 1975.[13]

The closure of the British Sugar Corporation's factory at Cupar in Fife in 1972 brought to an end the growing of sugar beet in Scotland. Although the area previously grown was less than 1 per cent of the tillage area, the crop was locally important on farms in Fife, East Perthshire and Angus. These farms responded to the loss of their market by increasing their cereal acreage and producing more stock-feed crops and temporary grass, geared to increasing cattle numbers. The growing of vegetables, and especially of peas, also increased greatly on beet-growing farms, and was facilitated by the setting up of co-operatives which made possible the purchase of expensive pea-vining machines.[14]

Horticultural crops account for 4 per cent of total agricultural output, compared with 11 per cent in England and Wales, but during the period since World War II the area of fruit and vegetable growing has tended to increase in Scotland while that in England and Wales has decreased. Some crops are relatively more important in Scotland than in other parts of the UK, and indeed Scotland accounts for as much as 85 per cent of UK production of raspberries. Raspberry growing began in the late nineteenth century in east Perthshire,[15] but over the last half century the neighbouring county of Angus, where most of the processing facilities are located, has had the largest acreage. Production also extends to Fife and south Kincardine, and in recent years there has been an increase in raspberry-growing around the inner Moray Firth. In the main growing area in Tayside, the crop is grown principally alongside agricultural crops on extensive farms and is geared to the processing market, especially to jam factories. Elsewhere it is grown mainly on small holdings and intensive units, and is intended for the fresh market. Scottish dominance in British raspberry production is attributed primarily to climatic conditions of rather cool, drought-free but sunny summers in the east of the country. The growing area became closely related to processing facilities and, once established, these facilities have helped to perpetuate raspberry-growing in the district, and have also encouraged the production of other horticultural crops such as peas, beans and carrots. The main area of production of other vegetable crops, such as the brassicas, is in East Lothian. As improvements in transport and in processing have freed vegetable-growing from the shackles of close proximity to urban markets, the pattern of concentration in the areas most favoured environmentally, such as Tayside and the Lothians, has become more clearly defined. The growing of tomatoes under glass, on the other hand, is still mainly located in the Clyde valley, where the growth of the industry in the nineteenth century was encouraged by the availability of cheap coal and proximity to the Clydeside market. Rising costs of heating have badly affected the glass-house industry in recent years, and the tomato acreage fell by as much as 45 per cent between 1970 and 1977.

Livestock

Livestock and livestock products account for around three-quarters of Scottish agricultural output, but this figure understates the livestock sector in land-use terms. Around 90 per cent of the agricultural area is used either as grazings or for the production of hay or silage, and two-thirds of the acreage of tillage crops is used to grow feedstuffs for livestock.[16]

The relative importance of different classes of livestock varies markedly across the country, and if the overall pattern of livestock density is to be depicted, then different types of animals have to be converted into livestock units, on the basis of their feed requirements. This procedure reveals that the areas of greatest livestock density are in south-west Scotland, notably to the north of Ayr and in Wigtown. Secondary areas of high density include much of north-east Scotland as well as the lowlands around Dumfries. Dairy cattle are the leading class of livestock in the south-west Lowlands, while beef cattle occupy primary position in the North-east. Sheep are dominant over most of the rest of Scotland, except for very small areas around cities such as Aberdeen and Edinburgh, where pigs are the leading livestock.

Cattle numbers have increased by more than 50 per cent since the end of World War II. This increase is accounted for by beef cattle: the beef-cow herd almost quadrupled between 1951 and 1975, although a decline set in after 1975. The most rapid period of growth was in the late 1960s and early 1970s; between 1968 and 1973, for example, the herd grew by approximately one-third. The dramatic increase in beef-cow numbers in the post-war period is attributable to a number of factors. Beef production was particularly encouraged under the selective expansion programme in the mid-1960s, and levels of support were adjusted to encourage increased production. A major factor throughout the period was the hill-cow subsidy and its level. In the early 1970s, over 86 per cent of the beef-cow herd were eligible for subsidy payment,[17] and more recently the proportion of beef cows in the Less Favoured Areas and hence eligible for Hill Livestock Compensatory Allowances (which replaced the subsidy payments after Britain joined the EEC) remains at over 80 per cent.[18] But comparatively few cows are found on hill farms; the majority are on upland farms, located in the straths, upland margins and poorer areas of lowland rather than highland country. Major concentrations of beef cows are located in the straths and basins of the Eastern Highlands, but the most rapid rates of growth of numbers in the late 1960s and early 1970s were in south-west Scotland, where there was a shift of emphasis from dairying to beef on many farms.

Beef-cow and calf-production systems are based on grass, grazed in summer and conserved as hay or silage in winter. The limiting factor is winter feedstuffs, and although there was overall a slight increase in Scottish self-sufficiency in animal feeding stuffs during the two decades prior to the early 1970s, much of the expansion in beef-cow numbers around the end of that period was on farms where hay and concentrates had to be bought in to supplement home-grown cereals and fodder. In recent years, cereal prices have tended to rise faster than stock prices, and the modest (10 per cent) reduction in beef-cow numbers at the national level has been accompanied by much more dramatic decreases

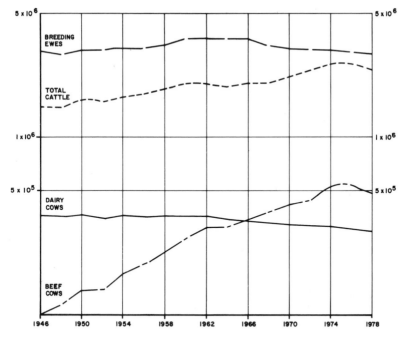

Fig 9.1b Livestock in Scotland, 1946–78

in the more vulnerable areas where expansion was most dependent on bought-in feed.

Approximately half the fat cattle output in Scotland is derived from the beef-breeding herd, with 30 per cent coming from the dairy herd. Imported calves or stores from England, Wales and Ireland make up the remaining 20 per cent.[19] Although the relative importance of the beef-breeding herd is much greater than in England and Wales, it does not determine the distribution of beef cattle. The main contrast between distributional patterns of beef cows and beef cattle is in the north-east Lowlands, where beef cattle densities are very high, unlike those of beef cows. This area has for many years had a reputation as the leading beef-producing region, employing a production system based on the combination of summer grazing and winter court-feeding.

Fat cattle are the biggest single component of Scottish farm output, and second position is occupied by milk and milk products. Dairy cattle are strongly concentrated in the South-west, which accounts for between two-thirds and three-quarters of the Scottish herd, and within this area, their concentration is mainly in a broad zone between the Clyde Valley and the Ayrshire coast, and in coastal parts of Dumfries and Galloway. Numbers of dairy cows have declined slowly since around 1960, and are now approximately 20 per cent lower than their early post-war peak. With this decline, the pre-eminence of the South-west has been emphasised. Nevertheless, some dairying is carried on almost throughout the Lowlands, and extends as far north as Caithness and Orkney, where much of the output is converted to butter and cheese.

During the period between 1969 and 1975, dairy farms declined from approximately one-quarter to one-fifth of full-time holdings,[20] and the number of producers registered with the Scottish milk marketing boards fell by 41 per cent between 1966 and 1976. In some peripheral areas, the decline in the number of producers was more dramatic – in Sutherland from 12 to 3, and in Caithness from 52 to 20.[21] But decreases were not confined to such areas, and numbers fell by around one-third in core counties such as Ayrshire and Wigtown. As numbers of producers fell, the average herd size increased from 39 in 1960 to 71 in 1975. In the area of the Aberdeen and District MMB, the average herd size is almost exactly twice that of England and Wales.

Dairying, like the production of beef cattle, is closely associated with grass, whose total area has been relatively static during the post-war period, although the mown area has steadily increased. Next to rough grazings, grass is the biggest component of the agricultural area. Rather more than half the total supplies of feedstuffs are usually derived from grass, which occupies more than three-quarters of the improved land on the west side of the country, and falls to under 50 per cent only in the tillage-dominated parts of Tayside, Fife, the Lothians and Borders. The spatial pattern of permanent grass has a stronger westerly emphasis than that of the rotational type. Little is grown in the North-east, but in extensive areas on the margins of the south-west Lowlands, where combinations of high rainfall and clay soils discourage cultivation, over three-quarters of the grass acreage may be in the permanent category. Nationally, the proportion is around one-third.

While a strong correlation exists between the distribution of grassland and cattle, the relationship with sheep is weaker. Sheep are found on all types of farms in almost every part of Scotland, but are most numerous on hill farms. These account for around 37 per cent of the breeding flock, with a further 28 per cent on upland farms. The major concentrations of breeding ewes are in the Southern Uplands and parts of the South-west Highlands, where the better quality rough grazings support higher stocking densities than the more barren hills of the Central or North-west Highlands. The calculation of ewe stocking rates and their spatial variation is hindered by problems of definition of rough grazings in the agricultural census, but it is known that the rate varies from more than one ewe per hectare on the better grazings to one ewe to more than 5ha in poorer Highland areas.

While the breeding ewe flock is strongly concentrated in the hills and uplands, the fattening of sheep has a stronger lowland emphasis, and major flows of lambs from Highland areas focus on the lowland parts of Tayside, Fife, the Lothians and Borders. Sheep represent the major and in many instances the only enterprise on hill farms, but fattening is carried on in a wide variety of farm types, usually as a subsidiary enterprise. In the post-war period, the size of the ewe flock increased steadily until the early 1960s but thereafter declined until recently. The downward trend in ewe numbers began at a time of low prices and depression in hill-sheep farming. In the mid and late 1960s, several Highland estates removed their breeding flocks, leaving the red deer as the only major grazing animal.[22] Since then, a continuing decline has accompanied afforestation, especially in parts of Dumfries and Galloway and the South-west Highlands. The afforestation of hill grazings is the biggest and most dramatic change in rural land use in Scotland in the post-war period and is likely to continue in the foreseeable future.

The Structure of Scottish Farming

Full-time farms in Scotland number around 20,000. There are in addition about 11,000 other 'significant' holdings (ie with a labour requirement in excess of the equivalent of one man-day per week) and a further 21,000 'insignificant' holdings, many of which are crofts in the north and west of the country. As in other parts of Britain, the number of farms has declined in recent decades, and in the first half of the 1970s the number of full-time units fell by around 10 per cent.[23] Since then, however, the number of full-time units has tended to stabilise, as some part-time units have undergone an expansion to full-time levels. Over 90 per cent of Scottish agricultural output comes from full-time farms. Of the full-time units, approximately 36 per cent are classed as of medium size (ie with a labour requirement equivalent to between two and four full-time workers). The remaining full-time units are almost evenly divided between the small and large classes, the latter accounting for around half the national output. The majority of hill sheep and upland farms are in the category of small units, while almost three-quarters of the cropping and dairy farms, which display a strong concentration in the eastern Lowlands and south-west Scotland respectively, are in the large category (ie with at least three full-time workers – or their equivalent – in addition to the working occupier).

Overall, 83 per cent of the full-time farms have working occupiers, but the proportion varies from only 60 per cent on hill sheep farms (many of which are run by estates) to 93 per cent on dairy units.[24] Occupiers contribute around 40 per cent of the agricultural labour input, and about 25 per cent of regular male workers are members of the occupier's family. Full-time hired labour contributes less than 40 per cent of the total labour input, and is represented on just over half of the full-time holdings,[25] despite the fact that approximately two-thirds of full-time units have labour requirements equivalent to more than two full-time workers.[26]

Since rough grazings are such an important element in the Scottish agricultural area, average farm size is higher than in other parts of Britain, and indeed the average size of Scottish full-time holdings is more than twice the UK average. If only crops and grass are considered, however, this disparity is greatly reduced. While 6 per cent of significant holdings extend to more than 500ha in total area, only 0.2 per cent have 500ha or more of crops and grass. Conversely, while 12 per cent of the units are under 5ha in total area, 21 per cent have under 5ha of crops and grass, and indeed almost 5 per cent have no crops and grass.

Strong regional and intra-regional contrasts in farm size exist. The hill and upland farms with substantial areas of rough grazings are generally much larger than other farm types, but contrasts also exist in low-ground farms. These are partly related to contemporary farming systems, but are strongly influenced by historical factors, and especially by the pattern of evolution during the early nineteenth century. The largest units (in terms of extent of crops and grass) are the cropping farms which dominate the agricultural landscape of parts of Angus, Fife and the Lothians. Farms of between 120ha and 400ha are also numerous in south-west Scotland, where the emphasis is on grassland husbandry rather than on cropping. In much of the North-east, on the other hand, the average farm size is smaller and in many parishes more than half of the holdings fall within the range of 40–120ha; here, farm amalgamation has proceeded more rapidly in recent years than in most other parts of the country.[27]

The interaction between land type, historical factors and land use is extremely complex, and marked variations in farm-size characteristics can occur in very small areas. In the Highlands, tiny crofts may be juxtaposed with sheep farms extending to thousands of hectares, while, in the lowlands, large cropping farms may lie alongside smallholdings created as a result of government policy during the early part of the twentieth century.[28]

Page 209 *(above)* Typical crofting landscape in north-west Tiree, Outer Hebrides; *(below)* attempts to stabilise coastal sand dunes by planting strips of marram grass, Eoligarry, north-west coast of Isle of Barra, Outer Hebrides

Page 210 *(above)* Banff, a Royal Burgh coastal town on the Moray Firth. Duff House stands in parkland now occupied by Duff House Royal Golf course on the banks of the River Deveron; *(right)* Crovie village, Banffshire. Traditional Scottish fishing villages such as this characteristically had the houses built as near the shore as possible. Boats were drawn up on the beach, and fish split, salted and spread on the beach to dry

The pattern of variation of farm tenure is even more complex. Approximately 53 per cent of the total agricultural area and of the significant holdings are owner-occupied. The great majority of insignificant holdings in the Highlands and Islands are rented, but no clear geographical pattern of tenure of full-time units emerges, and when rented land is considered as a percentage of agricultural land a very complicated pattern emerges. The proportion of rented land tends to reach its highest levels along the upland margins (as well as in the crofting districts), but pockets of tenanted farms rented from large estates are still to be found in most parts of the country. The twentieth century has witnessed a major decline in the area and number of holdings rented, and there is a continuing tendency for estates to take tenanted land in hand.

Scottish farming has undergone major changes since the war, and has seen a steady expansion in output, at least until the mid-1970s. These changes have had less effect on the rural landscape than in England. The trend towards specialisation which has resulted in the emergence of strong landscape contrasts between eastern and western England is not so prominent in Scotland. While there has been a growing concentration on grass-based cattle rearing on the upland margins and on cereals in parts of the east-central Lowlands,[29] there has been less specialisation than in England, and there are no Scottish equivalents of the barley prairies of districts such as Lincolnshire. Processes such as field enlargement and hedge removal have taken place in Scotland, but not as commonly as in England, and their impact on the generally more open Scottish landscape has been smaller. It is indeed rather surprising that the post-war changes in agricultural systems and output have been accompanied by so little change in the rural landscape, which in many parts of the country still bears a strong imprint from the early nineteenth century.

Forestry

Although the area of grouse moor may exceed that of forests, forestry is the second land use in Scotland in terms of value of output and employment. Around 9,000 people are employed in forestry, or about one-sixth of the rural workforce,[30] and there is further employment in transport and secondary wood-using industry. The forest area has expanded markedly during the twentieth century, and seems set to expand further during the latter part of the century and the early decades of the next.

The present forest area is around 820,000ha, or approximately 11 per

cent of the land surface. This figure is similar to the percentage in
Wales, but is far higher than in other parts of the British Isles: England
and Ireland have respectively 7 and 4 per cent of their land areas under
forest. Compared with other parts of the EEC, however, Scotland is not
well endowed, and its forest percentage is little more than half the EEC
average.[31] When the forest area per head of population is calculated, on
the other hand, Scotland emerges in a much more favourable position.
Only France and Luxembourg of the EEC countries are better
endowed, and the Scottish area per head is more than seven times that
of England.

Scotland also differs from England in the composition of the forest
area. In Scotland, approximately 54 per cent is in state (Forestry
Commission) ownership, while the remaining 46 per cent in the private
sector is divided between long-established private estates and more
recently established forestry investment companies. In England, on the
other hand, only 28 per cent of the forest area is in state ownership, and
of the other EEC countries, only Ireland has a larger proportion of its
woodland under state control. The predominance of state control is
associated with the generally young age of Scottish forests. The
Forestry Commission was established in 1919, and rapid state
afforestation has occurred since World War II. Only a small proportion
of Scotland's forests are mature and fully productive, and – with the
exception of some of the early Forestry Commission plantations located
in areas where conditions are favourable for rapid growth – these
mature forests are mainly in the private sector. They are located in the
straths such as Deeside, Speyside and Tayside in the eastern parts of
the Highlands. These estates have a long tradition of involvement in
forestry, dating back to the late eighteenth century or even earlier. In
some of these straths, small pockets of native pinewood survived from
early post-glacial times, and in some instances native strains of trees
were planted as commercial forests during the late eighteenth and
nineteenth centuries, when much of the rest of the country was already
almost treeless. Although some of these mature plantations were felled
during the two world wars, the forestry tradition survived, and many of
these estates still maintain active forestry enterprises.

Rapid expansion of the forest area, however, is a phenomenon of the
twentieth century. In the inter-war period, the Forestry Commission
began to acquire land for afforestation in several parts of the country,
but mainly in lowland heath or upland areas rather than in truly
highland or mountainous districts. Notable acquisitions during this
period included areas of sand dunes at Culbin near the mouth of the
Findhorn, and at Tentsmuir between St Andrews and the Firth of Tay.

The afforestation of these barren wastes was a notable sylvicultural achievement, but in terms of forest area the acquisition and afforestation of upland margins in a series of discontinuous arcs between Stonehaven and the Dornoch Firth were more important. Land was also afforested around Loch Lomond and Loch Long, in the South-west Highlands, and in a number of areas in the western half of the Southern Uplands. Acquisitions in the Central and Northern Highlands at this time were largely confined to the Great Glen and a few small properties on the west coast (such as Lael near Ullapool), where nuclei of forests had been established by private owners in the nineteenth century. Little afforestation was achieved in the private sector during the inter-war period.

In 1943, a White Paper on Post-war Forest Policy[32] was published, setting a target of 2 million ha of potentially productive forest in Britain by the end of the century. It was hoped that 40 per cent of this area would be contributed from the existing private sector, and the remaining 1.2 million ha would be afforested, mainly by the Forestry Commission. After the war, the Forestry Commission embarked on this major task of afforestation with the intention of allocating half of the target area to Scotland and dividing the remainder between England and Wales. But agricultural policies directed at greater self-sufficiency in food supply meant that farming was a stronger competitor for hill land than previously, and consultative procedures involving the Department of Agriculture hindered the flow of better quality hill land to forestry. The result of all this was not only that the Forestry Commission fell short of its land-acquisition targets, but also that much of the hill land acquired was of a poorer quality than had been usual before the war. From this early post-war period, a gradual shift towards the north and west has been apparent, especially in recent years.

By the mid-1950s, the urgency of the post-war planting programme had been largely dissipated, not least because of problems of acquiring land. But in 1955, a special planting programme was instituted in parts of the crofting counties, with the objective of creating employment.[33] This special programme was on a very small scale, but it marked the beginning of a trend. In the late 1950s and the 1960s, social objectives became increasingly important in forest policy, and increasing proportions of Britain's afforestation effort became concentrated in Scotland, Wales and the extreme north of England. This trend has continued to the present, and is reflected in the fact that over 80 per cent of state afforestation is now located in Scotland, and also in the relocation of the headquarters of the Forestry Commission from

London to Edinburgh. Planting rates were increased in the late 1960s, when a stated government objective of increasing employment opportunities in rural and upland areas coincided with a period of relative depression in sheep farming, which facilitated the flow of rough grazings into forestry. An increased proportion of the Scottish planting figure was directed to the crofting counties at this time, but south-west Scotland was also a major focus of activity. The moist mild climate of that district, with its long growing season, led to rapid tree-growth rates. The same was true of Argyll, where major concentrations of state forests were built up in mid-Argyll and Cowal.

The Highlands north of Argyll are generally less attractive for purposes of afforestation, because growth rates decline as exposure increases and larger proportions of the land are unplantable. Nevertheless, the relative importance of the north is growing as land becomes increasingly difficult to acquire in other parts of the country, and an increasing proportion of the planting effort is now located on blanket bogs and similar land types in Sutherland and Caithness. The distribution of state forest land in Scotland has a distinct westerly emphasis (Fig 9.2). This arises from a number of factors, including the greater suitability of the wetter west for tree growth and the better agricultural quality of land in the east. Another factor is the prevalence in the Eastern Highlands of grouse moors, which many estate-owners have been reluctant to release to the Forestry Commission for afforestation.

Although the greater part of post-war afforestation has been carried out by the Forestry Commission, rates of planting in the private sector increased rapidly in the 1960s and early 1970s. The fiscal advantages of forestry investment, combined with grant-aid, encouraged some long-established private estate owners to initiate or expand forestry enterprises, and forestry investment companies also became active.[34] These companies established very extensive forests in south-west Scotland, notably near Moffat, and also acquired and afforested sizeable areas in Argyll. The combined forests of the public and private sectors now occupy large proportions of the land area in these districts, and in recent years the private investment groups have been forced to look further north for planting land.

Deer Forests and Grouse Moors

Although hunting forests were a prominent use of land in medieval Scotland, the modern deer forest, like the grouse moor, dates from the Victorian period. The main phase of expansion was in the last two

POTENTIAL FOREST AREA
FORESTRY COMMISSION LAND
GRANT - AIDED PRIVATE FORESTS

Fig 9.2 Generalised distribution of existing forests and potential forest areas

decades of the nineteenth century when hill sheep farming took a steep
downturn, as a result of growing competition from Australia and New
Zealand. Deer forests continued to expand until 1912, when the total
area devoted solely to deer was 1.45 million ha.[35] Since then the area
has contracted, especially during the two world wars, during which
many extensive deer forests – from which sheep had once been cleared –
were restocked. The main zone of deer forests is closely associated with

the highest and most rugged parts of the Highlands and consists of a broad belt running northwards along the watershed from Loch Linnhe, with a secondary area running north-eastwards from Loch Linnhe towards the Cairngorms.

Since grouse-moor areas have never been monitored by official statistics, their extent can only be estimated very approximately. It seems likely, however, that their area exceeds 1 million ha, of which the greater part lies between the Moray Firth and the Firth of Tay. Grouse moors are closely associated with dry heather moors, and typical locations are on heather-clad plateaux on the drier, east side of the country. Like deer forests, the development of grouse moors, with their characteristic lines of shooting butts and mosaics of patches of burnt heather, took place in the nineteenth century. Together with shooting lodges, kennels, keepers' houses and game larders, they form important elements of the landscape in many upland and highland areas, and although their impact on local economies is now smaller than at the turn of the century, they still represent important sources of employment in many remote areas.

The area of ungrazed deer forest (Table 9.1), although not known precisely, is certainly small compared with the area over which red deer range. It has been estimated that land occupied or used by red deer may extend to around 3 million ha, or 37 per cent of the total land surface. Over most of that area, deer share the ground with sheep, and in some instances also with cattle. During the 1970s, the red deer population grew rapidly from around 180,000 to 270,000,[36] despite a loss of some deer wintering ground to forestry and, to a much lesser degree, to agricultural improvements. This rapid population growth occurred during a series of mild winters which reduced deer mortality, and may have been facilitated by the growing practice of feeding the animals with cobs or other materials during the periods of hard winter weather. During the 1960s and 1970s, feeding was stimulated by the high prices commanded by venison, which is the main product of some estates in the most rugged parts of the Highlands. Between 35,000 and 40,000 deer are shot annually,[37] of which just under half are stags. Most of the venison is exported, mainly to Germany.

The sport of stalking was the main reason for the creation and expansion of deer forests during the Victorian period, and meat production was unimportant. Today, venison production outweighs sporting value in most estates, although revenue from stalking rents is still an extremely important element in the economies of many properties. The traditional practice of letting a deer forest for the whole season has generally been replaced by shorter periods of letting, in some cases even on a daily basis.

Although some experiments in capital-intensive deer farming in Highland areas are currently being undertaken, the intensity of land use on most deer forests is extremely low. The employment density may be of the order of one man per 10,000ha or more, but, in the absence of this deer-based employment, the frontier of settlement would retreat far down valley in many Highland districts.

Grouse moors are usually managed at a higher intensity than deer forests, and considerable efforts are expended in heather burning to produce suitable habitats for the birds, and in the control of vermin and predators. Along with underlying rock and soil types, moor management is a strong influence on the density of grouse population, and hence on value for shooting.[38] Even on the best grouse moors, however, the annual crop in terms of grouse shot consists of only a few ounces of meat per acre. Sporting values are very much higher than those of meat production, and shooting rents represent the main source of income on many estates in the east side of the Highlands. Most grouse moors are also grazed by sheep, at least seasonally, and the combination of shooting and grazing values has proved a strong disincentive to the transfer of grouse moorland to forestry.

Outdoor Recreation and Nature Conservation

Since World War II, and especially since 1960, there has been a great increase in recreational activity in the countryside, and in interest in conserving wildlife and scenery. Plans for a system of national parks in Scotland came to nought in the early post-war years,[39] although the areas identified as suitable for national park status were designated as National Park Direction Areas (Fig 9.3), for which the Secretary of State for Scotland was empowered to determine the outcome of planning applications. More recently, the Countryside Commission for Scotland drew up a framework for a hierarchical system of recreational parks in Scotland – including a small number of special parks (with some similarities to English National Parks) in the most outstanding scenic areas – as well as regional parks, country parks and urban parks.[40] Legislative provision exists for urban parks, country parks and regional parks. Two regional parks have been established in the Pentland Hills near Edinburgh and in the hills behind Greenock. As yet, no provision exists for special parks, although the government in 1976 accepted in principle the proposals set out by the Countryside Commission.[41] Some existing regional and district authorities may oppose the setting up of special parks, within which they would lose

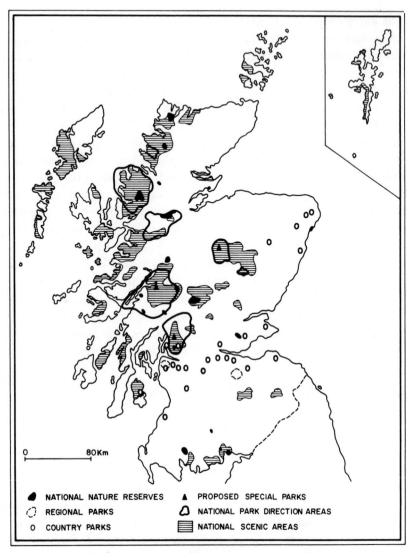

NATIONAL NATURE RESERVES   ▲ PROPOSED SPECIAL PARKS

REGIONAL PARKS   △ NATIONAL PARK DIRECTION AREAS

O COUNTRY PARKS   ▤ NATIONAL SCENIC AREAS

Fig 9.3 Areas of countryside recreation and conservation

planning and development-control powers to park authorities.

By 1980, a total of 21 country parks were on the register of the Countryside Commission.[42] As Fig 9.3 indicates, there is a broad correspondence between country parks and the national distribution of population, with the majority lying in the central belt and the remainder in the North-east. Several of these parks have been established in the park lands of large mansion houses, for example at Culzean in Ayrshire, Aden House near Peterhead and Haughton House on Donside.

Although the number of country parks and similar facilities has grown in recent years, much outdoor recreation is still set in countryside used also for other purposes. Activities such as climbing and hillwalking have higher participation rates in Scotland than in England and are widely distributed over the Highlands. Areas such as Ben Nevis and the Cairngorms are major foci for mountain sports, while during the 1960s and 1970s the provision of facilities led to the rapid growth of skiing at Cairngorm, Glenshee and Glencoe, and more recently at the Lecht between Donside and Speyside. In contrast to mountaineering, the development of skiing, or at least of its infrastructure of ski-lifts and ski tows, has had considerable impact on the mountain environments in which it is located.[43]

Increasing attention has been paid during the 1970s to the need to conserve the outstanding landscapes of Scotland, and in 1978 the Countryside Commission for Scotland defined a number of National Scenic Areas[44] (Fig 9.3), where it is hoped that appropriate development-control policies can be operated. Scotland also has many areas of outstanding quality for wildlife and geological features, and the largest national nature reserves in Britain are located in the Highlands. Some of these reserves, such as the island of Rum and Beinn Eighe, are owned by the Nature Conservancy Council, and nature conservation and research are the dominant land uses, but the majority are under private ownership, and management for conservation continues alongside deer husbandry, sheep farming or forestry. Indeed, both nature conservation and recreation are commonly found alongside other land uses, rather than as sole or primary uses of extensive areas of land.

Contemporary Issues

A number of issues relating to the use of rural land in Scotland have attracted attention and controversy in recent years. These include the loss of farm land to urban development, the impact of afforestation on land uses such as hill farming and deer enterprises, and the more general and long-standing issue of the ownership and control of rural land, especially in the Highlands and Islands.

Land Transfer from Agriculture to Urban Use

Both the percentage of urban land and the rate of land transfer are small compared with the total extent of agricultural land in Scotland. During the 1960s and early 1970s, transfers averaged around 2,400ha per year, equivalent to around 0.04 per cent of the total agricultural area or 0.2 per cent of the area under crops and grass. The concern is not with the amount of land lost to agriculture, but rather with the quality of the land. During the 1970s, over 20 per cent of the land lost by agriculture to urban uses was in land grades A+ and A (ie first quality arable land). Such land is less than 3 per cent of the total agricultural land. By contrast, the poorest grade (largely rough grazings) occupies around three-quarters of the agricultural land yet contributes only 1 per cent of the land flow to urban uses.[45] This disproportionate loss of better quality agricultural land is an inevitable consequence of the distribution of urban areas in Scotland: few are surrounded by rough grazings, and several, including cities such as Edinburgh and Dundee, are at least partly encircled by top quality land. The problem has been particularly acute around the inner Moray Firth, where rapid industrial and urban development in the late 1960s and the 1970s abstracted substantial quantities of high grade agricultural land.

In 1977, guidelines were issued by the Scottish Development Department to regional and district planning authorities, drawing attention to the need to conserve good quality farmland and suggesting a policy of refusal of planning permission relating to development on the top grades of land.[46] Even before then, there was a downturn in the rate of land transfer, but it is too early to judge whether this is temporary or permanent.

The Impact of Afforestation

Since the end of World War II, the forest area has more than trebled, and the forest density in parts of Argyll and Galloway is now very high. Afforestation was particularly rapid in the late 1960s and early 1970s, when over 30,000ha were planted annually, almost equally divided between the state and the private sector. Since then rates have fallen to around half that figure. In the state sector, problems of land availability have meant that target acreages have not been achieved, and in any case targets were reduced compared with the late 1960s. In the private sector, the decline in planting rates has been more dramatic, with the achievement in 1978, for example, being only one-third that in 1971. This reduction followed the replacement of estate duty (under which forestry investment was favourably treated) by Capital Transfer Tax, together with a more general loss of confidence in the industry. But although planting rates have fallen in recent years, Scotland has had a growing share of the British planting area in both sectors. In 1978, 78 per cent of private afforestation and 86 per cent of state planting were in

Scotland. Furthermore, 98 per cent of the land acquired for afforestation by the Forestry Commission was in Scotland,[47] so that Scotland's share of afforestation seems set to increase in the future. Therefore it seems probable that sizeable areas of hill land in Scotland will continue to be afforested, even if policies for more rapid afforestation in Britain in general are not adopted. If these policies are adopted, rapid and extensive afforestation will have a major effect in much of the Highlands and uplands. Scotland will probably continue to have a major share of new planting, not least because the strength of opposition (on aesthetic grounds) to afforestation is less than in most upland areas in England and Wales.[48]

If Scotland's forests do continue to expand, the greatest effects will probably be felt in areas of hill sheep farms and deer forests. The breeding ewe flock has declined since the mid-1960s, although it continued to increase, despite steady afforestation, for the first two decades after World War II. The effect of continuing afforestation on sheep numbers is difficult to predict, and depends on the form and pattern of afforestation as well as on the state of sheep farming. In recent years, the Hill Farming Research Organisation has reported major technical improvements, whereby the livestock carried by hill farms, and their output of livestock, can be greatly increased. As yet, these innovations have been adopted by few hill farmers,[49] perhaps partly because of the time required for the ideas to spread, but probably also because farmers are reluctant to make the considerable capital investment required. It is possible that the sale of part of a hill farm might provide the capital for the improvement of the remaining part, so that sheep output might be little affected. On the other hand, if prospects for hill farming were to appear gloomy, then the existence of a ready market for hill land for afforestation might accelerate the demise of hill-sheep farming.

The impact of afforestation is also felt by red deer. In many parts of the Highlands, the proportion of plantable land is small, and the plantable land is often the wintering ground for the deer. If this wintering ground is afforested the deer population is adversely affected, and hence the primary land use over extensive areas is threatened. Until recently, planting was carried on without consultation between forestry and deer interests, but recently it has been agreed that the Red Deer Commission should be consulted before afforestation occurs.[50]

If afforestation continues at its present or increased rates, then the main land-use changes will probably be felt in the Central and Northern Highlands, where reserves of plantable land are relatively large. If past patterns of afforestation are continued, the main grouse moor areas on the east side of the Highlands will be relatively little affected.

Ownership and Control of Rural Land

The nature of the ownership and control of rural land in Highland Scotland has long attracted controversy. For more than a century, large parts of the Highlands have been owned by absentee landlords, some of whom value their Highland estates more for sport than for purposes such as agriculture or forestry. During the 1970s, the controversy came to a head when several overseas buyers entered the land market. Only a small percentage of the Scottish agricultural land area is in the hands of overseas owners, but their number and the area owned increased markedly during the third quarter of the 1970s. Previously most absentee owners had their permanent residence in the south of England. While it is widely accepted that few Highland estates can be run profitably, and that employment provided by stalking, angling and other sporting activities is welcome in many areas with few other employment opportunities, the view has repeatedly been expressed that land in some sporting estates could be used more productively. The Highlands and Islands Development Board produced detailed plans for land-use changes which would increase land production and employment in Mull and in the Strath of Kildonan,[51] but these suggestions for the intensification of land use were not adopted by the local landowners. Eventually in 1978, the Highlands & Islands Development Board (HIDB) sought increased powers[52] from Parliament which would enable it, under stringently defined conditions, to require a landowner to co-operate in land-use changes. In some cases a landowner could be required to accept a tenant or lessee who would implement an acceptable land-use system, or in the final resort his land could be compulsorily acquired. Powers of compulsory acquisition are already held by the Forestry Commission for land for afforestation, and by the Department of Agriculture and Fisheries for Scotland for land settlement and for preventing the under-use of agricultural land, but these powers are seldom employed. The new powers sought by the HIDB have not been granted, but the application was simply a reflection of the long-established problems surrounding the ownership and use of Highland land. Land allocation between the major uses and between owners in the Highlands, as in the Lowlands, is controlled by the market, but in the context of the very large ownership units of poor Highland land, the effects of the quirks of the market and of ownership are greater than in many lowland areas. Repeated calls for systems of zoning or planning which would ensure a more rational and efficient allocation of land between competing uses have largely gone unheard by government, but the experience of the HIDB plans would suggest that such systems would be successful only if means of ensuring their implementation can be devised. In the meantime, conflicts and controversies over land-use questions may be expected to continue in at least some parts of the country.

Notes to this chapter are on pages 311–13.

10

Fisheries

J. R. Coull

ALTHOUGH the early record is sparse, it is clear that fishing has been important in Scotland from the time of earliest human settlement. For thousands of years the main activity must have been the catching of fish for local subsistence, though there were certainly commercial fisheries by the medieval period. Subsequent expansion of the commercial effort, especially in the modern period, has made the fisheries of Scotland of major importance in the European context, and the Scottish fishing fleet is now one of the most advanced to be found anywhere.

The Earlier History

The earliest settlers in Scotland were food-gatherers rather than farmers, and depended on hunting and fishing along with the collecting of vegetable food material. Most of their known settlements are in shore-side locations on both the west and east coasts, although they are also known inland beside rivers like the Tweed and the Aberdeenshire Dee. A big component of the diet of the coastal communities was shell-fish, collected especially in estuaries, but there is also evidence for fishing by line and harpoon. The earliest date so far obtained for this from the archaeological sites is before 6500BC on the island of Jura.[1] It appears that subsequently both coastal and river fishing were adjuncts to farming. It is well known that, until the great economic advance of the Industrial Revolution, most people rarely had meat in their diet. In these circumstances, fish from inland waters or from the sea was one of the most important sources of protein. This becomes forcibly evident from the more plentiful written records of the seventeenth and eighteenth centuries, and is well recorded in MacFarlane's Geographical Collections.[2] For a long period, most of the more densely populated parts of Scotland have been within relatively easy reach of the sea, and the origins of the practice of fish-wives from coastal villages exchanging fish for such farm products as eggs and cheese are lost in history.

Despite the proximity of much of the population to the sea, for much of the past fresh-water fish had relatively greater importance. Pike, perch, trout and eel were all extensively caught, but undoubtedly the most important and most highly prized species taken in fresh water was the salmon. Salmon were caught mainly in the summer-time in the lower reaches, as they came in from the sea to ascend the rivers for spawning. So important were the salmon fisheries that from medieval times they were a Crown prerogative, and there is far more early legislation on the Scottish statute book relating to salmon than to any other fish species. Friction was also common between coastal and upstream proprietors over the number of salmon actually allowed to ascend the rivers. Salmon were usually caught by net and coble in the estuaries, or at the cruives – the weirs set across the rivers, with gaps in them where the fish could be caught as they moved upstream. The bigger eastward-flowing rivers were particularly important, especially the Tweed, Tay, Dee and Spey. In practice the fishings of these were in the hands of royal burghs and religious houses, although after the Reformation the latter category passed into lay hands. As well as going for local consumption, salmon was also one of the most important national exports. There are many complaints on record of the poorest classes having too much salmon in their diet, partly no doubt because it was preserved for out-of-season consumption by pickling in barrels.

From the late eighteenth century, the value of salmon was enhanced, as contact was established with bigger centres (especially London) to which catches were conveyed in the fresh state in ice. In the nineteenth century the modern catching pattern was established,[3] by which most salmon are caught in trap nets along the coast as they approach the rivers. Although it has inevitably decreased in relative importance, the salmon is still a high-value fish, prized in the markets of the present-day affluent society.

Sea-fishing was dominated for most of the historical period by inshore operation in small open boats; and indeed there were various catching methods deployed at the coast which did not require boats at all. Herring fishing is relatively well recorded from medieval times. There was considerable commercial exploitation of it and it was an important export even in the days of a simpler economy. The catching of white fish is not so well recorded. While it entered less into organised commerce, it appears clear that there was a comparatively steady yield of fish like cod and haddock around the coasts, in contrast to the more seasonal, and in any case less predictable, herring.

Although their earlier growth is frequently obscure, there was by the eighteenth century a series of fishing villages on the east coast, as well as some on the Clyde where fishing was largely a specialised occupation. This contrasted with the crofter-fishing still characteristic of the Highland coasts. Fishing was largely by line for white fish, and the women of the fishing communities played an important role by baiting lines and curing the part of the catch not for immediate consumption. Activity in earlier times was dominated by settlements in the Firths of Forth and Clyde. These provided sheltered waters on which open boats could operate more freely, and around the shores of the firths the most densely populated part of the country provided a market.

While undeniably important to Scotland, the fisheries provided a level of yield which by any modern comparison was very small. It was long realised that, properly exploited, the fisheries held great potential for increasing national wealth, and it was also clear that other nations were better organised to harvest the sea than the Scots. Particularly important were the Dutch, who pioneered the more productive technique of catching herring by drift-net from bigger boats on the open sea. Ironically most of the Dutch fishing was done much nearer to the Scottish coast than to their own, and for centuries it was a Scottish national ambition to develop a fishery to rival the Dutch. The various enactments and measures directed to this end were for a long time of limited effect. The main provisions were the Royal Fishery Companies established in the seventeenth century,[4] and the schemes of the Board of Trustees in the eighteenth.[5] The Scots had neither the skill nor the resources of the Dutch, and their early attempts were mostly directed at developing a 'buss' (large boat) fishery in the Minch. However, the main Scots ports – places like Dunbar and Crail on the Forth and Greenock and Rothesay on the Clyde – never really developed the organisation for boats to operate at a distance like the Dutch. It appears that in Scotland the busses mainly acted as mother or carrier ships for the less effective small boats which continued to do most of the fishing. In the days before telephone and radio, there were also constant problems caused by the necessity of having barrels and salt for curing herring in the right place at the right time, since the herring were to be found in different lochs in different seasons. The clumsy administrative measures allowing exemption from salt duties were also inhibiting.

The Herring Fishery

There was some expansion in herring fishing in the eighteenth century, with government help, notably in the form of tonnage bounties for fitting out the necessary vessels. However, Adam Smith pointed to a serious weakness in this policy when he noted vessels fitted out to catch

Page 227 (above) Herring curing station, Lerwick, Shetland c1885. There was a great boom in the Shetland herring fisheries at the close of the nineteenth century. Women can be seen gutting at the pier-side "farlanes", in the foreground women are topping up barrels of herring before the lids are put on; (left) landing herring at Mallaig. Ports on the mainland side of the Minch have the advantage of direct road access to market. Mallaig is now one of the most important ports in Europe for mackerel and herring

Page 228 *(left)* Production
platform in the Forties oilfield.
This large field was one of the
first to be developed in the
North Sea. The oil is
transported by pipeline to a
landfall at Cruden Bay, south
of Peterhead *(below)* the Sullum
Voe terminal in the Shetlands
receives oil by pipeline from
several fields in the East
Shetland Basin

not herring but the bounty.[6] At the end of the century another system was introduced giving a bounty per barrel of herring produced, and this proved an important stimulus to increased effort. By this time an important fishery had been established in Caithness, where over a two-month summer season boats went out nightly and brought their herring back next day to be cured ashore – an important advantage over the Dutch who had to cure the herring in the restricted space aboard ship. At this stage boats might only carry about ten nets apiece, and they engaged with a curer to land herring at a fixed price through the season. The work of processing herring ashore, which involved gutting and packing in barrels, was largely done by the womenfolk.

After this beginning, the nineteenth century is an impressive story of expansion in the herring fishery.[7] It was taken up on more and more parts of the coast, and by mid-century the Aberdeenshire ports of Peterhead and Fraserburgh were outdistancing Wick as leading fishery centres. Success touched off a spiral of expansion and improvement, probably best seen in the herring fleet itself. More boats were built and, in addition, the boats got bigger as fishermen accumulated more capital. Bigger boats could carry more nets, which could catch more herring, to provide the finance for still bigger boats. By the end of the century, boats of 60ft or 70ft long (about 20–30m) were being built, now decked instead of open, although still powered by sail. Steam power first made its appearance with small engines and boilers to relieve the crew of the heavy work of hauling the leader rope and of hoisting the heavy main sail. Around 1900, however, steam power was installed to propel the herring drifters. Although this certainly increased their catching power and made them much less limited by wind and tide, the cost of a first-class boat tripled from about £1,000 to about £3,000.

In the early days of the herring fishery, crews had generally worked a two-month summer season and reverted for the rest of the year to lining for white fish. However, the success of the herring fishery, and especially the investment in bigger boats, led them to extend their operations till they encompassed in many cases the whole working year. This was made possible by a widening mobility. It was possible to fish in the late spring in the Minch, and in the latter part of the nineteenth century there was a rapid expansion of the Shetland fishery which began in May. In late summer it was possible to fish around the Isle of Man, and the climax of the whole herring year became the autumn fishery from the East Anglian ports of Great Yarmouth and Lowestoft. There was also a more restricted winter fishery in the Minch and off the Firth of Forth.

The Scottish herring fishery was in its hey-day in the early years of the twentieth century before World War I. By this time the auction system of selling had almost completely replaced the old contract cure, operations had become substantially centralised at the bigger harbours, and the total cure at the peak exceeded 2,500,000 barrels, in addition to substantial landings by Scottish boats in England. In addition, from the late nineteenth century kippering provided another market product; and from the same time 'klondyking' (temporary preservation in ice and salt) allowed the supplying of Continental processors with Scottish herring. Thousands of boats and tens of thousands of men and women were involved, many of them engaged in substantial migrations around the coasts through the year. A range of countries were supplied with exports, and to many in Central Europe herring were a staple part of the diet, reaching them through the Baltic ports.

The story of the herring fishery after World War I is one of hardship and contraction. Markets were disorganised, rival nations were expanding their catches, and on top of this came the slump of the Great Depression, when the Scots fishery communities were as hard-hit as any in the country. Even so, herring continued as a substantial fishery until after World War II, when the main development became the adoption of the pair-trawl and then the purse-net, which replaced the labour-intensive drift-net with gear which could be power-hauled. However, the catching power around the North Sea has built up so much – especially in Denmark and Norway – that the herring stocks have been subjected to serious over-fishing, and since 1977 there has been a complete ban on catching them, apart from the restricted fisheries on the Clyde and at the Isle of Man.

White Fishing

Although overshadowed by the herring fishery in the nineteenth century, white fishing has always been important. As well as being caught for local consumption, traditionally part of the catch was also gutted, salted and dried, frequently on the shingle beaches around the coast above which the fishing villages were situated. Dried and salted fish (especially cod and haddock) also entered into local, inter-regional and even international commerce, and this trade was certainly expanding in the eighteenth century.

Most active in commercial fishing in early modern times were the Shetland Islands, where the 'haaf' fishery[8] was organised by the landlords and their agents, and prosecuted mainly in six-man open boats with long-lines in a two-month summer season. Fishing stations were usually at outlying points on the islands so as to be near the fishing grounds, and most exploited were grounds off the north-west of the islands where, at the edge of the continental shelf, good catches of ling as well as cod could be obtained. It has been estimated that in this fishery, at its peak in the early nineteenth century, about 2,500 tons of cod and ling were caught annually; at one time it may have accounted for nearly 90 per cent of the Scottish catch of those species.[9]

Although there were some ventures in bigger smacks to operate more safely and further off-shore, white fish were caught mainly by fishing from small boats during most of the nineteenth century. From 1882, however, there was a prominent new departure, especially in the city of Aberdeen, with the beginning of steam trawling. Throughout the nineteenth century, trawling with sailing vessels had been developing from English ports in the North Sea. Given favourable conditions, it was considerably more productive than the traditional line-fishing, fish being caught *en masse* in the trawl bag, although before the use of steam-power the raising of the trawl from the sea-bed was very heavy work. Aberdeen effectively started in trawling at the time when steam-power was being successfully applied to power the vessels as well as to haul the gear by winch, and indeed Aberdeen largely owes its origin as a trawl port to English fishermen settling there. This occurred too when the national railway network was substantially complete, and there was a fast-expanding market for fresh fish in the growing cities. Expansion of trawling in Aberdeen (and to a lesser extent Granton) took place under boom conditions, and by the time of World War I Aberdeen was established as one of the half-dozen main trawling ports of Britain.

Although the number of trawlers operating from Aberdeen reached over 300 in the inter-war period, the main growth phase had already passed; in later decades trawling has generally been economically marginal and struggling, although there was a prominent phase of fleet renewal around 1960, prompted by an aid scheme of the White Fish Authority. The trawler fleet in recent times has been increasingly handicapped by restrictions in distant- and middle-waters, and for the Scottish fleet (which has been largely middle-water) the limitations on freedom of operation around the Faroe Islands has had serious effects. Although Aberdeen is still the main organising and processing centre in Scottish fisheries, landings at the port are now past their peak, and the inshore port of Peterhead now leads in Scottish landings.

Since the inter-war period the inshore sector of the fleet has had a growing involvement in the catching of white fish. The use of the ground-seine, which is a bag-net but operated with ropes rather than the steel works used in the trawl, was adapted from a Danish method and pioneered by Lossiemouth men from 1921. Lossiemouth was well established as a seine-net port by World War II. The technique was subsequently taken up more generally in Scotland and by the 1960s most of the white fish were caught by the seine. Landings were made at a series of points around the coasts; the great part of those on the west coast, at such ports as Oban and Lochinver, were made by boats based on the east coast. The increased use of the more flexible medium of road transport allowed this fish to be delivered to market. As seine netting grew, the older labour-intensive method of lining dwindled to very small proportions.

More recently a considerable section of the inshore fleet has adopted the light trawl, which allows some saving of labour and also the working of rougher sea bottom than is possible with the ground-seine. A progressive increase in engine power, necessary to pull the trawl, has allowed this to happen. The inshore fleet in the last decade has concentrated much of its landings at Peterhead. This sector of the fleet is now one of the most efficient to be found anywhere. The 'inshore' designation is in fact misleading, as many of the vessels are around 80ft (about 25m) and may fish 200 miles (320km) or more from land.

Scottish fishing has for over 150 years included the luxury item of lobsters. This fishery is still largely prosecuted by small craft which can get close inshore, and is widely dispersed around the coasts. There has been a considerable expansion of the effective resource base for Scottish fishing in the last quarter-century with the rise of considerable fisheries for other shell-fish – especially nephrops (scampi), but also crab, scallops and shrimps. There has also been some exploitation of species for reduction to meal and oil – mainly Norway pont and sand-eel, although other species can go to this outlet when markets are glutted.

Conclusion – Intractable Problems

Overall, recent times have seen far-reaching changes in Scottish fisheries, with the adoption of a series of fishing aids as well as new techniques and new fisheries. Echometer and radio telephone have become standard accessories, and nearly all boats of over 40ft (about 13m) have the Decca navigator which can pin-point position at sea. Catching power has been considerably increased, and the industry has become much more capital-intensive, employing about one quarter of the fishermen recorded in the peak days before World War I. The traditional curing methods have almost completely given way to other forms of processing, and there is increasing emphasis on quality products.

However, the fisheries now have to face serious new problems. Catching power has been increasing fast in other countries, and around the north-east Atlantic has reached a level considerably in excess of the reproduction capability of the fish. There is now a constant tendency to over-fishing, which even in the best of circumstances is difficult to contain. There are very great additional complications for Britain as part of the EEC, which is now ultimately responsible for fisheries policy for its members. The fact that the principle of exclusive 200-mile fisheries zones is now generally accepted has meant that fishing by non-EEC nations within the EEC 200-mile 'pond' has been largely phased out, although this is counterbalanced by the loss or restriction of access for EEC distant-water fleets, especially around Iceland and in the Barents Sea. There is also a marked divergence of interest within the Community, where the island positions of the UK and Ireland contrast with those of Continental members. On a basis of division of the EEC 200-mile zone by median lines between states, Britain would have within its national zone about 60 per cent of the entire Community 'pond'; this prompted fishing interests here to campaign for a big share of available fish. However, existing catching patterns developed in circumstances of open access and freedom of the seas, and with the inevitable ceiling on yield from fish stocks there is simply not enough for everybody. It is clear that the new regime of regulation must be one which incorporates TACs (total allowable catches) for individual species, or groups of species, together with quotas to allocate the shares of the TACs between nations. The fact that it took more than ten years of difficult and protracted negotiations to reach an EEC fishery policy is a measure of the difficulty of the modern position. This is an illustration of the formidable problems encountered when, within expanding countries, a resource ceiling is reached.

Notes to this chapter are on pages 313–14.

11

Energy Resources

Keith Chapman

INDIGENOUS energy sources, such as water power, coal, hydro-electricity, oil and natural gas, have played an important role in the economic development of Scotland since the advent of the Industrial Revolution. The availability of water power was the principal factor controlling the distribution of cotton manufacture which, by the close of the eighteenth century, 'had become Scotland's greatest industry'.[1] Although the introduction of the steam engine was relatively slow in Scotland, partly due to the abundance of water power, the new technology brought about a radical shift in the geographical pattern of economic activity, as the Lanarkshire coalfield in particular became the focus of the new iron-making and engineering industries which formed the basis of the nineteenth century prosperity of the Central Belt. The linkages between these activities and coal mining, established during the Industrial Revolution, have had a dominating influence upon the country's industrial geography. By comparison with the historical significance of coal, the impact of offshore oil and gas has so far been minimal but, in terms of providing a new focus for economic development related to the exploitation of an indigenous energy resource, parallels may be drawn between the contemporary activities of the oil companies in the North Sea and those of the mine-owners and canal-promoters 200 years earlier in the Forth-Clyde valley.

This chapter seeks to identify the causes and consequences of decline and growth in Scotland's primary energy industries since 1945. For convenience it is divided into three sections concerned with coal, oil and natural gas, and other energy sources. Such a division is arbitrary to the extent that events in the coal industry, for example, cannot be explained without reference to trends in the prices of competing fuels. Nevertheless, this structure is logical from both a temporal and a geographical point of view. Thus, whilst coal declined from its immediate post-war monopoly to approximately 33 per cent of primary fuel consumption in Scotland by 1978, oil and natural gas increased their combined shares to almost 55 per cent of the energy market.[2] The remaining 12 per cent was divided more or less equally between hydro-electric and nuclear power.[3] Looking ahead, it is probable that both natural gas and nuclear energy will increase their relative contributions whilst, in the long term, Scotland has considerable potential for such renewable energy sources as wind and wave power. Implicit in these changes in the structure of the energy market are associated changes in the geography of energy production. Thus, whilst the Central Belt has experienced the problems associated with the decline of coal, the North-east, the Orkneys and the Shetlands have attracted most oil-related activities and the North-west and Western Isles seem likely to be most closely involved with any future development of alternative energy sources.

Coal

The Scottish coal industry has been in more or less steady decline in terms of production, employment and number of mines ever since the mid-1950s (Figs 11.1 and 11.2). This experience has been shared with other coal-producing areas, but the contraction has been especially severe in Scotland as its share of total United Kingdom production fell from 13.4 per cent in 1937 to 7.4 per cent in 1979–80.[4] This has meant that Scotland has changed from a traditional exporter of coal, notably to the power stations of Northern Ireland and south-east England, to a significant net importer. The deterioration in Scotland's position with respect to the other coal-mining areas of the United Kingdom reflects the poorer productivity of Scottish pits, which is in turn related to more difficult geological circumstances as compared with the coalfields of Yorkshire and the East Midlands. Thus whereas output per manshift in Scottish mines exceeded the national average in 1937, by 1980 it was only 64 per cent of the levels achieved in the highly productive North Nottinghamshire coalfield, and Scotland ranked eleventh out of the twelve National Coal Board areas for which data is collected.[5] In view of these statistics, it is not surprising that the Scottish industry should have been especially hard hit by competition from imported oil, the real price of which fell steadily from 1957 to the end of the 1960s. With the widening of the price differential between the fuels, petroleum derivatives rapidly displaced coal in most of its traditional markets as domestic and industrial consumers switched fuels, British Rail phased out its steam locomotives, and oil gasification technology was introduced to Scotland's gas works in the latter half of the 1960s.

The expanding needs of the electricity-generating industry are the only exception to this picture of absolute decline in the markets for

Scottish coal. The volume burnt annually in the power stations of the
South of Scotland Electricity Board (SSEB) has increased from 3.4
million tons in 1960 to approximately 8 million tons twenty years later.
The Longannet complex has been an important factor in this trend.
The complex consists of three separate mines linked by a conveyor belt
which comes to the surface at Longannet Mine. The coal is treated and
crushed before being supplied to the adjacent power station of the
SSEB. The latter became fully operational in 1972 and the co-
ordination of investment in power generation and coal-mining facilities
at Longannet underlines the close relationship between the electricity
supply and mining industries in Scotland.

The importance of this relationship is demonstrated by the fact that
the proportion of the total output from Scottish mines destined for use
in the power stations increased from less than 20 per cent in 1960 to
almost 75 per cent in 1980. These figures suggest that the fortunes of the
Scottish coal industry have become progressively more dependent upon
decisions taken by the SSEB. The relationship between the
nationalised coal and electricity supply industries has long been a
sensitive political issue in the United Kingdom. Public funds have, at
various times, been used to subsidise the use of coal rather than other
fuels and pressure has been placed upon the electricity-generating
authorities to construct coal-burning stations. Under the terms of the

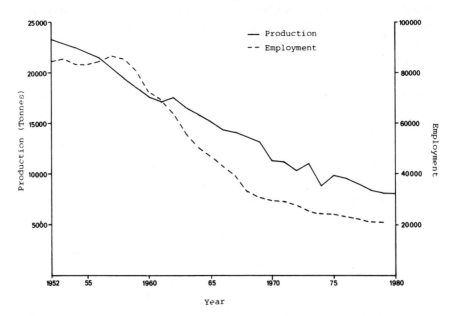

Fig 11.1 Production and employment in the Scottish coal industry, 1952–80 (compiled from data
in annual reports of National Coal Board)

Coal Industry Act 1977, the government agreed to provide up to £7m annually to the National Coal Board (NCB) over a period of five years to enable it to supply coal at a price acceptable to the SSEB, which in turn undertook to maximise its use of coal up to a level consistent with the efficient operation of its generating facilities. A more specific short-term arrangement was negotiated in 1978 to persuade the SSEB to continue operating the coal-burning station at Kincardine during the winter of 1978–9. This also involved payments to the NCB to subsidise coal production.

Despite such measures, the contribution of coal-burning stations to total generating capacity has declined significantly over a ten-year period beginning with the commissioning of Longannet in 1972 and ending with the expected full operation of the new Peterhead unit in 1982. Thus coal-burning stations accounted for over 80 per cent of the SSEB's installed output capacity in 1972 and approximately 62 per cent of generating capacity in Scotland as a whole; the corresponding figures for 1982 will be 55 and 38 per cent.[6] These changes are a consequence of the construction of three large non-coal-burning power stations at Inverkip, Peterhead and Hunterston.

The oil-fired plant at Inverkip on the Clyde was officially opened in 1979. It was originally planned towards the end of the 1960s at a time when trends in the relative costs of coal and oil clearly favoured the latter as a fuel for electricity generation in thermal stations. The oil price increases of 1972–3 disrupted this trend and therefore affected the economics of the Inverkip project. Power stations are ranked in a so-called merit order on the basis of unit production costs which are determined by a combination of fuel price and thermal efficiency. New stations with higher efficiencies usually go to the top of the merit order and are used for base-load generation, whilst older units which are displaced down the order tend to be operational for progressively shorter periods and are relegated to performing a 'topping-up' function at times of peak electricity demand. This pattern has not occurred in the case of Inverkip which, from an early stage in its life, has operated on a two-shift basis supplying the grid for the morning and evening peaks. The withdrawal from service of two of the three generating sets at Inverkip within two years of the official opening of the station further emphasises its subsidiary role within the national generating system – a status which is unusual for such a large modern plant.

Peterhead power station becomes fully operational in 1982. Although designed to burn both oil and natural gas, it will initially use gas from the Brent Field. The operation of the Peterhead station will be closely tied to offshore developments affecting the supply of natural gas.

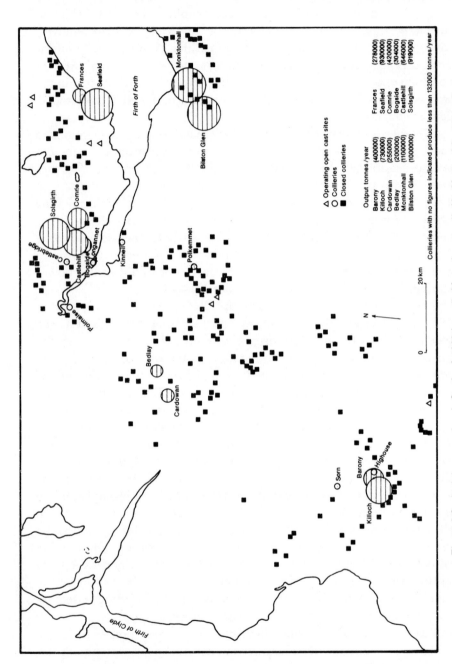

Fig. 11.2 Coal mining operations in Scotland, 1980 (compiled from data supplied by National Coal Board)

Frances
Seafield

Firth of Forth

Monktonhall

Bilston Glen

Solsgirth
Comrie
Castlehill
Bogside
Longannet
Kinneil

Polmaise

Polkemmet

Bedlay

Cardowan

N

20 km

0

Sorn

Barony
Highhouse

Killoch

Firth of Clyde

△ Operating open cast sites
○ Collieries
■ Closed collieries

Output tonnes/year
Barony   (400000)   Frances   (278000)
Killoch   (730000)   Seafield   (930000)
Cardowan   (255000)   Comrie   (420000)
Bedlay   (200000)   Bogside   (304000)
Monktonhall (1100000)   Castlehill   (646000)
Bilston Glen (1000000)   Solsgirth   (919000)

Collieries with no figures indicated produce less than 132000 tonnes/year

There is ample evidence that very substantial quantities of gas will be yielded as a co-product of oil from many North Sea fields. The Department of Energy expects that natural gas availability will tend to fall away during the 1990s, but others have argued that this peak may be deferred into the next century.[7] However, there remains considerable doubt regarding the development of a trunk pipeline system to bring potential gas supplies ashore. If such a system is constructed, it will almost certainly make its landfall at St Fergus, 11km north of the new Peterhead power station. The price and availability of natural gas to this plant will be influenced by the nature and extent of any gas-gathering pipeline system. In view of the experience of Inverkip, it seems likely that Peterhead's contribution to total electricity supply in Scotland will depend upon the extent to which it is fired by natural gas rather than oil. Despite these uncertainties, the operation of Peterhead implies some contraction in the overall contribution of the coal-fired stations in central Scotland which, together with the nuclear plants at Hunterston, have been accounting for a growing proportion of the electricity supplied to consumers in the North of Scotland Hydro-Electric Board (NSHEB) area since 1971.

The decline in the significance of coal-fired plants relative to total generating capacity in Scotland has been further encouraged by the growing importance of nuclear power. After the commissioning of the Hunterston 'A' Station in 1964, the contribution of nuclear power to total output increased to 21.1 per cent in 1979–80.[8] Most of this power is derived from Hunterston 'A' and Hunterston 'B', which was commissioned in 1976, although the Dounreay and Chapelcross facilities of the United Kingdom Atomic Energy Authority and British Nuclear Fuels respectively also supply the grid. The commitment to nuclear power was further emphasised with the confirmation in 1980 of government approval for the construction of a 1220 MW station at Torness.

The NCB regards the power station market as crucial to its investment plans.[9] However, Manners[10] has presented convincing evidence to suggest that, contrary to the predictions incorporated within the NCB's *Plan for Coal*,[11] this market will contract during the last twenty years of the century. Although framed at the UK scale, the arguments employed by Manners may be applied to the situation in Scotland. Notwithstanding the difficulties involved in predicting future trends in the relative prices of coal and oil and in forecasting the demand for electricity, the simple fact that all of the most recently commissioned generating plants in Scotland use fuels other than coal

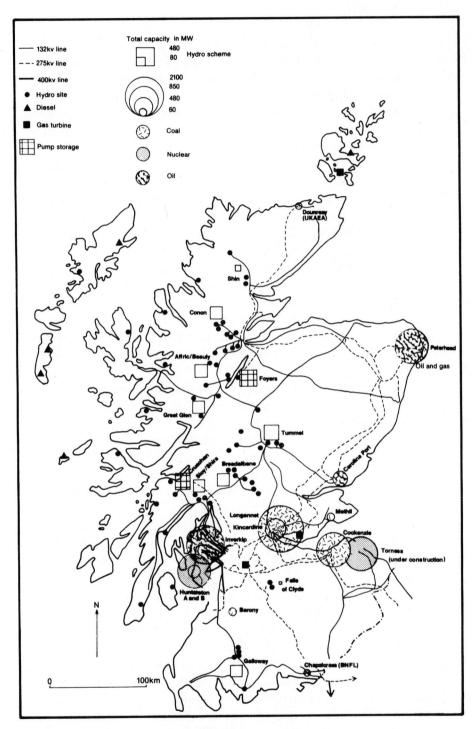

Fig 11.3 Electricity generation in Scotland, 1980. (compiled from data in annual reports of South of Scotland Hydro-Electric Board. Base map provided by John Bartholomew and Son Ltd

suggests that the Scottish coal industry is in a vulnerable position.

In these circumstances, the proven reserves of coking and other coals at Canonbie in the Borders are unlikely to be mined and there is little prospect of any completely new developments in Scotland apart from the cyclical exploitation of opencast sites. Even if demand can be maintained, deep-mined production will come from the extension of existing collieries. Kinneil colliery is currently being linked under the Forth with the Longannet complex which is capable of expansion in the direction of Clackmannan and Alloa (Fig 11.2). The only other significant scheme under consideration involves the sinking of a new shaft at Musselburgh to permit the exploitation of reserves under the Bay from Monktonhall colliery. Even if these schemes materialise, they will not prevent a further reduction in the relative contribution of Scottish mines to total UK production. Most of the major new coal reserves which have been established by an intensive exploration effort since the publication of *Plan for Coal* lie outside Scotland and, although there is considerable uncertainty regarding the level of production which will be achieved by the NCB in future years, there is little doubt that the bulk of this output will be derived from Yorkshire and the East Midlands of England.[12]

Oil and Gas

The contrast between the fortunes of the Scottish coal industry during the 1970s and those of the offshore oil and gas industry during the same period could not be more pronounced. Whatever yardsticks are employed, the speed of development in the latter has been impressive. Between 1967 and 1979 a total of 931 exploration, appraisal and development wells were drilled in the UK sector off Scotland.[13] Official estimates of oil reserves, which are notable for their caution, have steadily increased, whilst discoveries of natural gas in the northern North Sea are making major additions to the already substantial reserves contained in the earlier developed southern basin off the coast of eastern England. Not only have discoveries been made, but they have also been rapidly developed. UK oil production, almost all of which is derived from the waters off Scotland and the Shetlands, exceeded, in terms of energy equivalent, indigenous coal output for the first time in 1979, and the country became self-sufficient in petroleum in the following year.[14] These developments had made the UK the twelfth largest oil producer in the world by 1979, with an output greater than such established producers as Mexico and Nigeria.[15]

Despite the rapidity of development, it is possible to distinguish

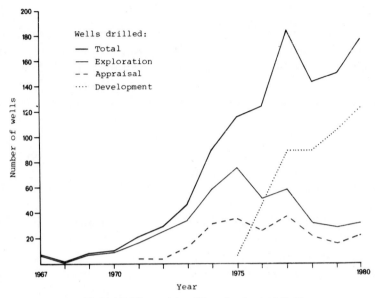

Fig 11.4 Drilling activity offshore Scotland, 1967–80

between successive stages in the exploitation of North Sea oil and gas, as the emphasis has shifted from a concern with exploration to the problems of development, production, processing and the ultimate impact upon patterns of energy consumption. These stages overlap, but their associated impacts upon the economy and environment tend to differ in their timing and spatial distribution. It is therefore convenient to review the events of the last ten years within the framework provided by this sequential process of exploitation.

The first exploration well on the Scottish side of a hypothetical line dividing the UK sector along a parallel extending eastwards from the mouth of the Tweed was drilled in 1967. The level of activity was limited in the late 1960s, but accelerated rapidly following the allocations of territory in the third and fourth licensing rounds to reach a peak in 1975 (Fig 11.4). Apart from a number of unsuccessful wells in the Moray Firth Basin, the search was initially concentrated along the southernmost segment of the median line between the UK and Norwegian sectors. Since 1971, however, the drilling rigs have funnelled northwards along the structural trough formed by the Viking Graben, which straddles the median line from the Maureen field in the south to Magnus in the north (Fig 11.5). The greatest number of exploration wells have been concentrated in the East Shetlands area, but the West Shetland and Moray Firth Basins continued to attract strong interest in the applications for the seventh licensing round announced in 1980. The sharp decline in the exploration effort in 1978

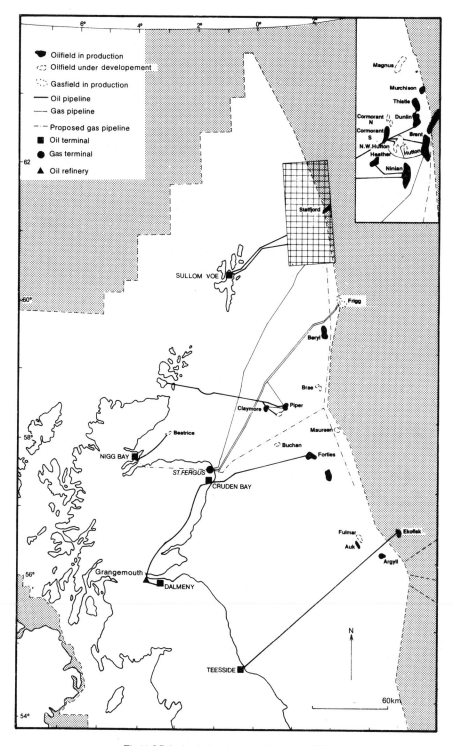

Fig 11.5 Principal oil and gas developments, 1980

and 1979 will probably be arrested for a few years during the early
1980s. BP's discovery of heavy oil to the west of the Shetlands seems
likely to stimulate renewed efforts in this area despite otherwise
disappointing results. Furthermore, the previous exploration of an area
does not preclude subsequent efforts on lesser prospects in the same
general location. Thus exploration may be expected to continue at or
above its 1979 level as long as the high international price of oil is
sustained.

Early exploration stimulated the development of several small
service bases along the east coast from Leith in the south to Lerwick in
the north. However, Aberdeen rapidly established itself as the principal
centre as the development phase proceeded. Although Sumburgh
airport and the associated marine bases in the Shetlands continue to
play an important role in channelling men and materials to the
northern rigs, the importance of other harbours such as Peterhead and
Montrose has declined relative to Aberdeen, which has elevated its
position from that of a service base to a centre of administration and
control over all aspects of offshore operations. By the end of 1979, these
operations were particularly concerned with the exploitation of earlier
discoveries and more than two-thirds of the wells drilled were devoted
to field development (Fig 11.4). Despite a tendency for the time-lag
between the announcement of a discovery and the commencement of
production to increase steadily during the 1970s, resulting in successive
downward revisions in official estimates of output,[16] sixteen oilfields
plus the Frigg gasfield were on stream by the end of 1980 and a
succession of others will follow in the early years of the decade.

With few exceptions, most of the discoveries lie considerable
distances from the coast and the most important development decision
involves the method of bringing the oil ashore. In the case of oil, two basic
alternatives exist – a pipeline or a shuttle-service of tankers from
offshore loading facilities. Both strategies have been employed in the
North Sea, with pipelines generally preferred for larger fields and
offshore loading used for smaller accumulations which cannot easily be
linked into existing networks.[17] Just over 90 per cent of the oil landed in
1979 was delivered by pipeline, with the balance shipped directly by
tankers from offshore loading systems to the refineries.[18] Several
pipelines were in operation by the end of 1980, with the most complex
system serving several fields in the East Shetlands area (Fig 11.5). The
terminals at the pipeline land-falls are perhaps the most visible impacts
of the development phase, although on-shore facilities may be minimal
as at Cruden Bay. The major terminals are at Sullom Voe, which
receives oil from the East Shetlands fields, and at St Fergus, which

processes gas from Frigg, supplemented by small quantities from the Piper Field which are fed into the Frigg pipeline. Supplies to St Fergus were augmented during 1981 with the commencement of flows of associated gas from Brent and other oilfields in the East Shetlands complex. These developments will ensure that St Fergus will, by the mid-1980s, replace Bacton in East Anglia as the most important terminal node on the transmission network of the British Gas Corporation (BGC).

The production phase technically commenced in 1975 when the Argyll and Forties fields came on stream, but this stage in the exploitation of the oil and gas resources of the northern North Sea only became firmly established by the end of the decade. The utilisation of these resources is obviously the next step in the development sequence, and some of the issues raised by their processing and utilisation may be considered by reference to oil, natural gas, and natural gas liquids (NGL) in turn. Grangemouth is Scotland's only major oil refinery. Events in the North Sea have inevitably stimulated proposals for additional facilities to enable the export of refined products rather than crude oil.[19] Continuing speculation surrounding specific sites at Sullom Voe and the Cromarty Firth had failed to produce any tangible developments by mid-1981. This is not surprising in view of the chronic overcapacity problems of the refining industry in Western Europe.[20] Most of the major operators in the North Sea already have refineries either in the UK or elsewhere in the EEC. Thus in 1979 just under 50 per cent of British North Sea oil production was refined in the UK, with a further 28 per cent delivered to other EEC member countries and the USA taking the largest single share of the remainder.[21] These figures suggest that the oil companies are successfully resisting political pressures to refine the bulk of North Sea production in the United Kingdom and that there is little prospect of any major greenfield site development in Scotland.

Unlike oil, natural gas requires very little processing before delivery to the final consumer. Apart from the construction of the St Fergus terminal itself, the major investments have been concerned with the development of a pipeline system for the onward transmission of the gas from this landfall. The southward penetration of gas from the northern North Sea is a notable reversal of the flow pattern of the early 1970s. Scotland first became a significant importer of natural gas from England in 1970 and, by 1975, supplies ultimately derived from the southern North Sea had virtually displaced the output of manufactured gas from the gasworks of the towns and cities. With the start of production from Frigg in 1977, flow patterns within the transmission system of the BGC were radically altered. As the output of fields in the southern North Sea declines and the production of those in the north increases, the contribution of gas from offshore Scotland to total UK requirements will increase steadily during the 1980s, and the areas served from the terminals in eastern England will steadily contract as new supplies from St Fergus, probably reinforced by contributions from Morecambe Bay by 1985, penetrate farther south.

The product supplied by the BGC and generally referred to as natural gas is methane. Several other gases and light petroleum fractions are frequently found in association with both natural gas and oil deposits. These co-products, of which ethane is the most important, have considerable potential as raw materials for petro-chemical manufacture.[22] Successive UK governments have declared a desire to encourage petro-chemical manufacture based on North Sea feedstocks, and Scotland is best placed to take advantage of this political commitment. The first major scheme will take place at Mossmorran in Fife using raw material piped from St Fergus. The prospects for any further development, probably at Nigg on the Cromarty Firth, depend to a large extent upon the construction of a gas-gathering pipeline system designed to tap the associated gas of many oilfields which would not individually justify the costs of bringing their products ashore. Fig 11.5 indicates the general alignment of such a system as originally proposed in 1978.[23] However, the government's decision in 1981 not to participate in funding this system has led to more delay in the implementation of the idea, but not necessarily to its complete abandonment.

This discussion of North Sea oil and gas has so far been structured with reference to the successive phases from exploration to consumption. It is obvious that this structure is somewhat artificial, since exploration continues at the same time that the Auk field, for example, is nearing exhaustion. It is also obvious that the various impacts of these operations are not necessarily specific to a particular stage in the sequence of development. Concern regarding the environmental effects of oil-related developments has been expressed from the very beginning and particular attention has been focused on the coastline.[24] Oil spillages have occurred at Sullom Voe and, in 1976, the Department of the Environment estimated a 50 per cent probability of a blow-out in the UK sector by 1981.[25] In addition to these continuing risks, there has been an environmental price to pay for North Sea oil. A wide range of facilities have been required to bring the oil and gas ashore and it is legitimate to trade the economic benefits against the loss of amenity involved in the construction of coastal terminals, petro-chemical units and so on. However, there have been unnecessary environmental sacrifices. In particular, pressures to accelerate development and to minimise imports of expensive capital equipment resulted in a proliferation of platform fabrication yards at deep-water west coast sites in the mid-1970s. Even at the time, Department of Energy estimates of the demand for such platforms were regarded as too high by many observers,[26] and subsequent events have demonstrated that the 'pressing national need' used to justify the establishment of yards such as Portavadie was an illusion.

There is no doubt that events in the North Sea have created new jobs in Scotland which, although still experiencing higher unemployment than the UK average and suffering from the effects of the recession, has nevertheless significantly improved its position *relative* to the rest of the country during the 1970s.[27] However, these jobs are very unevenly distributed. In 1980, the Grampian region accounted for over 70 per cent of the total of 45,820 jobs in Scotland estimated as being directly related to the North Sea oil industry.[28] Whereas the number of such jobs in Grampian has increased in every year since 1974, the only other areas which have shown a similar trend have been Tayside and the Islands. Although the regional contrasts are less pronounced when indirect oil-related employment is included, Grampian's overall dominance is likely to be accentuated as the production phase continues and service and administration functions replace the manufacturing jobs associated with the construction of capital equipment during the development stage. Thus most of the new jobs have been and will be created in areas outside the Central Belt which has traditionally been the focus of Scotland's unemployment problem. This situation has inevitably raised questions regarding the use of revenue derived from the taxation of offshore production. It is not only the Scottish National Party which has recognised that the immediate economic effects associated with oil-related employment are much less significant than the longer-term benefits accruing from balance of payments savings and royalty income.[29] These matters are beyond the scope of the present chapter, but they do emphasise that the effects of the exploitation of North Sea oil and gas upon the landscape of Scotland are perhaps less significant than its impact upon the country's economy and society.

Other Energy Sources

Despite the historical significance of coal and the contemporary attention focused on oil and natural gas, awareness of the existence of alternatives to these fossil fuels and to nuclear power has increased in recent years. In the case of the UK, it is envisaged that an expanded research programme into new energy technologies will be financed by income derived from North Sea oil.[30] Most of these technologies relate to the exploitation of renewable energy sources in an attempt to promote an energy future unconstrained by the problems of dependence upon a dwindling resource base. Preliminary research suggests that certain parts of Scotland could play an important role in such an energy future for the UK. However, before assessing these new technologies, we will consider the role of two more familiar alternative energy sources in Scotland – peat and hydro-electric power.

Peat

Peat has long been used as a source of fuel by the crofters of the Highlands and Islands where it is available in abundance. More than 50 per cent out of an estimated 1.58 million ha of peatland in the UK is found in Scotland.[31] Most of this proportion is concentrated in the north and west with the counties of Sutherland, Ross and Cromarty and Caithness accounting for just under half of the Scottish total, although significant concentrations are found as far south as Dumfries and Wigtown.[32] Apart from the traditional domestic use of this peat, the possibilities for commercial energy production fall into two general categories – conversion to other fuels and the generation of electricity.

Peat is like any other hydrocarbon material in that it can be used both as a source of energy and as a chemical raw material. Although the technology exists to produce high-BTU gas such as methane from peat, gasification of this material normally yields a low- to medium-BTU product. This could be used on a local scale either as a fuel in industrial furnaces and gas engines or as a source of such chemicals as methanol and ammonia. However, whilst the technical feasibility of such operations is not in doubt, their economic prospects are very dubious.[33]

The generation of electricity in peat-fired thermal power stations is a familiar and well-established technology by comparison with gasification. Approximately 19 per cent of Irish electricity output in 1979 was produced in this way.[34] An experimental station was established at Altnabreac in Caithness in 1956, but shut down only four years later as a result of severe fouling problems in the gas turbines. This experience prompted the Scottish Peat Committee to dismiss as 'slight' the prospects of large-scale exploitation of peat for fuel.[35] This assessment remains essentially valid in the early 1980s. The capital and generating costs of peat-fired plants are approximately 30 per cent higher per unit of installed capacity than oil-fired plants.[36] Furthermore, major subsidies have been required in the USSR,

Finland and Ireland to finance the establishment of large-scale programmes. Even allowing for the continuing rise in the price of conventional fuels, there is little prospect that electricity could be generated more cheaply from peat on the Scottish mainland. However, consumers in the Orkneys, Shetlands and the Hebrides are not linked to the mainland system and derive most of their electricity from diesel generating sets (Fig 11.3). These are expensive to operate and the costs per unit of electricity from such equipment quadrupled between 1971 and 1979. In these circumstances, the substantial peat deposits of Lewis and the Shetlands (notably Yell) offer an opportunity to replace the diesel sets which rely on imported fuel with small power stations based on a local resource. The recent fall in the price of oil, however, makes such developments less likely.

Hydro-electricity

Hydro-electric power makes a more important contribution to electricity supply in Scotland than anywhere else in the UK. Several factors have contributed to the intensive exploitation of the opportunities presented by the country's physical geography.[37] Attempts to promote the aluminium smelting industry at the turn of the century stimulated the integrated development of manufacturing and generating facilities at Foyers on Loch Ness in 1895, at Kinlochleven in 1909 and later at Lochaber during the 1920s and 1930s. The subsequent widespread introduction of hydro-electricity into the public supply system depended upon the concept of a national grid which was officially endorsed in the Electricity Act of 1926. This significantly increased the possibilities for hydro-electric development, since it removed the necessity both for co-ordination with industrial projects and also for maintaining a continuous output since several stations feeding into a grid could operate intermittently in response to water and demand fluctuations. The establishment of the NSHEB in 1943 provided a further impetus to hydro-electric development and the Board retained its overall responsibility for electricity supply north of the Clyde and Tay when the industry was nationalised in 1947.

The integrated nature of the Scottish electricity system has ensured that hydro-electric developments in the north have been influenced by demands from the south. By comparison with thermal generating sets, hydro-electric power stations can be brought into operation very rapidly and are therefore useful for meeting peak demands. Consequently, there is a tendency for stations such as Sloy and Errochty on the southern margins of the NSHEB area to operate on much lower load factors than those further north which have to meet a greater proportion of local demand. The flexibility provided to the Scottish electricity system by hydro-electric power is further reinforced by the pumped storage schemes at Cruachan and Foyers which consume electricity at night when demand is low and generate power when demand is high. Such schemes also provide a measure of insurance against loss of output from other sources.

Throughout the 1950s and 1960s, the NSHEB was a net exporter of electricity to its southern neighbour. The reversal of this relationship during the 1970s has already been noted. Associated with this change has been a decline in the contribution of hydro-electric power to the total electricity system requirements from 27.1 per cent in 1961 to 13.2 per cent by 1979.[38] The relative contribution of hydro-electricity seems likely to be further diminished in the future as any increases in the demand for power are taken up by new thermal stations such as Peterhead and, eventually, Torness. Any absolute increases in the output of hydro-electricity will be small in view of the fact that extensive surveys for new hydro-electric sites in the NSHEB area 'indicate that there is limited potential which may be economically and environmentally acceptable'.[39]

Wind and Wave Power

Hydro-electricity is not, however, the only possible renewable source of power in Scotland. Official surveys of the prospects for developing wind[40] and wave[41] power in the UK indicate that north and west Scotland offer the most favourable sites for any commercial development of both these technologies. It is very difficult to reach conclusions regarding the economic feasibility of wind and wave power. Both technologies have their proponents,[42] but the Department of Energy[43] regards wave power as the more promising of the two. Official enthusiasm remains muted, however, and the most encouraging assessment does not envisage any commercial operation before the end of the century. Technical studies indicate that the greatest potential energy from this source lies along a line parallel to the west coast of Scotland at a distance of approximately 150km beyond the Outer Hebrides, although other areas have been identified extending from the Pentland Firth south-eastwards to the Buchan coast and also off south-west England. The Scottish sites have the disadvantage of being more remote from the national grid, but since 'the size of the potential contribution from wave power is sufficiently large . . . that it is worth considering as an insurance against the consequences of failure of one of our existing supplies',[44] it would be surprising if the Atlantic coast of the Outer Hebrides were not guarded along at least a small part of its length by an experimental array of wave-energy converters by the end of the century.

New energy sources not only imply a new geography of energy production, but also new patterns of related developments.[45] Generally speaking, alternative energy technologies are more suited to the establishment of local supply/demand systems, whereas the scale of production and relative mobility of conventional fuels have favoured a nationwide form of organisation and planning. For example, the best prospects for wind power appear to lie in the construction of small windmills serving the water- and space-heating needs of individual consumers in remote areas,[46] and Ross[47] argues that the principal contribution of wave power will lie in meeting the energy requirements of 'distant' communities. Wave power could influence the economic development of the Hebrides in a number of ways. Labour would be required to maintain and operate the converters offshore. Depending upon the conversion system used, it may be necessary to locate generating facilities on-shore and it is conceivable that the availability of low-cost electric power might be used to stimulate certain types of industrial development. More specifically, energy-intensive processes involving the desalination and subsequent electrolysis of sea water may enable the large-scale production of such basic chemicals as ammonia and methanol. The establishment of such a chemical complex in the Hebrides remains highly speculative in view of the uncertainties surrounding the development of wave power, but there is no doubt that agencies such as the Highlands and Islands Development Board will be very interested in promoting this technology.

Scotland has been very fortunate in its endowment of energy resources. In certain quarters, this endowment is regarded as a mixed blessing in the context of the pit byngs of the Central Belt and the unwanted environmental debris of the oil boom. However, the renewable alternative energies are by no means devoid of impact upon the landscape. Hydro-electric schemes have often provoked fierce opposition and any major wave energy project off the Hebrides, for example, would almost certainly be linked to the national grid via transmission lines routed across Skye. Despite such adverse consequences of exploiting Scotland's energy resource base, it would be an extreme view which regarded this base as anything other than an asset – an asset which has exerted a powerful influence upon the country's modern history and which continues to affect its contemporary geography.

Notes to this chapter are on pages 314–15.

12

Manufacturing Industry

Michael Cross

EVER since the Industrial Revolution in the eighteenth century, Scotland has played an important and distinguished role in the manufacturing economy of Great Britain. This long involvement with manufacturing industry can loosely be divided into three periods. First, the pre-1914 period when Scottish engineering and shipbuilding were pre-eminent throughout the world. Second, the inter-war period, when many of the weaknesses of Scottish-based industry began to appear. The third period dates from 1945, and is the one with which this chapter is mainly concerned.

Since 1945 the nature of manufacturing industry in Scotland has undergone two major changes: a decline of industry in the major cities and an increase in the level of external ownership. An examination of these changes may help to indicate the possible future patterns and trends of industrial employment in the country. This chapter examines the processes underlying these changes at the national and regional levels and reveals the sources from which new employment is likely to arise. Special attention is therefore given to employment created by the opening of new plants by either new or existing (Scottish and non-Scottish) firms, for it can be argued that the continued existence of manufacturing industry in Scotland depends upon having a constant supply of employment created in new plants, rather than on, say, the on-site expansion of existing plants. This source of new employment can be identified as Scottish and non-Scottish and an examination of each forms a major part of this chapter. The final section speculates as to the likely state of manufacturing employment over the next few years and suggests several policy initiatives which the Scottish Development Agency could adopt.

However, the discussion is opened by an historical perspective. Several arguments are presented which indicate that the historical legacy of the Industrial Revolution has had a profound influence on present-day Scottish affairs. It also becomes apparent that the industrial structure of the late nineteenth century is not too dissimilar in some respects from that of today; this parallel might act as a warning, rather than a forecast, of what could happen to manufacturing industry in Scotland.

An Historical Perspective

The Industrial Revolution affected all areas in Britain with the necessary resource base of fuel and labour, and eventually, with developments in transport systems, major regional industrial centres emerged – several existed by 1870. During the initial stages of the revolution, say, 1750 to 1830, Scotland, and especially the West of Scotland, was well placed to take a lead in these developments. Five main factors acted to promote the area as an initial focus for development and ultimately led to its success as a major industrial centre: a dramatic increase in population (despite the area having the highest infant mortality rate in Great Britain) provided the initial labour force for the first mines and factories; improved transportation helped link both fuel and labour within the region and then with other regions, giving the area an initial comparative advantage; world markets opened-up with the already expanding foreign trade centred upon Glasgow; agricultural reform aided the situation by increasing farm output from the potentially productive hinterland; and finally, the area had become an almost natural home for the newly created machine-powered manufacturing industry.[1]

The West of Scotland therefore had many initial advantages, and adapted from being a major textile region to one based on chemicals, iron and steel shipbuilding and heavy engineering. Why then, in the post-1945 period, did it fail to adapt again and develop a new industrial base? Why has it failed to develop new industries? It is answers to these and similar questions which would help reveal why the area has declined, and more especially, why it has failed to unite new methods and products in new firms. A review of existing literature on Scotland's manufacturing industry provides some understanding of its present plight. From such a review the following reasons help to explain the failure of the economy to adopt new methods and products; significantly, they all stem from the industries upon which the region had based its earlier prosperity.

First, both the control and ownership of the major traditional industries were concentrated in the hands of a few men;[2] when allied to a community of interest,[3] this led to a situation where most of the 'entrepreneurial' (risk-taking) decisions were taken by the same few men. Such a situation did not allow many people to experience key managerial roles and hence deprived them of the necessary training to become entrepreneurs. It should be noted, however, that the industries for which Scotland was best suited and in which it specialised were ones in which there was a low ratio of management to operative and therefore a narrow decision-making (managerial) base.

Second, the growth of industry in Scotland was not only largely based upon local enterprise, invention and discovery, but also upon imported English capital.[4] This combination of resources tended to inhibit diversification by directing funds to those projects with the greatest short-term gain. Both the nature of control and the source of capital were favoured by the type of industry (small batch and unit production) and the markets served. The final product, and this is the third point, was delivered in the first years to the British, and then later to an international market. Local production was mainly geared to either the single unit production of ships and heavy engineering goods, or to the manufacture of low level technology items, eg railway track. During the nineteenth and early twentieth centuries these industries relied on captive markets (based on the lack of competition and a community of interests), which to some extent guaranteed their continued existence. With the growth of foreign competition and product substitution these industries could not compete as effectively because of their now inherent high operating costs and relative inefficiency.[5]

The influence of the captive market possibly went beyond simply encouraging inefficiency, because its form may have removed a necessary interface between the traditional and the new industries.[6] In a market where a single product is delivered, the contact between producers and buyers is minimal. Thus in the highly specialised manufacturing industries of Victorian Scotland the chance of the flow of ideas between the market and the production site was greatly reduced. Awareness of competition and changing market requirements was also minimal. When demand finally did change, the existing managerial and production procedures were in no position to meet this new challenge. Furthermore, a single contract may not only occupy all of the productive capacity available in a plant, but may also demand large capital resources. This situation would tend not to encourage a plant owner to find new markets for any excess capacity he might have. Also the effect of producing a specialised item with limited market demand (ie products that were mono-purpose and mono-market) meant that surplus production could rarely be channelled into new markets. Finally, the captive market ensured a steady income with minimum effort and investment. Abrupt changes in the requirements of a major shipbuilder can have a costly and disruptive effect on other firms in the production chain.

These factors, amongst others, led to minimal contact between the Scottish producers and their markets. Furthermore, these markets were rapidly changing and demanding new products made by new methods and from new materials. The large concentration in final products (eg shipbuilding), employing many thousands of workers, also militated against the survival and development of new industries in Scotland. In contrast, in the English West Midlands greater efforts lay with component production that allowed swift market changes and involved investment on a smaller scale. This region's products could also serve many markets. For example, locks and chains would be required in some form for many basic end-products, whether engines, ships or cars. The English West Midlands was also an area which was more accustomed to the new large batch and continuous production methods that were to become common during the inter-war period.[7]

The three factors – nature of control, source of capital, and type of market served – acted together further to stifle the emergence of a new industrial base. For example, captive markets encouraged the slow adoption of new methods of production because of the highly interlinked nature of production and the reliance upon a common final market. This led to an almost complete failure to 'include' new industries, eg motor vehicles, in the region's trading network.[8] Furthermore, '. . . in adversity, retrenchment won out over new enterprise',[9] with, for example, Beardmore, a major Scottish industrialist of the day, choosing to cease his involvement in both aircraft and motorcar production. Beardmore's reaction was unfortunately typical of the response of other industrialists to the government's desire to reduce its involvement in industry after 1918.[10]

Throughout this discussion, it is interesting to note that Scotland was not the only part of the UK failing to secure a major foothold in the new industries. In fact, Britain as a whole failed to attract and develop many of the emerging new industries of the 1900–14 period.[11] However, after 1918, the South East and the West Midlands, and especially London, rapidly developed as major locations for the new industries. Many of these were also dominated by new concerns, often huge in size, operating vast production lines with low unit costs, and organising labour in new ways. Such concerns were alien to existing practices in Scotland (J. & P. Coats was an exception) and much of Scottish management was not familiar with the new production techniques and planning procedures.[12]

The development of industry based on local reserves of coal was also challenged as new forms of power (eg electricity) released much of industry from such resource-based locations. This switch meant that new centres could develop in Britain whose growth was enhanced by the extensive transport network already in existence. The industrial structure of Scotland, however, was neither well placed nor equipped for twentieth century industry and this position was still further compounded by the physical (environmental) legacy of the Industrial Revolution.

In the early decades of the twentieth century factors impeding the progress of manufacturing industry in Scotland were location, a poor physical environment, and problems created by a centrally controlled industrial base, dependent upon native invention and largely external capital, and specialising in narrow and declining international markets. Two questions now arise. First, is the present industrial structure greatly different from its pre-1945 form? And second, is it better placed than its predecessor for future development?

The Structure of Manufacturing Industry in the 1970s

During the 1952–75 period employment in manufacturing industry in Scotland declined by a little over 100,000. The brunt of this decline was borne by the traditional Scottish industries, ie iron and steel, shipbuilding, and textiles. Others managed to maintain their employment levels throughout the period, and these include the food and drink, chemicals, and mechanical engineering industries. Perhaps the most encouraging sign in the overall picture of decline and stagnation was the growth of the instrument and electrical engineering industries. Yet, despite these changes, some of which have been dramatic, the *relative* employment structure of manufacturing industry does not appear to have greatly changed since World War II (see Table 12.1).

However, beneath each of the aggregate industrial employment totals in the table are hidden some of the more important features of manufacturing industry in Scotland. For example, if the vehicles employment total is split into its constituent parts two distinct trends are immediately recognisable. One is the continuing decline of employment in locomotive and railway carriage manufacturing; the other is the growth of the motor vehicle industry which has almost totally offset the whole of the railway industry's decline. This illustrates the danger of referring only to aggregate employment totals for an industry; it can hide many of the features of a nation's industrial structure. The following discussion therefore attempts to highlight

Table 12.1

Manufacturing employment in Scotland, 1952–75

Industry by S.I.C.	1952	1956	1960	1966	1971	1973	1975
03 Food & drink	93.6	91.6	100.5	103.0	103.5	101.9	99.0
04 Coal & petroleum products	37.5	37.9	36.9	33.6	32.5	30.1	31.8
05 & chemicals							
06 Metal manufacture	66.8	66.5	58.7	52.0	45.8	44.0	43.2
07 Mechanical Eng.	107.0	118.7	120.7	128.7	104.4	94.3	104.8
08 Instrument Eng.	10.5	11.5	11.5	16.2	18.9	17.7	17.7
09 Electrical Eng.	18.8	20.5	28.3	42.7	50.2	52.9	51.7
10 Shipbuilding	77.2	79.6	68.9	47.7	44.8	42.4	41.5
11 Vehicles	40.3	48.0	42.8	44.7	37.1	37.6	35.8
12 Other metal goods	27.8	27.8	27.8	27.5	26.2	26.5	24.9
13 Textiles	117.2	120.0	109.8	98.6	76.0	75.7	62.4
14 Leather	4.7	4.5	4.3	3.7	3.4	3.6	3.1
15 Clothing & footwear	33.3	33.9	31.6	32.2	33.5	37.5	34.4
16 Bricks & pottery	26.0	25.9	22.7	24.0	22.5	21.4	19.5
17 Timber & furniture	31.2	30.5	26.9	25.6	25.7	26.0	22.7
18 Paper & printing	51.5	54.9	58.0	59.6	53.9	50.8	48.9
19 Other manufacturing	16.3	15.6	16.2	15.6	16.2	17.5	16.1
Total	759.7	787.4	765.6	755.4	694.6	679.9	657.5

Source Fothergill, S., and Gudgin, G. H., *Regional Employment Statistics on a Comparable Basis 1952–75*. Occ. Paper No. 5. (Centre for Environmental Studies 1978)

some of these hidden features and places strong emphasis on their geographical distribution.

Each industry is made up of a large number of plants, ranging from the small family business to the massive car assembly plant (Table 12.2). The size and number of plants in each industry varies, but almost without exception plants employing 500 or more employees dominate each industry. While having a high concentration of employment in large plants may ease the monitoring of industry and the implementation of an industrial strategy, it may not be in the long-term interests of the economy. Of course, not all areas are dominated by large plants. In fact, the number of labour market areas in Scotland dominated by a single plant in 1973 was fourteen (45 per cent).[13] In many respects the structure of industry and the future prospects for growth depend upon the fortunes of these large plants. Admittedly, the smaller plants play a vital role, but it is these larger plants that will determine the short-term prospects for employment growth or decline, and may in turn influence the long-term viability of the economy. So, what are the characteristics of these large plants?

Nearly 70 per cent of manufacturing employment is in plants whose ownership lies outside Scotland (Table 12.3), and over the 1973–7 period the level of external ownership rose by a few per cent. This shift has been due to the higher closure rate of Scottish-owned plants, the heavy reliance upon incoming branch and subsidiary plants for new

Table 12.2

Manufacturing units* by employment size, Scotland 1975

Employment size of manufacturing units

Industry by S.I.C.	11–19	20–99	100–199	200–499	500 and over	Total
03 Food & drink	4,111[a]	19,310	9,607	23,181	43,641	99,850
	(283)[b]	(461)	(69)	(72)	(37)	(922)
04 Coal & petroleum	91	250	150	245	1,443	2,170
products	(7)	(6)	(1)	(1)	(1)	(16)
05 Chemicals	492	2,578	2,173	5,059	16,917	27,219
	(34)	(57)	(15)	(16)	(15)	(137)
06 Metal manufacture	592	3,141	3,834	6,590	25,604	39,761
	(41)	(72)	(27)	(21)	(20)	(181)
07 Mechanical Eng.	2,589	10,336	8,085	16,220	48,046	85,276
	(179)	(246)	(55)	(54)	(34)	(568)
08 Instrument Eng.	360	321	872	2,727	13,871	18,151
	(25)	(16)	(6)	(9)	(10)	(66)
09 Electrical Eng.	794	4,008	2,650	8,383	33,029	48,864
	(54)	(73)	(20)	(24)	(25)	(196)
10 Shipbuilding	513	1,947	1,179	4,938	30,177	38,754
	(36)	(44)	(8)	(15)	(14)	(117)
11 Vehicles	558	1,992	619	1,076	30,457	34,701
	(41)	(47)	(5)	(3)	(9)	(105)
12 Other metal goods	2,164	7,850	3,111	5,561	7,765	26,451
	(151)	(186)	(23)	(19)	(10)	(389)
13 Textiles	1,331	12,968	13,801	18,843	11,815	58,758
	(93)	(268)	(96)	(63)	(13)	(533)
14 Leather	254	1,136	591	203	—	2,184
	(16)	(28)	(4)	(1)	(—)	(49)
15 Clothing & footwear	827	7,207	7,791	10,361	6,305	32,491
	(58)	(157)	(56)	(35)	(8)	(314)
16 Bricks & pottery	596	5,357	2,541	3,820	3,802	16,116
	(41)	(128)	(19)	(11)	(5)	(204)
17 Timber & furniture	2,855	9,497	3,310	3,175	—	18,837
	(205)	(222)	(25)	(10)	(—)	(462)
18 Paper & printing	1,593	8,161	6,423	11,830	16,274	44,281
	(113)	(184)	(46)	(36)	(19)	(398)
19 Other manufacturing	717	3,564	2,103	2,872	6,870	16,126
	(49)	(80)	(16)	(9)	(7)	(161)
Total	20,437	100,288	68,563	125,010	295,711	610,000
	(1,426)	(2,276)	(490)	(399)	(227)	(4,818)

a Employment b Number of units * A unit is any factory or plant, etc, at a single site or address
Source Business Statistics Office and Scottish Council (Development & Industry)

Table 12.3

Location of ultimate ownership of Scottish manufacturing plants and employment, 1973 and 1977

Location of ultimate ownership	Plants Number	%	Employees Number	%	Average size of plant (Employees)
Scotland	2,886[a]	68.6	202,560	36.1	70.2
	(2,176)[b]	(71.6)	(243,440)	(41.2)	(111.9)
England	994	23.6	248,280	44.2	249.8
	(644)	(21.2)	(235,150)	(39.8)	(365.1)
Europe	82	1.9	14,240	2.5	173.7
	(44)	(1.4)	(12,560)	(2.1)	(285.4)
North America	222	5.3	86,400	15.4	389.2
	(148)	(4.9)	(87,730)	(14.9)	(592.8)
Other world	6	0.1	630	0.1	105.0
	(5)	(0.2)	(370)	(0.1)	(74.0)
Joint venture	18	0.4	9,090	1.6	505.0
	(24)	(0.8)	(11,450)	(1.9)	(476.7)
Total	4,208		561,200		133.4
	(3,041)		(590,700)		(194.2)

Source   a Scottish Council (Development and Industry) – 1977 figures
         b Firm, J. R. 'External Control and Regional Development The Case of Scotland', *Environment and Planning*, 7, 4 (1975). Table 3 – 1973 figures

employment, and the acquisition and take-over of previously Scottish-owned plants. The long-term impact of the last process is not known, but it would appear that a large proportion of the English-owned sector has developed by this means.

Perhaps of greater significance is the split in ownership of plants by employment size. Just over 70 per cent of plants with fewer than 100 employees are under Scottish ownership. Conversely, fewer than 30 per cent of plants employing 100 or more employees are under Scottish ownership. This level falls to around 20 per cent for plants employing 500 or more employees (Table 12.4). If the future prosperity of Scottish industry lies with these large plants, it is unlikely that either regional or national policies will have any major effect. In the main, these large, externally-owned plants represent a part of either a national or an international company, and their performance and future must be assessed within the overall strategy of the company. Some of the possible implications of this issue are considered later.

It is now worth considering how industry is spread amongst the regions and sub-regions of Scotland. More than half of all manufacturing employment is in the Strathclyde region (Table 12.5). The Clydeside conurbation still maintains its dominant position with over 70 per cent of all the employment of this region. However, Glasgow city is of secondary importance to its surrounding area. It is this latter

Table 12.4

Manufacturing units* by employment size and location of ultimate ownership, Scotland 1977

Employment size of manufacturing units

Location of ultimate ownership	1–10	11–24	25–99	100–199	200–499	500 and over	Total
Scotland	3,655[a]	10,236	47,078	30,324	46,887	64,382	202,562
	(640)[b]	(599)	(947)	(224)	(157)	(59)	(2,626)
England	267	1,953	15,844	19,849	45,410	164,957	248,280
	(41)	(111)	(301)	(143)	(144)	(115)	(855)
North America	47	367	2,999	5,232	12,520	65,231	86,396
	(7)	(22)	(49)	(37)	(36)	(45)	(196)
Europe	40	203	1,496	1,792	3,239	7,470	14,240
	(7)	(12)	(28)	(13)	(11)	(8)	(79)
Other world & joint venture	0	33	303	772	1,075	7,535	9,718
	(0)	(2)	(6)	(6)	(4)	(5)	(23)
Total	4,009	12,792	67,720	57,969	109,131	309,575	561,196
	(695)	(746)	(1,331)	(423)	(352)	(232)	(3,779)

a Employment *b* Number of units * A unit is any factory or plant, etc, at a single site or address
Source Scottish Council (Development and Industry)

area which received nearly 80 per cent of all incoming branch and subsidiary plants entering Scotland during the 1945–65 period.[14] This influx of new, externally-owned investment is reflected in the build-up of employment in electrical engineering, vehicles and clothing in the outer areas of the conurbation. An important feature of this development has been the successful growth of the new towns of East Kilbride and Cumbernauld designated in 1947 and 1955 respectively.

From the mid-1960s the flow of firms into the Glasgow area began to decline, and many of those entering after 1965 were seeking new locations. Prior to the mid-1960s only a few major investments failed to locate in the Clydeside area. Notable exceptions are the plants of Clarkson Tools (formerly Cleveland Twist Drill) and General Motors in Peterhead, and Uniroyal's plant in Dumfries (now owned by Continental Gummiwerke of West Germany). The area to gain most during the post-1965 period was Fife, whose share of the electrical engineering industry, for example, grew dramatically and now employs around 9,000 people. Since a large percentage (55 per cent) of these 9,000 jobs are held by women, however, this new industry has not directly aided the situation resulting from the rundown of coalmining in the region. Similarly, the Borders gained over 1,000 jobs in new electrical engineering plants during the late 1960s and early 1970s.

The growth of the electronics and electrical engineering industries since 1945 has been largely the result of the establishment of externally owned branch and subsidiary plants. As the UK and European

Page 261 *(above)* Longannet is
one of the largest coal-fired
power stations in Europe and
its continued operation is
crucial to the fortunes of the
Scottish coal industry. The
conveyor belt supplying coal
direct from the mines may be
seen in the foreground; *(left)*
Sloy hydro-electric power
station. Such facilities are more
important contributors to
electricity supply in Scotland
than anywhere else in the
United Kingdom, but their
relative significance is
declining. Further major hydro-
electric developments are
unlikely

Page 262 *(above)* The nuclear power stations at Hunterston on the Firth of Clyde contributed approximately 20 per cent of total electricity output in Scotland in 1980. Another nuclear plant is under construction at Torness; *(below)* St Fergus gas terminal, 1981. Gas from the Frigg and Brent fields is piped ashore here where it receives the necessary treatment before entering the transmission system of the British Gas Corporation

markets of these two industries have grown, so has their involvement in Scotland; thus these growing industrial sectors in particular have come to be dominated by externally owned plants (Table 12.6). However, the presence of a large external ownership element in an industry does not necessarily imply that it either has, or will have, any growth potential. For example, the near complete dominance of metal manufacturing and shipbuilding by English-based concerns is because of the nationalisation of these industries in 1967 and 1977 respectively.

Because the distribution of incoming branch and subsidiary plants has not been even, some areas have a greater proportion of employment in Scottish-owned plants than others. These variations in the level of internal and external ownership are detailed in Table 12.7, and several features emerge. First, employment in North American-owned plants is highest in areas surrounding the major cities, the city of Dundee being an exception.[15] Second, in contrast, the level of employment in Scottish- and English-owned plants is markedly higher in the major cities; again, Dundee is the exception. These inner city locations were some of the first to be developed, hence the greater involvement of Scottish- and English-owned firms. Furthermore, if the average age of all manufacturing employment is calculated, it is found that the inner city areas have by far the oldest industrial stock.

Overall, the numbers employed in manufacturing industry in Scotland have fallen dramatically since the early 1950s. Between 1952 and 1980 180,000 jobs were lost, and although this averages only 6,000 jobs per year, it represents a reduction of about 25 per cent of the 1952 manufacturing employment stock. The bulk of this decline has not been evenly distributed throughout the period. As stated earlier, just over 100,000 manufacturing jobs were lost between 1952 and 1975, whilst between 1975 and 1980 the figure was around 80,000. However, beneath this outward appearance of relatively gradual aggregate employment decline, several significant changes have occurred. For example, there has been a marked build-up of externally owned plants which have concentrated mostly in new industries and in new locations. But how different is the present-day industrial structure from its pre-1945 predecessor?

Taking one element, that of the control and ownership of industry, as an example, one could argue that there has been little material change between the two periods. The highly concentrated form of control and ownership which existed during the nineteenth and early twentieth centuries has come to be replaced by a more diffuse, but equally remote form of control and ownership; a broad management structure has therefore not been allowed to develop in either period in large sections

Table 12.5
Manufacturing employment by region/sub-region and industrial order, Scotland 1977

Region/ Sub-region	03 Food & Drink	04 Coal & Petroleum Products	05 Chemicals	Industry by S.I.C. 06 Metal Manu-facture	07 Mech-anical Eng.	08 Instru-ment Eng.	09 Elec-trical Eng.	10 Ship buildin
STRATHCLYDE	34,710	379	12,180	25,970	54,539	7,943	20,907	28,08
Clydeside Conurbation	27,509	283	4,978	23,667	45,988	5,233	17,218	13,95
Glasgow City	15,830	93	1,982	5,300	17,806	2,153	1,987	7,83
Outer Clydeside	11,679	190	2,996	18,367	28,182	3,080	15,231	6,11
Outer Strathclyde	7,201	96	7,202	2,303	8,551	2,710	3,689	14,13
LOTHIAN	11,542	8	3,657	805	4,713	1,187	11,394	1,34
Edinburgh City	8,369	—	3,204	315	2,152	474	8,273	1,32
Outer Lothian	3,173	8	453	490	2,561	713	3,121	1
TAYSIDE	4,506	254	100	120	6,318	8,092	2,573	1,04
Dundee City	1,965	245	58	69	2,509	8,039	2,264	1,04
Outer Tayside	2,541	9	42	51	3,809	53	309	
GRAMPIAN	12,097	9	204	38	5,387	29	871	1,94
Aberdeen City	7,050	9	191	38	3,108	29	366	1,51
Outer Grampian	5,047	—	13	—	2,279	—	505	42
CENTRAL	2,945	1,443	5,679	5,537	2,053	940	205	18
FIFE	2,548	60	713	779	4,635	663	9,387	17
BORDERS	812	—	47	9	282	56	1,195	9
SOUTH WEST	2,414	—	1,698	210	735	—	—	—
HIGHLANDS & ISLANDS	2,102	—	88	1,407	4,677	101	89	5
Total	74,051	2,153	24,366	34,875	83,589	19,024	46,619	33,05

Source Scottish Council (Development and Industry)

of manufacturing industry. In the earlier period this was a function of the product made, eg boilers, vessels, etc, while in the later period it was a function also of the organisational structure of the firms involved. It could be suggested, then, that both the historic and the contemporary forms of ownership exhibited by manufacturing industry in Scotland have had much the same result.

The analyses presented in this section have only succeeded in

11 Vehicles	12 Other Metal Goods	13 Textiles	14 Leather	15 Clothing & Footwear	16 Bricks & Pottery	17 Timber & Furniture	18 Paper & Printing	19 Other Manufacturing	Total
26,047	14,661	21,906	1,174	19,798	10,040	6,285	14,244	7,618	306,501
22,678	10,347	10,312	1,115	12,270	6,910	4,811	13,407	5,926	266,618
8,051	4,118	4,376	326	7,752	4,209	2,535	9,086	2,223	102,503
14,627	6,229	5,936	789	4,518	2,701	2,276	4,321	3,703	124,115
3,369	4,314	11,594	59	7,528	3,130	1,474	837	1,692	79,883
5,840	3,666	2,466	103	1,321	3,256	1,373	8,209	1,739	62,622
—	1,532	703	103	552	399	1,015	6,683	468	35,571
5,840	2,134	1,763	—	769	2,857	358	1,526	1,271	25,051
81	1,264	13,353	67	1,046	374	1,050	4,931	1,506	46,682
22	608	9,599	—	856	68	821	4,356	1,461	33,981
59	656	3,754	67	190	306	229	575	45	12,701
328	1,393	3,671	33	370	1,444	1,706	6,743	491	36,758
148	704	2,500	33	337	1,141	980	6,368	266	24,785
180	689	1,171	—	33	303	726	375	225	11,973
1,063	1,316	2,266	—	1,686	4,997	1,836	1,956	482	34,667
20	1,124	1,706	—	2,020	1,174	998	4,003	3,112	33,121
10	656	9,140	147	367	151	167	411	279	13,826
8	56	1,222	137	874	230	299	138	1,192	9,213
9	225	1,474	26	140	2,904	1,069	1,205	91	15,657
33,406	24,362	57,930	1,690	27,801	24,635	14,768	41,856	17,008	561,198

describing the overall form and structure of manufacturing industry in Scotland. It has not considered, for example, how the overall changes described came about. The next section therefore examines the processes of manufacturing employment change and a number of general questions are addressed. For example, are the present trends of employment change likely to continue? Are the present locations of industry likely to remain the same?

Table 12.6

Location of ultimate ownership by major industrial sectors, 1973 and 1977

Location of ultimate ownership (%)

Industry by S.I.C.	Scotland	England	N. America	Europe	Other world	Joint venture
03 Food & drink	47.7[a]	40.7	9.7	0.2	—	0.1
	(48.3)[b]	(44.5)	(5.7)	(1.5)	(—)	(—)
04 Coal & petroleum products	11.8	88.2	—	—	—	—
	(15.4)	(80.2)	(—)	(—)	(—)	(4.4)
05 Chemicals	6.9	70.3	13.9	8.3	—	0.04
	(11.8)	(63.2)	(12.1)	(10.7)	(0.3)	(1.9)
06 Metal manufacture	17.1	80.5	1.3	—	—	1.0
	(18.3)	(70.4)	(2.2)	(—)	(—)	(9.1)
07 Mechanical Eng.	38.9	24.9	30.9	2.2	—	3.1
	(39.0)	(29.2)	(29.3)	(1.9)	(0.4)	(0.3)
08 Instrument Eng.	6.1	33.0	60.4	—	—	—
	(16.9)	(21.0)	(60.7)	(—)	(—)	(1.3)
09 Electrical Eng.	12.8	45.8	31.1	10.3	—	0.1
	(7.8)	(52.4)	(31.4)	(8.3)	(—)	(0.1)
10 Shipbuilding	14.4	78.8	1.9	0.04	—	—
	(53.3)	(29.8)	(11.8)	(—)	(—)	(5.1)
11 Vehicles	7.7	65.3	24.9	0.4	—	—
	(9.8)	(53.3)	(36.4)	(0.5)	(—)	(—)
12 Other metal goods	52.6	37.4	6.9	2.7	0.2	0.2
	(58.6)	(25.2)	(10.9)	(0.4)	(0.1)	(4.8)
13 Textiles	74.1	21.8	3.2	0.8	—	—
	(64.2)	(28.8)	(3.0)	(3.6)	(—)	(0.4)
14 Leather	72.5	23.3	—	2.5	—	—
	(88.0)	(12.0)	(—)	(—)	(—)	(—)
15 Clothing & footwear	46.0	37.8	15.6	0.1	—	0.4
	(48.2)	(38.0)	(13.8)	(—)	(—)	(—)
16 Bricks & pottery	27.9	45.6	1.4	0.3	1.9	22.9
	(37.1)	(48.1)	(1.2)	(—)	(—)	(13.6)
17 Timber & furniture	78.0	17.4	0.8	3.8	—	—
	(87.2)	(12.4)	(0.4)	(—)	(—)	(—)
18 Paper & printing	47.1	47.9	3.4	1.5	—	—
	(55.0)	(39.4)	(2.5)	(0.8)	(—)	(2.3)
19 Other manufacturing	25.7	35.9	27.5	9.2	0.7	0.9
	(28.4)	(43.2)	(26.1)	(1.5)	(0.1)	(0.8)
Total	36.1	44.2	15.4	2.5	0.1	1.6
	(41.2)	(39.8)	(14.9)	(2.1)	(0.1)	(1.9)

Source a Scottish Council (Development & Industry) – 1977 figures
b Firn *op. cit.* Table 6 – 1973 figures

Table 12.7

Percentage location of ultimate ownership by region/sub-region, 1977

Region/ Sub-region	*Location of ultimate ownership (%)*					
	Scotland	*England*	*N. America*	*Europe*	*Other world*	*Joint venture*
STRATHCLYDE	30.9	48.5	17.6	2.4	—	0.4
Clydeside						
Conurbation	32.0	48.6	16.3	2.4	—	0.5
Glasgow City	41.2	54.5	2.6	0.8	—	0.7
Outer Clydeside	24.4	43.7	27.6	3.7	—	0.4
Outer Strathclyde	27.9	48.2	21.3	2.6	—	—
LOTHIAN	37.6	53.1	7.4	1.3	0.2	0.3
Edinburgh City	38.8	56.5	4.1	—	—	0.5
Outer Lothian	35.9	48.7	11.8	3.1	0.5	0.5
TAYSIDE	53.0	21.2	23.0	2.8	—	0.1
Dundee City	47.4	21.8	27.3	3.7	—	—
Outer Tayside	68.1	19.6	11.6	0.2	—	0.4
GRAMPIAN	45.0	41.7	9.6	3.2	—	0.3
Aberdeen City	43.1	47.6	7.2	1.5	—	0.5
Outer Grampian	48.9	29.9	14.5	6.5	—	—
CENTRAL	39.5	43.4	6.1	2.7	0.8	7.5
FIFE	32.1	44.1	19.6	3.4	—	0.8
BORDERS	67.7	18.1	9.6	4.6	—	—
SOUTH WEST	35.8	42.6	19.5	2.1	—	—
HIGHLANDS & ISLANDS	28.6	28.4	11.0	2.9	—	28.9
Scotland	36.1	44.2	15.4	2.5	0.1	1.6

Source Scottish Council (Development and Industry)

Manufacturing Employment Change – A Components-of-Change Approach

The shape, form and purpose of manufacturing industry are constantly changing, because of a number of factors, eg product development, process innovation etc, and this results in some companies expanding at the expense of others, one outcome being that employment levels can change throughout an industry. Each change is made up of various responses made by individual plants. Some plants will require a larger workforce, while others will shed surplus labour. Other firms may be forced to close because they cannot respond to the new conditions. A further cause of employment change comes from the opening of new plants by either new or existing firms. These are the four main components of employment change, and any analysis attempting to consider the source of new employment in either the short or the long term requires information on the recent trends of these components. It is this information which is presented here.

During the 1951–74 period nearly 350,000 new manufacturing jobs were created, while over 380,000 were lost. Of the new jobs, 221,500 came from the opening of new plants. This total divides almost equally between incoming (101,400) and non-incoming plants (120,100). However, most of the new jobs created by plant expansion occurred in non-incoming plants (102,000 of 125,300), the remainder coming from the expansion of pre-1952 incoming plants (23,300). Nearly all the employment lost was the result of closure (195,700) and contraction (173,900) of non-incoming plants. Incoming plants lost only 1,100 jobs by contraction and a further 11,200 from closure. These individual employment gains and losses have meant that the level of employment in incoming plants has increased from 28,700 to 141,000, while employment in their non-incoming counterparts has declined from 648,900 to 500,700.[16]

These figures are illuminating, but they do not give any indication of how these various employment components differ within Scotland – a situation which is complicated. Not all areas are suffering from a decline in manufacturing employment. Some areas, the new towns of East Kilbride, Glenrothes, Irvine and Livingston, for example, have all increased their manufacturing employment levels over the 1968–76 period. However, only Livingston gained most of its new employment from the opening of new plants, while the other three relied on the expansion of plants already operating in 1968. The fifth new town, Cumbernauld, perhaps surprisingly, remained virtually static throughout the period. Furthermore, the greatest proportion of any

Table 12.8
Components of manufacturing employment change, 1968–76

Region/ Sub-region	Employment[a] 1968	1976	Shift	Closures	Cont- raction	Openings
STRATHCLYDE	421,290	341,170	−80,120	75,790	78,300	18,810
Clydeside Conurbation	330,500	255,420	−75,080	58,000	58,190	14,420
Glasgow City	167,030	119,630	−47,400	31,160	22,090	3,960
Outer Clydeside	163,470	135,790	−27,680	26,840	36,100	10,460
Outer Strathclyde	90,790	85,750	−5,040	17,790	20,110	4,390
LOTHIAN	83,210	65,480	−17,730	12,410	7,030	4,550
Edinburgh City	56,230	36,330	−19,900	6,640	2,660	1,400
Outer Lothian	26,980	29,150	+2,170	5,770	4,370	3,150
TAYSIDE	57,760	45,850	−11,910	11,300	12,980	3,550
Dundee City	42,680	31,110	−12,570	8,280	11,520	2,230
Outer Tayside	15,080	14,740	−340	3,020	1,460	1,320
GRAMPIAN	39,940	36,510	−3,430	4,130	4,540	3,070
Aberdeen City	27,300	23,380	−3,920	3,030	2,750	2,320
Outer Grampian	12,630	13,130	+500	1,100	1,790	750
CENTRAL	41,560	36,140	−5,420	6,900	6,320	2,940
FIFE	30,090	38,820	+8,730	3,850	7,800	6,850
BORDERS	16,300	13,300	−3,000	2,980	2,780	4,350
SOUTH WEST	10,770	11,360	+590	970	900	1,070
HIGHLANDS & ISLANDS	7,950	14,370	+6,420	3,110	4,320	8,570
Scotland	708,870	603,000	−105,870	121,440	124,970	53,760

a All figures rounded to nearest ten

Source Cross, M. *New Firm Formation and Regional Development* (Gower 1981), 58

employment lost in all five of the new towns was the result of the contraction of employment in plants already open in 1968.

Of course, it is possible to make similar observations for each of the Department of Employment's local office areas.[17] Such an analysis would be informative, but at the same time would not readily indicate the overall patterns and trends of employment change. Obviously a balance must be struck between the very local and the national levels of analysis, and so two intermediate scales are used – the regions and sub-regions. Their components of manufacturing employment change are detailed in Table 12.8.

Perhaps the most striking feature of Table 12.8 is the decline of employment in Scotland's four major cities. Collectively these four cities have lost nearly 84,000 manufacturing jobs and suffered by far the largest relative declines. The most disturbing case is that of Glasgow, the largest manufacturing centre in Scotland, where the closure of plants was the largest contributor to its decline. In fact, Glasgow had a markedly higher rate of plant closure compounded by a relatively low birth rate of new firms.[18] However, Glasgow not only lost jobs; it also gained some, but a much lower number. Again the source of new employment is important. Most of the new employment in Glasgow came from the expansion of existing plants, and the employment created by the opening of new plants was mainly in plants of non-Scottish origin. It is a knowledge of these various components and their relative importance which gives some indication of how the regions and sub-regions will fare in the coming years.

The areas surrounding both Aberdeen and Edinburgh have expanded their level of manufacturing employment, but around Dundee and Glasgow the level of manufacturing employment has declined. However, the decline of the last two areas is less in both absolute and relative terms than that of the cities upon which they are centred. In Strathclyde region, excluding the Clydeside conurbation, the level of decline has been less severe than in either the city or its surrounding areas. Of the remaining regions, Fife, the Highlands and Islands, and the South-west have all shown increases in their levels of manufacturing employment, whereas the Borders and the Central regions have suffered some decline from their 1968 levels. A distinct pattern thus emerges with the traditional manufacturing centres suffering the largest declines, but this is partially offset nationally by the growth and less severe decline of the more recently established manufacturing centres.

It would therefore appear that the future employment prospects of an area are largely dependent upon the continuous opening of new manufacturing plants. The employment provided by these can be split into three phases: employment created immediately on opening; the growth of the initial labour force; and the generation of employment external to the new plant. (This last may be in local firms providing goods and services directly or indirectly to the new plant. It may also be in new firms established by employees previously employed in the new plant.) The job generation process is obviously more complex than this, but the division of employment growth into these phases enables the process to be easily conceptualised. If the general proposition is accepted that the future of manufacturing employment in Scotland largely depends on the opening of new plants because it is new plants that have the greatest growth potential in the long term, several questions arise. For example, what are the prospects for Scotland given the apparent low birth rate of new *indigenous* firms and the present changes in the location of industry? Such a question can probably be best tackled by considering new employment as coming from either Scottish or non-Scottish sources.

Sources of New Employment
Scottish Sources

There are two sources of new manufacturing employment from a Scottish base – the opening of new plants by completely new, and by already existing, firms, and the on-site expansion of existing plants (though existing plants may expand by way of opening new plants elsewhere which are then included in the first category). It is the first source which is considered here. Of the 16,502 new jobs created by the opening of Scottish-owned plants during the 1968–77 period, 12,194 were in new firms and the remainder, 4,308, were in Scottish-owned branch and subsidiary plants. It is the 12,194 jobs in new firms that are of greatest interest here. Are they in the growing industrial orders? Are they likely to expand and create more jobs? And, perhaps of more importance to the places in decline, which areas are either producing or attracting these new firms?

The picture is not encouraging either industrially or spatially. Four industrial orders dominate the supply of employment from new firms (Table 12.9). Three of the industries – food and drink, mechanical engineering, and metal goods not elsewhere specified – traditionally have a high birth rate because it is relatively 'easy' to set up a business in these industries. Hence, one would expect a large number of new firms in these industries. The employment such firms create, whilst welcome, is unlikely to further diversify the Scottish economy. Furthermore, most of these new firms are geared to local markets and in many cases they will be replacing firms which are closing. The fourth industrial order, the miscellaneous group, gives some encouragement in that it includes the plastics industry. This industry has a large growth potential, notably in product substitution (many products at present made of metal being replaced by products in glassfibre reinforced plastics) and in packaging (eg expanded polystyrene). Again the markets for these products are mostly local.

The remaining employment from new firms is spread amongst the other thirteen industries. However, there are several industries that

Table 12.9

Manufacturing employment change in each industrial order in the UK and Scotland, 1966–75,
and employment created by new firms in Scotland, 1968–77

Industry by S.I.C.	UK employment '000		Change %	Scotland employment '000		Change %	Change %	Employment in new firms Absolute Totals	Net %
	1966	1975		1966	1975				
03	826.8[a]	743.6	−10.06	103.0	99.0	(15.06)	−3.89	1,422[b]	11.83
04 & 05	548.0	521.8	−4.78	33.6	31.8	(4.84)	−5.36	140	1.15
06	626.0	498.5	−20.37	52.0	43.2	(6.57)	−16.92	342	2.80
07	1,276.7	1,125.2	−11.87	128.7	104.8	(15.94)	−18.57	2,116	17.35
08	158.2	149.1	−5.75	16.2	17.7	(2.69)	+9.26	178	1.46
09	926.7	859.8	−7.22	42.7	51.7	(7.86)	+21.08	711	5.83
10	220.1	194.0	−11.86	47.7	41.5	(6.31)	−12.99	424	3.48
11	857.9	760.3	−11.38	44.7	35.8	(5.44)	−19.91	263	2.16
12	590.1	517.7	−12.27	27.5	24.9	(3.79)	−9.45	1,681	13.79
13	801.1	558.0	−30.35	98.6	62.4	(9.49)	−36.71	1,171	9.60
14	60.6	46.6	−23.10	3.7	3.1	(0.47)	−16.22	74	0.61
15	560.0	443.8	−20.75	32.2	34.4	(5.23)	+6.83	759	6.22
16	360.7	296.2	−17.88	24.0	19.5	(2.97)	−18.75	282	2.31
17	318.7	291.7	−8.47	25.6	22.7	(3.45)	−11.33	967	7.93
18	650.6	590.2	−9.28	59.6	48.9	(7.44)	−17.95	403	3.30
19	336.5	342.8	+1.87	15.6	16.1	(2.45)	+3.21	1,241	10.18
Total	9,118.7	7,939.5	−12.93	755.4	657.5		−12.96	12,194	

Source a Fothergill and Gudgin *op. cit.*
      b Cross *op. cit.*

stand out, notably electrical engineering, textiles, clothing, and wood
and timber. Probably of greatest significance are the new firms in the
electrical engineering industry (Fig 1). It is this industry, along with
instrument engineering, that is seen as an area for future employment
growth.[19] In fact, it is these new firms, and not existing Scottish-owned
firms, that are supplying the bulk of employment in these two
industries. Yet, even this total of 889 new jobs is greatly overshadowed
by the employment created by non-Scottish firms in the two industries.

Another source of employment from Scottish-owned industry exists
in the establishment of branch and subsidiary plants. This source
provided 4,308 new jobs, chiefly in the food and drink, mechanical
engineering and textile industries (3,774 or 87.6 per cent of all
employment created by this source). Again, the employment is
undoubtedly needed, but it does not represent a radical attempt by
existing Scottish industry either to move into new markets or to
introduce new products or processes.

In terms of location, the new firms tend to be found in two types of
area. The first is around the major existing industrial centres, where
they can take advantage of the facilities available in the new towns and
on the many industrial estates around the major cities. Concentrations
are thus found in all the new towns, and places such as Dalkeith and

Musselburgh near Edinburgh. Of course, large numbers of new firms are still found in the major cities. Yet, in relation to the total manufacturing employment in the cities, new firms play a relatively lesser role in employment provision than they do in the outerlying areas; ie the birth rate of new firms is lower in the cities than it is in the outerlying areas.

The second locational trend of new firms is their creation and movement into the rural areas. Areas of outstanding natural beauty have acted as a focus for new firm founders looking for a new life-style. One area gaining greatly from this trend is the Highlands and Islands. Here, well over half of the new firms established during the 1968–77 period were set up by founders moving into the area.[20] This is where the major difference lies between the two types of location chosen by new firms. The first one represents a very much localised production and retention of new firms, while the latter relies not on its own industrial base to produce new firms, but on the attracting of the founders of new firms to the area.

It is here that a key question lies. Does the present reliance upon non-Scottish sources for new employment matter? Does the large number of non-Scottish-owned plants provide the necessary conditions for new-firm formation? The latter question of course assumes that new firms are important;[21] that is, important not only in providing much-needed employment, but also in creating new products and forming the basis for self-generated growth in Scotland. At the moment there is little evidence that the formation of new firms is able, even remotely, to provide the bulk of new employment opportunities. Furthermore, many of these new firms are not introducing new products, nor are they exploiting new markets. Nevertheless, a reliance upon incoming plants, even if the flow is diminishing, will remain for the foreseeable future. But how wise is this, and where do these plants come from?

Non-Scottish Sources

Scotland has relied since 1945 upon a constant supply of branch and subsidiary plants, largely from the rest of the UK and North America, to offset the employment lost by the continual decline of the traditional industries. The sources and industrial activities of those plants opening during the 1968–77 period are detailed in Table 12.10. The in-flow of these plants has been encouraged by the regional policies implemented by successive governments.[22] Recently, the wisdom of this dependence has been questioned, especially with the drop in the availability of mobile investment.[23]

Table 12.10

Manufacturing employment created by incoming plants by industrial order, 1968–77

Location of ultimate ownership

Industry by S.I.C.	England Number	%[b]	N. America Number	%	Europe Number	%	Rest of the world [a] Number	%	Total %	
03	1,252	7.8	154	0.9	74	1.4	—	—	1,480	(3.9)[c]
04	—	—	—	—	—	—	—	—	—	—
05	1,135	7.1	79	0.5	13	0.2	—	—	1,227	(3.3)
06	1,276	7.9	—	—	—	—	—	—	1,276	(3.4)
07	2,713	16.9	5,899	37.0	169	3.2	—	—	8,781	(23.3)
08	160	0.9	1,321	8.3	—	—	—	—	1,481	(3.9)
09	1,045	6.5	3,103	19.5	1,389	26.2	21	6.6	5,557	(14.8)
10	15	0.1	655	4.1	231	4.3	—	—	901	(2.4)
11	128	0.8	198	1.2	—	—	—	—	326	(0.9)
12	2,037	12.7	729	4.6	53	0.9	—	—	2,819	(7.5)
13	2,035	12.7	785	4.9	172	3.2	—	—	2,992	(7.9)
14	119	0.7	—	—	42	0.8	—	—	161	(0.4)
15	2,488	15.5	2,084	13.8	31	0.6	130	40.6	4,733	(12.5)
16	698	4.3	442	2.8	1,796	33.8	—	—	2,936	(7.8)
17	108	0.7	—	—	70	1.3	—	—	178	(0.5)
18	547	3.4	362	2.3	84	1.6	—	—	993	(2.6)
19	326	2.0	112	0.7	1,658	31.2	169	52.8	2,265	(6.0)
Total (net)	16,082		15,923		5,311		320		37,636	

a also includes joint ventures. *b* column percentage. *c* row percentage.
Source Cross *op. cit.*

One of the main problems with these branch and subsidiary plants is that in many cases they represent 'truncated' firms. As the main purpose of establishing a branch is usually to expand the productive capacity of the firm, its *raison d'être* is production. Hence, it does not usually possess the full range of management functions on opening. It is from this situation that many of the disadvantages stem. The level of managerial decision-making is of a routine, rather than of the 'innovative-entrepreneurial', type. This tends to limit the independence of the plant and inhibits its involvement in the local economy. The range of employment opportunities open to employees is also limited, and often the key managerial positions are held by non-locals. It is also possible that the opening of a new plant and the introduction of new production methods, new wage rates etc, to an area have led to strained labour relations which may disrupt the operations of other local firms. And, while the new plant may benefit the local people by providing employment that might not otherwise have been there, it might be less secure and less skilled than in other locally owned plants. In fact, the main benefit of these plants is that they do provide employment, but this may be only for a short time.[24]

Given these possible disadvantages of branch plants and the current dependence of a large measure of the Scottish manufacturing economy upon externally owned plants, the degree of self-generation within the economy may be under threat. It would appear that the employment opportunities offered in many of the branch and subsidiary plants are not likely to be those that encourage 'entrepreneurial' behaviour. In fact, it is possible that those employees exhibiting 'entrepreneurial' talents in the Scottish plant of a company might be transferred to the company's divisional headquarters outside Scotland.[25]

It is against this background that external investment must be considered. Furthermore, as mobile investment declines and as the ageing branch plants close, the true benefits, if any, to the Scottish economy will begin to emerge. Research has indicated that, while the survival rates of branch plants are no worse than those of the parent plants, those in Scotland would appear to have a higher closure rate than their counterparts in the other UK regions.[26] The benefits from these branch plants could therefore be regarded as being short-term, and as only one element in an industrial development strategy. Unfortunately, government industrial regional policy has been almost solely devoted to attracting mobile investment, rather than helping either existing or new indigenous firms, despite the provisions of the Industry Act of 1972. It is to these possible policy options that we turn in the next section.

Prospects for Future Growth and Policy Directions

From the foregoing comments the outlook for manufacturing industry in Scotland can only be regarded as gloomy, and possibly depressing. And, with the closure of the Singer plant at Clydebank, Peugeot's at Linwood, and the British Aluminium smelter at Invergordon, and the cessation of harvester production by Massey Ferguson at Kilmarnock, and with the future of BL's plant at Bathgate in question, the need for new policy initiatives becomes even more acute. This situation is further exacerbated by the thousands of redundancies which are being declared annually. But what of the future?

Over the next few years unemployment in Scotland may reach, and will probably remain close to, 300,000. The numbers employed in manufacturing industry will also continue to decline and remain less than 30 per cent of the total working population. Of course, the geographical intensity of these changes will vary, but by far the greatest hardship will be felt in west central Scotland. Other areas, such as Fife, will also experience employment decline, but Fife's current and relatively new industrial base will tend to afford it some protection against the more severe aspects of future industrial decline.

Even though the picture being presented for the foreseeable future is undoubtedly bleak, there are some positive aspects. For example, one of the most encouraging moves made by central government has been the creation of the Scottish Development Agency. The Agency, with a wide-ranging remit, has been entrusted with the task of regenerating industry in Scotland. At the moment it is operating in both a proactive and a reactive manner, and its presence is being felt particularly in the East End of Glasgow. Here, central government, Strathclyde Regional Council, the Scottish Special Housing Association, the Greater Glasgow Health Board, the Housing Corporation, the Manpower Services Commission and the Agency are organising the investment of over £150m in the almost complete renewal of the area.[27] The GEAR (Glasgow Eastern Area Renewal) Project is an integrated one with six key elements: (i) helping residents to secure employment; (ii) retaining and creating jobs; (iii) improving the quality of life; (iv) improving the environment; (v) creating better housing; and (vi) involving the community. The roles of the bodies involved vary within each of the six elements, with the Agency taking a leading role in the economic regeneration aspects and factory building. Leith, a part of Edinburgh, is another area receiving similar attention and where the symptoms of an area having suffered long-term decline are evident. In other areas, such as Clydebank and Glengarnoch, a reactive response has come from the Agency to deal with immediate problems created by the closure of a major employing plant. The main difference between the planned and reactive responses is the time period over which they operate.

Another area of the Agency's activities has been investment in Scottish-based companies. While this latter policy has not been completely successful, it represents a more direct approach to aiding local industry than that afforded by existing government assistance.[28] Since 1975 the Agency has invested £23.7m in forty-eight companies based in Scotland and employing about 10,000 people. The type of company invested in ranges from a household name like Henry Ballantyne and Sons Ltd (the Agency share has now been sold to Dawson International) to Edinburgh Instruments Ltd, who are at the forefront of a specialised part of laser technology.

It is this active side of the Agency which could have the greatest impact upon industry in Scotland. What freedom the Agency will be allowed remains an open question, but there are several exciting policy options. Initially the Agency could concentrate upon the existing industrial base and attempt to increase the efficiency of the existing medium-sized companies (ie those with 250–500 employees). This policy would expand the already extensive assistance afforded by the Agency to small businesses. Assistance is already offered directly to many such firms, with loans towards the purchase of new plant or towards the costs of management training. How active a role the Agency should play is debatable, but its success also relies to a large extent upon the co-operation (as opposed to intervention) of local industry.

Less traditional policies could also be tried. For example, in areas where the economy is notably lacking, say, in the technology of numerically controlled machines, the Agency could offer assistance to firms in order that they may acquire it. The Agency at the same time could also act as an 'innovation co-ordinator'. Here, rather than relying upon the passive transfer of technology between firms, the initiative could be taken actually to market new ideas to local industry. Several possibilities exist. One is to sponsor the development of a new item using Scottish resources, eg the Wolfson Micro-electronics Research Institute, and then offer it under licence to an existing local firm for manufacture. In one major respect this has a distinct advantage over establishing a new firm. The depressed areas of Clydeside already have a number of large companies that might be able to introduce a new product to their present range; whereas, if a new firm was established it is unlikely that the founder would readily locate it in a depressed area. A second source of new ideas could come from the co-ordination of excess ideas (products or processes) generated by industry, not necessarily in Scotland, and an assessment of the potential of implementing them in Scotland. Such a policy could revolve around the principles adopted by General Electric in the USA, where they try to sell off ideas surplus to the company's requirements. Not only do they sell off the idea, but also offer considerable assistance in putting it into practice.[29] Such a policy could be used by existing large companies, but, if so, it is likely that the South-east of England would benefit to the exclusion of Scotland. The South-east already exhibits a greater production and implementation of new ideas than any other region,[30] and this position would only be enhanced without the Agency's direct involvement for the benefit of Scotland.

Of course, there remains the more traditional policy of attracting foreign investment to Scotland, which will continue for the foreseeable future. In Scotland the attracting and handling of inward investment is dealt with by 'Locate in Scotland' – an umbrella organisation formed between the Agency and the Scottish Economic Planning Department.

It is possible that the terms of investment offered to incoming firms could be further weighted in favour of the recipient region, Scotland. For example, investment grants could be geared to the level of training offered to the local labour force, and the number of higher management and research posts created. Further incentives could also be given in order to attract full marketing, sales and purchasing functions to the new plant.[31] These policy elements could be combined with an emphasis on joint ventures either between the Agency and the incoming firm, or between an existing local firm and the incoming firm. Obviously in an ideal world all of the items might be sought, but in a time of little mobile investment Scotland's bargaining position is not particularly strong.

A final area the Agency could attack is the low level of new-firm formation. Such a policy is closely linked to the policies of aiding existing firms and of tailoring inward investment more to Scotland's long-term advantage. Here, the Agency might directly assist those people wishing to leave local firms to establish their own firms, and also those individuals wishing to move to Scotland for the same purpose. Such a policy is probably a short-term one, and it assumes that the supply of new firm founders can be encouraged. The two policies discussed earlier represent an attempt to create an occupational and industrial mix of conditions which would favour new-firm formation. They are an attempt to create and to mobilise sufficient local skills and expertise to ensure the economy's buoyancy and continued existence.

All these policies will take time to perfect and to implement, and their results will only become apparent over a thirty- or forty-year period. Before that time several difficult questions remain to be answered. How far will the policies pursued by the Agency in the interests of Scotland be allowed to impede UK policies?[32] Will a greater degree of local control be required for those parts of the nationalised industries and publicly-owned corporations operating at present in Scotland?[33] On what criteria will the allocation of new employment through public investment, if it exists as an option, be based? Will Glasgow gain at the expense of the Highlands? Clearly many issues remain to be resolved, but while the immediate outlook in the short term is bleak, the long-term future of manufacturing industry in Scotland seems assured. However, the shape and size of that industry would appear largely to depend on the freedom given to the Scottish Development Agency and the growth of the UK economy which will itself depend in part upon the revenue generated by North Sea oil.[34]

Notes to this chapter are on pages 315–18.

Page 279 *(above)* Prestwick Circuits Limited, Ayr — Scottish entrepreneurship in the booming electronics industry; *(below)* nursery factory units in Broad Street, part of the Glasgow East End Redevelopment Project — a breeding ground for tomorrow's Scottish entrepreneurs?

Page 280 *(above)* Dunrobin Castle, seat of the dukes of Sutherland, owners of vast areas of the county of Sutherland. Built mostly in the Victorian period following the Highland clearances when the clans were dispossessed of their lands; design shows considerable French influence; *(below)* modern land use on blown sand and raised beach deposits near Lochinver, Sutherland; backed by ice-scoured Lewisian gneiss bedrock and the spectacular mountain, Suilven, an isolated mass of Torridonian sandstone.

13

Scotland's Future Development

E. A. Smith

THIS chapter seeks to identify themes significant to the fabric and character of the Scottish environment and, by analysing the relevant factors and processes, tries to indicate possible developments to the end of this century.

The physical environment is often changed by such developments as afforestation, which clothes former moorland and farmland in timber, or major recreational projects like those proposed for the Cairngorms (Lurcher's Gully) and Ben Wyvis, or open-cast extraction of minerals such as uranium in Orkney. However, the main geographical changes are likely to occur in the human sphere, with a continuing redistribution of people from the traditional and often shabby urban–industrial centres to more pleasant urban localities on their periphery, to the new towns and particularly to the strengthening economic environment of the east coast. This chapter therefore emphasises economic and political trends providing the initiatives, the stimuli and the constraints which will influence the shaping of Scotland and Scottish life over the next two decades. In this respect the greatest challenge of all is the transition from an insecure and unhappy dependence on declining traditional industries to a new industrial revolution based on new technologies and offshore energy industries. Some of these technologies, especially nuclear power, are a source of great disquiet, and these concerns may increasingly hallmark the remaining years of this century with dissent and civil protest.

Restructuring the Scottish economy is neither easy nor painless. The need for major change has for long been recognised, but the social and political implications of stimulating and assisting that change have caused governments to exercise a cautious delay which has allowed the strength of the Scottish economy to be eroded like a form of economic osteoporosis. Scotland has thus been over sensitive to the vagaries of national and international trading cycles.

But the country's problems, whether in town or countryside, cannot be resolved, nor the aspirations of the Scots fulfilled, wholly by indigenous Scottish or even British effort. An increasing proportion of available investment capital is directed by trans-national corporations and institutions, while increasingly the ground rules of development and trade are supervised by international agreements and organisations. Not only do national and local government, together with the numerous agencies such as the Scottish Development Agency and the Highlands and Islands Development Board, help shape the future patterns but so too do the directives, institutions and agencies of the European Community.

Scotland still suffers from excessive dependence on declining industries of the past and a lack of emphasis on, and capital investment in, existing or new firms with potential for future growth. This situation has been exacerbated by decisions, often politically motivated, to allocate large sums to propping up the declining industries in order to save jobs in the short term, even though they are not viable in the long term. At the same time, the long-term possibilities for creating secure jobs by identifying opportunities in the growth sectors of the market have not been fully exploited.

The previous chapter has outlined the structures and entrepreneurial attitudes which have served to undermine the security and well-being of many traditional Scottish industries. Moreover, important trends in recent industrial developments have been the significant dependence on non-Scottish capital and the increasing control of Scottish industry from non-Scottish headquarters. This then is the uneasy base from which to view the future prospects for Scottish industry and industrial employment, and the character and condition of Scotland's urban–industrial fabric. However, there are encouraging signs for the future. The North Sea oil industry occupies the premier place in offshore oil technology and possesses long-term opportunities to export both know-how and hardware to new areas of oil exploration and production in other parts of the world. Scotland also already has a major stake in the electronic revolution, with some 40 per cent of Europe's production of micro-chips; on a global scale it may be exceeded only by California's 'Silicon Valley'. However, much has yet to be done by government and the development agencies to attract to Scotland the manufacturers who produce the devices utilising this sophisticated micro-chip circuitry.

The following sections identify the main issues that are fundamental to the future well-being of Scotland's industrial fabric. Later sections widen the horizon to examine other key issues which will influence the character, condition and harmony of the Scottish environment.

Coal

The European Community meets only 18.6 per cent of its energy requirements from coal and is 53.2 per cent (in 1978) dependent on oil, the vast proportion of which is imported from politically sensitive or unstable areas. It is thus desirable that, wherever and whenever economically possible, imported oil should be replaced by indigenous energy sources. World oil supplies are likely to plateau in the 1990s and thereafter to decline, although by the year 2000 oil should still be providing half the world's energy. Even without considering the oil price rises as a tool of economic or political policy on the part of the major world producers, prices will rise substantially as demand begins to exceed supply and as technologically and economically more difficult deposits are exploited. This will help to reinstate coal as a major energy source and the fact that, at present rates of consumption and with existing technology, European Community resources will last 300 years seems to afford some optimism for the coal industry.

Most of the Community's deposits are in West Germany and the UK, but Scotland is unlikely to be an early beneficiary from any shift towards coal. By comparison with Yorkshire and the East Midlands of England, the geology of the Scottish coalfields makes exploitation difficult and productivity too low. (In 1974–5 the loss per ton of Scottish coal was £0.96 compared with £0.29 in the UK as a whole.) The massive investments from Community funds needed to refurbish and expand Europe's coal industry would first benefit the economically attractive fields, although the slowly changing attitudes towards coal may give greater momentum to the expansion of the Scottish deep mines north of the Forth and the seams under the Forth; this would further enhance the eastward drift of Scotland's industrial centre of gravity. The immediate prospect, however, is for the continued decline in the use of coal, except for electricity production, and unless some of the new generation of power stations (most of which are planned for nuclear fuel) are coal-fired, then even the 8 million tons consumed by the South of Scotland Electricity Board will decline, with serious implications for the industry. Reduced demand as a result of major consumer closures, such as Invergordon's British Aluminium smelter in early 1982, is clearly a cause for concern.

North Sea Oil and Gas

The exploration and exploitation of North Sea oil and gas deposits is a familiar and well-documented feature of recent Scottish geography and has been concisely covered in Chapter 11. It has helped to reinvigorate a flagging industrial structure, contributed substantially to the exchequer and reduced the balance of payments deficit, given an eastward jolt to the Scottish industrial centre of gravity, and provided the inspiration and credibility for a short-lived surge of nationalistic political aspirations in the first half of the 1970s.

In 1979 the energy value of oil produced from the British sector of the North Sea exceeded that of UK coal production, and in 1980 statistical self-sufficiency was achieved, creating directly and indirectly 60,000 jobs. Self-sufficiency can be sustained into the next century, but maintaining this level of production will be a very costly operation and will present Scotland with still further challenge and opportunity. Within the North Sea sector exploration will be revitalised and new production is expected throughout the 1980s and 1990s. The Chairman of Shell UK, speaking at a seminar in September 1980 on 'Energy in the 90s', predicted an investment in the British sector of the North Sea of £60,000m during the next 15 years; since this will largely be devoted to the discovery and development of smaller fields, he said that it could mean drilling 500 exploration wells (400 were drilled in the 1970s). The implications for Scotland of such developments are immense. Direct employment in the oil industry, which in 1980 stood at about 45,000, could reach 70 or 80,000 by 1995. While the east-coast service ports would obviously expand to support increased offshore activity, the engineering sector of Scottish industry in central and west central Scotland, increasingly familiar with the needs of the oil industry, would also stand to gain substantially. Ongoing research and development of the necessary new technology should give Scotland a commanding position in this field, which could open up new industrial opportunities for Scottish companies as the worldwide hunt for oil gathers momentum.

Although the opportunities are great, and extend far beyond the period of indigenous oil production, the problems are also great, not least in providing the necessary skilled manpower. In the late 1970s there was already a worldwide shortage of trained engineers and oil technicians. Without a substantial increase in the supply of such personnel, it is a problem which could become a very serious constraint on the industry. Far greater efforts are going to be required by government, other agencies and the educational institutions to encourage recruitment into the appropriate fields and to provide the required forms of training.

At the end of the day much depends on the profitability of the enterprise. It should not be forgotten that over 90 per cent of capital invested in North Sea developments is private and only justifies its presence if the project remains viable. Of considerable significance in any assessment of profitability is the level of the Petroleum Revenue Tax. Clearly oil company strategy is greatly influenced by taxation levels and the scope of the tax-free allowances. Most important is that, given the long and increasingly extenuated lead times for oil field development, the companies require stable conditions in which to plan and implement their operations.

The oil industry has tapped a resource whose revenues and technological requirements should provide the initiatives and investments for what has been called Scotland's second industrial revolution. The opportunities exist and present a challenge to industry, entrepreneurs and especially to government which must create the right environment in which innovation and expansion can thrive. In this respect it can only be hoped that pressure will be brought to bear on the oil companies to refine the greater part of the North Sea production in the UK and encourage downstream developments.

Much of the pace and character of oil and gas developments in the last two decades of the century will depend on the rate and pattern of extraction and on the taxation structures and levels to which the industry is subject. These are all susceptible to the vagaries of political decision; yet more than anything else what the industry needs, with its long lead times and technical constraints on production, are firm and stable policies on which it can base its continuing major investment programme.

Natural Gas

Natural gas provides about 20 per cent of UK primary energy consumption (oil, 40 per cent) and the southern North Sea began production in 1967. Since then the country has been largely converted from coal gas to North Sea gas. St Fergus receives and processes gas from the Frigg and Brent fields, together with smaller quantities from the Piper and other fields in the East Shetland Basin which feed into the Brent pipeline. This latter pipeline, and the separation plant for the natural gas and gas liquids at St Fergus, are part of the Far-North Liquids and Associated Gas System (FLAGS), which will pipe the gas liquids to Mossmorran in Fife where they will be fractionated into components. While the resultant propane balance and natural gasoline will be liquefied and shipped out by tanker, the ethane will be used as feedstock for an adjacent ethylene plant. The FLAGS project offers some prospect of attracting other processing plants but, while the gas-gathering plans are likely to proceed, the decision by the Norwegian Government to pipe their massive reserves to a Continental landfall, rather than participate in FLAGS, is a serious blow to the economies of the programme and to prospects of new processing plant being sited at Nigg on the Cromarty Firth.

In late 1981 the government-sponsored gas-gathering pipeline project was abandoned largely due to objections from the participating companies to the British Gas monopoly purchase rights. However, individual gas pipeline projects are anticipated, the first having been announced at the end of 1981.

Just as natural gas progressively replaced manufactured gas, so too will supplies from the northern North Sea progressively replace the declining southern North Sea supplies by the end of the century. Confirmation of this trend will be the replacement by the mid-1980s of Bacton in East Anglia by St Fergus in Grampian as the major terminal of the British Gas Corporation.

Nuclear Power

In 1978 just over 10 per cent of UK electricity was generated by the nine Magnox and two Advanced Gas-cooled Reactors (AGR) currently in operation. Three more AGRs are under construction and should be operational in the early 1980s, while work began in the late 1970s on two further AGRs at Heysham II and Torness in East Lothian. Nuclear power has a particularly important role in Scotland both in terms of the technological frontiers and the commercial and economic aspects. However, the recent commitment of both Labour and Conservative Governments to continuing substantial investment in nuclear power installations is likely to face mounting opposition. Indeed, the attitude of the Labour Party on this whole question has become distinctly ambivalent. For although it is a fact that nuclear power generation has a better safety record than any other major method of power production, its complexity and the emotional correlation with means of destruction and genetic damage have aroused great disquiet which over secretive or politically inept nuclear agencies have done little to dispel. Anti-nuclear views are gaining acceptability, the anti-nuclear campaign is well organised and well funded and is pursued for a variety of motives. It cannot be disregarded, and it may undermine the determination of some governments to maintain the nuclear generation programme. That this programme is vitally necessary, however, there is little doubt. Although world growth in energy demand will not expand as rapidly as earlier forecasts suggested, energy demand could still require an extra 50 million b/doe (barrels per day oil equivalent) of supply. More than two-thirds of this would have to be met from non-oil sources. When one couples this with diminishing UK oil production towards the end of the century, the expected substantial rise in oil prices over the same time scale, and the difficulty of raising coal production within acceptable cost limits, the need for nuclear power generation is revealed. According to figures published for the UK's Magnox nuclear stations, they produce electricity more cheaply than either coal- or oil-fired plant. Some sources would suggest that the cost per therm is only half that of the conventional plant, but controversy still surrounds the true cost efficiency of nuclear stations.

Given the long lead times, a rapid sequence of decisions to construct nuclear stations is likely in the 1980s. Scotland will probably play a significant role in any nuclear programme, and the protest surrounding each announcement is likely to be fierce, even violent. Already there has been substantial protest at the decision by the SSEB to construct the Torness nuclear generating plant, at the request for permission to test bore in the Southern Uplands (refused in late 1981) to assess suitability for nuclear waste disposal, and in Orkney at the prospect of extensive open-cast extraction of uranium ore. All the indicators would suggest a strengthening of such protests and of the attitudes which underlie them. Certainly the argument that the use of nuclear power allows the conservation of our valuable fossil fuels is unlikely to achieve much acceptance, even though to substitute the electricity produced annually from the nuclear stations already commissioned and those under construction (1981) would require the total annual production from a large North Sea oil field like Piper.

Other Energy Sources

Wind, wave and sun provide renewable energy sources much wanted by the environmental energy lobby. Certainly they can meet certain limited local needs of a largely domestic variety but are unlikely ever to replace the major energy sources. Although improved technology will increase efficiency, it is worth noting that, under existing methods, to replace a 1 Gigawatt power station (which would occupy about a quarter of a square mile) would require 40sq miles of wind generators or, in British latitudes, 100sq miles of solar panels below which the land would be made sterile. None the less, experiments will go ahead and in 1981 the North of Scotland Hydro-Electricity Board announced an experiment with wind generators on Orkney. There is every chance that such schemes could play an important role in electricity supply to remote and island communities, at present dependent on increasingly costly diesel generators.

Wave power offers more hope and the North-west of Scotland provides the best environmental opportunities for both wave and wind generators. Unlike solar and wind power, the conversion of wave power into electricity does afford wider economic opportunities, but the favoured areas of northern Scotland are disadvantaged by their remoteness from the national grid. It is unlikely that experimental wave power units will be operational in northern Scotland before the end of the century, the speed with which this and any subsequent commercial development occurs depending on the patterns of energy demand and cost.

Peat as an energy source was the unsuccessful focus of the ill-fated Altnabreac peat gasification project of 1956. However, Scotland's peat resources are considerable, and the changing energy cost structures and the experience of the USSR, Finland and Eire indicate that the large peat deposits of Caithness, Sutherland and Ross and Cromarty may be viewed as a potential source of energy.

Hydro provided 13.2 per cent of the electricity generated in the UK in 1979. Its contribution in Scotland is unlikely to increase, irrespective of energy demand, as there are few remaining sites which would be economically or environmentally suitable.

In the longer term the emergence of a European Community 'Common Energy Policy' may influence the patterns of energy supply, investment and consumption. This could be of particular significance to the future of the coal industry, while the high-technology, high-cost North Sea oil and gas industry will remain highly sensitive to world price structures and national taxation policies. On the other hand, the future of nuclear power is uncomfortably susceptible to popular and political pressures unrelated to its economic characteristics or technical feasibility.

The strength of Scotland's energy base, and a potential source of substantial industrial power, lies in its broad spectrum of energy sources which surpasses that of any other European country and which extends to include the interesting opportunities for energy generation from wind and wave.

Farming

The future prospects for Scottish agriculture are inexorably bound up with agricultural policy and practice in the European Community.

Through the instruments of the Common Agricultural Policy the very laudable aim of restructuring and modernising a generally backward continental industry is pursued against a background of unseemly national self-interest, especially in those countries where the farming population comprises a significant part of the electorate or where there are strong emotional ties with the small farm holdings. The problems of devising an effective and fair policy for the diverse structural and environmental conditions within Community agriculture are immense. Coupled with this are the problems of inflation which have pressured the agriculture industry at a time when government seeks to restrain price rises in the vital food sector. Between 1976 and 1980, farm income in Scotland fell in real terms by over 50 per cent and by 24 per cent in 1980 alone (mainly as a result of costs rising faster than prices). One result of this has been a major increase in the industry's indebtedness to £2,900m in 1980 – an increase of 30 per cent over 1979. Certainly recovery from the recession of the late 1970s and early 1980s will help to restore the fortunes of farming, but any expected upturn in consumption will also be matched by an increase in temperate food imports, most of which could be produced domestically; their value in the late 1970s was of the order of £3,000m.

In recent years investment and production have declined as a result of poor returns and the disparity in the value of the Green Pound. The 1981 round of the EEC Common Agricultural Policy negotiations helped temporarily both this currency disparity and the prices received by the farmer, but constant vigilance will be necessary from government and from farming interests to ensure that Scottish farming is not disadvantaged by the application of common policies whose aims are noble but whose practices could jeopardise our highly efficient farming industry. In particular, opposition must be maintained to those parts of the EEC's proposed package for agricultural improvements which would be likely to put UK agriculture at a special disadvantage through the differential regional application of incentives and disincentives. However, the efficiency of Scottish agriculture provides considerable hope for the future, given the expected levels of world and EEC prices for major foodstuffs and the present government's blueprint for an annual expansion in the agricultural industry of about $2\frac{1}{2}$ per cent. But to fulfil this requires a reversal of the trend of the late 1970s, which itself will contribute to a wider economic revitalisation. It should be remembered that, in order to achieve the 1980 contribution to the GDP of £4.1bn, farmers purchased some £5bn worth of products from the rest of the economy.

Output in Scotland can be increased, especially in beef and sheep, and it is worth noting that, for every additional £2m of additional output, approximately 150 jobs can be created in ancillary industries. However, realisation of this potential will depend on a number of variables, including world food price levels and both government policy and the Common Agricultural Policy. A further complication could be changes in dietary patterns as medicine increasingly identifies the relationships between diet and the cause and cure of certain ailments.

In general, however, it is unlikely that Scottish farming will alter radically in the last two decades of this century. More aggressive marketing may expand opportunities at home and in Europe, although dairy farming, with its inbuilt structural surplus in Europe, may fare less well, despite Scotland's efficiency in having the largest average herd size in Europe – seventy beasts, compared with England's fifty and an average of ten in the remainder of the Community. Efficiency in farming has not been the dominant criterion for success or acceptability in Europe in the past and national self-interest is unlikely to allow it to become so in the near future.

Forestry

Some 10 per cent of Scotland is under managed woodlands (half the EEC figure) and, of these, 790,000ha (54 per cent) are state-owned as compared with 28 per cent in England. Approximately 70 per cent of new planting has taken place since 1945 and thus a great many of the plantations have yet to reach a productive state. Consequently, large volumes of timber and timber products still have to be imported to meet 92 per cent of UK requirements, and this costs more than £3,000m annually.

The opportunities for expansion of the woodland area are considerable, while still being consistent with good land use, especially with regard to agricultural needs, and of benefit to rural community viability. In the United Kingdom there are about 2.1 million ha of land suitable for forestry, of which 1.6 million are in Scotland. Much of this land is only marginally viable for agriculture and the balance of use is strongly influenced by some marginal hill-farming being sustained through subsidy. If such land were transferred from the agricultural to the forestry sector, the loss in production to the former, assuming no increased production elsewhere as a result of technological improvements or by other means, would be of the order of only 1.5 to 2.0 per cent by the year 2000. The benefits would be substantial. Not only would there be extra rural employment, but the multiplier effect would generate activity in other industries. There would be greater scope for amenity and public recreation and a large renewable resource would be established from which, among other things, chemical feedstock can be derived. Further, there would be considerable benefits to the balance of payments, although planting, at the most optimistic level, would still only meet 20 per cent of estimated future demand. Some areas of demand could never be met, for example hardwoods and construction timber, where for certain purposes the home-grown soft woods do not have the strength and durability of the slow-growing Scandinavian or Russian timbers.

Compared to most other industries, forestry is dependent on government decision. Government forest policy is at present under review and the decisions reached will determine the planting rate in the state sector, just as taxation policy has immense influence on the private sector. Forestry gives a relatively low yield on a very long-term investment. It is highly susceptible to taxation policy, as illustrated by the reduction of private planting to one third of the pre-1975 Finance Act level as a result of the introduction of Capital Transfer Tax as a substitute for the more favourable estate duty.

Forestry will nevertheless continue to be a major component in the Scottish landscape. This view is endorsed by the fact that, in 1978, 86 per cent of state planting and 78 per cent of private planting was in Scotland; 98 per cent of the land acquired for state afforestation is in Scotland, much of it in the Central and Northern Highlands. Irrespective of planting rates, and the long-term contributions of state and private forestry, the debate on the relationships between farming and forestry will continue. The economic well-being of hill farming, itself subject to many influences, will in part determine the nature of the relationship. Loss of hill grazings to forest can be compensated for, but only through considerable capital investment, while the reduction of the flock or herd size would have serious implications for the livestock industry. The red deer population would also be affected as their winter grazings coincide with the more desirable land for planting.

Although the long-term return of forestry does not make it attractive to the politician, the benefits of a major afforestation programme are clear. In the late 1970s the European Community with a larger acreage under timber met only half its requirements, and those requirements are expected to grow at twice the rate of planned output. All signs suggest an increasing worldwide shortage up to the end of the century and prices are likely to quadruple relative to other prices. Timber-exporting countries will increasingly wish to process their own timber, thus adding to the costs of the importing country. Yet Scotland has the land available for afforestation with a production potential at least one and a half times as high as the Community average, and production costs are only about two-thirds of the average. Whether or not we exploit these opportunities is largely a matter for government decision.

Land Use and Land Ownership

Competition for land between forest and farm interests is not the only area of concern. Throughout the 1960s and 1970s there was mounting anxiety and criticism expressed on developments in land use and land ownership; the latter in particular is likely to become a major issue in the last decades of this century, both in terms of the principle of extensive land ownership and also its implications for land use, especially in the Highlands. Concern has also been expressed over the loss to urban and industrial developments of some of Scotland's best agricultural land, which accounts for less than 3 per cent of the total agricultural land area. The problem of good agricultural land being built over is all too familiar around the central belt cities and the expanding urban and industrial coastal ribbon stretching from the Tay estuary to the inner Moray Firth. The planners have all too late become aware of this land misuse, but, directed by guidelines from the Scottish Development Department, it is likely that much less A+ and A—grade agricultural land will be utilised for such purposes in the future. This is of major significance as new industrial developments in the Central Belt seek greenfield sites and as much urban—industrial vitality is focused in the East and North-east, where the highest grades of agricultural land are even more scarce than in other populous regions of the country.

It is in the Highlands that large estates of low-value land are most characteristic. Few are economically viable and some are purchased and maintained as much for taxation as for sporting purposes. Maximising production on these marginal lands and expanding the limited employment opportunities is difficult and does not necessarily occupy a high priority with the owners, whether individuals or institutions. The fact that these tend to have their permanent homes or headquarters outside Scotland merely serves to intensify the sense of exploitation, and the feeling that the interests of Scots and Scotland are not being well served. These attitudes are partly born of a genuine concern for the Highland communities but also of a fundamental political objection to ownership of land in general and to ownership on a large scale in particular. Concern and criticism tended to harden in the 1970s as the relative weakness of sterling and relatively low land prices attracted a number of foreign buyers into the estate market.

Arabs and Dutch have been among the more publicised buyers but foreign purchases still account for a very small component in the total ownership pattern. Their real effect is to focus wider public attention on the problem and to generate a wider base of popular support for some review of land use and its relationship to local communities.

Both the Forestry Commission and the Department of Agriculture and Fisheries for Scotland possess compulsory purchase powers to ensure that the best use is made of the land, but these powers are rarely exercised. The Highlands and Islands Development Board has yet to be granted equivalent powers by Parliament that would enable it to insist on improved schemes of land use management.

The future of land use and of land ownership, while most acutely observed in the Highlands, affects the whole of Scotland and will depend in large measure on government initiatives. If a Labour government were to nationalise all land, then consequences would be very far-reaching. However, even without such draconian measures, the pressure of public concern may mean greater use being made of existing statutory rights to intervene to improve land-use practice, and in this context it may be hoped that the Highlands and Islands Development Board will also be granted the powers which it is now seeking; without them its efforts to improve conditions in the Highlands can be thwarted by uninterested and intransigent landowners.

As regards foreign ownership, it is highly unlikely that any constraint will be placed on owner nationality unless the patterns of ownership were deemed to pose a threat to the national well-being. Any action is particularly unlikely for as long as investment capital remains in short supply. The implications of any controls would be particularly acute in London and other major urban areas since it is unthinkable that any such controls would apply only to Highland estate ownership.

Fishing

Since the mid-nineteenth century the Scottish fishing industry has undergone substantial adaptation and change in adjusting to the opportunities and the challenges of new technologies of catching and of processing, and changes in the balance of species and of markets. Although the fishing industry is of only minor importance in the UK's GDP, it is of considerable importance in some regions. About half of the industry's workforce in Scotland is in Grampian, but it is also significant in many east-coast and island communities and elsewhere where alternative employment opportunities are often scarce; and for every fisherman there may be anything from four to seven ancillary jobs.

New types of gear and the use of electronic detection equipment have greatly increased catching efficiency; the resultant overfishing has threatened some species, such as herring, and has put at risk other varieties through reducing the number of fish available to breed. Exacerbating the situation has been the growth of industrial fishing to produce fish meal for animal feed and fertiliser. This is largely to compensate for the decline in supplies of these commodities from South America, and Europe has in recent years been industrially fishing two million tons per year for animal feed. Although pout fishing is the main source of this raw material, large quantities of edible and endangered species are included through inadequate protection and the loop-hole of the 'allowable bye-catch'.

To the combination of overfishing and the depletion of stocks must be added the extension of state control over traditional fishing grounds. Scotland was less affected than the English deep-sea fleets by the Icelandic extension of national control over its fishing and fish breeding grounds, but an equivalent action by the Faeroese was of considerable significance to the Aberdeen-based middle-distance trawler fleet. The restrictions on foreign fishing fleets imposed by the Norwegians and Russians within their unilaterally declared 200-mile limits have further intensified the difficulties.

Clearly these several problems cannot be resolved unilaterally, but the attempts to formulate a fair, practical, long-term European Community Common Fishing Policy proved very protracted and difficult while there has been only limited success in negotiations with non-Community states. Interim arrangements for the fishing industry in the Community introduced in 1972 ran out in 1982 and efforts by the UK to introduce its own conservation measures resulted in action being taken in the European Court. Eventually a Common Fishing Policy was agreed in early 1983. This is particularly vital to the Scottish fishing industry, and for the many fishing-dependent communities where alternative means of livelihood are difficult to come by. With Scotland in 1978 contributing 60 per cent of the UK's fish by weight and 53 per cent by value the wider significance is clear. Scotland has only a few large trawlers left and the great part of the modern fleet depends on grounds most affected by the Common Fishing Policy.

The future well-being of the Scottish fishing industry is dependent on the effectiveness of this policy. The combination of national self-interest, historic rights quite unrelated to the present circumstances, and current levels of fish stocks and the modern catching methods, together with aggravated mutual suspicions, do not auger well. The British fisherman used to draw 40 per cent of his catch from grounds from which he is now excluded; as a result he must become more dependent on his home waters in which some 60 per cent of European Community fish swim. The principle of equal access by Community members has been established with other restrictions to limit the pressure on stocks. Only the zone within the 3 mile limit remains exclusive while special controls apply within the 'boxes'. The way forward lies in the effective operation of the quota system with the eventual matching of catching power to sustainable yield. Fishing plans with local preferences may help some remote areas highly dependent on fishing while the fuller development of co-operative ventures embracing the catching, processing and marketing sectors will also bring about improvement. European money will be necessary for restructuring, administration and for the surveillance of the Common Fishing Policy without which there can be no confidence in the future of the fishing industry.

Even with the highly sophisticated technology available to the fishing industry, it is in essence the last 'hunting and gathering' component in our modern economic society. As a result it faces more uncontrolled and uncontrollable vagaries of the biological cycle and environment than any other. Although successful commercial fish farming has faced many problems, the techniques are becoming more fully understood and by the end of this century more and more fish for human consumption should be produced in the more controlled environments of tank, pond, loch and sea loch; to which developments Scotland can make a major contribution with her sheltered western sea lochs, numerous inland lochs, opportunities to use waste heat from power stations, and the growing scientific expertise in this highly specialised biological field.

Tourism

Scotland has already established a considerable reputation in the tourist and recreation industry. The combination of beautiful and often challenging environments, intriguing history, a distinct culture and much sought after sport, help explain its popularity, while the emotional attachments of people of Scottish descent and the international reputation of such diverse products as the Edinburgh Festival and whisky add to its attraction.

In the context of increasing prosperity and leisure in the Western world and the greater ease of travel, and in most cases a relative or even absolute reduction in the cost of that travel, Scotland has great potential for further tourist and recreation development. Not only does the increase in leisure time provide greater opportunities for home-based holidays, but cheaper international travel opens up a vast market in 'nostalgia' visits. Although foreign visitors account for a relatively small part of the total money spent by tourists in the UK, the contribution it makes to our invisible export earnings is very significant. Furthermore, holidays in less highly developed environments are growing in popularity, although by definition this intensifies the problems of pollution and environmental damage in the widest sense. Increased delimitation of areas of supervised and controlled environment is vitally necessary if recreation seekers are not unwittingly to destroy the very assets they seek to enjoy.

But the problems for Scottish tourism, and all the benefits which a largely non-urban-oriented industry is able to bring to areas in need of employment and economic opportunities, are in part the creation of the tourist industry itself. Certainly some of the costs of internal travel, and especially internal air fares, act as a deterrent to potential visitors to Scotland and especially to the Highlands and Islands, but the inability of many sectors of the hotel trade to give value for money must also be regarded as a major obstacle. The vast majority of foreign visitors enter the UK through London, and the exceedingly high price of London hotel accommodation, and the poor value for money by comparison with most other countries, was given as a significant factor in the drop in the 1980 number of visitors. Nor is Scotland blameless in this respect. Although Scotland suffers more than most areas of the UK from the fact that tourist traffic is seasonal, that season is extending both into spring and autumn. However, even taking into account the problems of season, a high proportion of Scottish hotels are regarded as too costly for the amenities and services provided. This reputation is, and will remain, a major deterrent to the expansion of tourism. It is probably, for example, a much more significant factor than the price of petrol, except for the caravan motorist who, in the main, contributes relatively little to the local economy. Certainly the tourist travelling by road is increasingly tempted by the fast trunk routes from the South which lead to the southern edge of the Highlands.

Tourism in Scotland has been slow to identify the needs, expectations and paying ability of its clients. However, awareness of the need for raising standards of such things as hotel rooms, catering and souvenirs is reflected in the slowly increasing number of rooms with bathrooms and of attractive handicraft items and woollen goods. The provision of a bed and breakfast service remains, and is likely to remain, an important contributor to the tourist industry, injecting an unquantifiable element into the local economy. There are already a number of areas where population decline has made available houses which can be renovated into holiday homes. Some landowners and farmers are also entering this market, but there are already a number of warning signs to suggest that a repetition of attacks on lowland or English-owned holiday homes might be pursued by a lunatic nationalist fringe, with serious repercussions for this albeit temporary increase in population. As to the larger-scale developments of the Aviemore variety, there has been considerable discussion and much opposition from environmental interests which regard Aviemore as having placed intolerable strains on the fragile mountain environment. They fiercely and unreasonably object to any further extension of skiing facilities beyond the existing Speyside ski area, they objected to the tentative proposals in the 1970s to develop skiing on Ben Wyvis, and they generally oppose all developments which are likely to threaten the wilderness qualities of the Scottish upland environment.

The Urban Fabric

Most Scots will continue to live in towns but the well-established post-1945 redistribution trends are likely to continue. The central belt urban areas which grew with the nineteenth-century industrial developments will continue to lose population as the old industries decline and new industries are discouraged by the scars of urban dereliction and by histories of industrial labour discord. The physical, economic and social environments of the new towns and of sites around the earlier urban heartlands have proved, and continue to prove, much more attractive to many industrial and commercial employers. Initially, much of this dispersal was motivated by a need to provide new homes and new opportunities for those living in the decaying centres of the traditional urban areas. Now the initiatives of the people, born of their ambitions, desires and needs, can be added to the initiatives of the various agencies involved.

Efforts continue to improve the urban environment of the traditional centres and revitalise their economies. Successive governments have given cash aid to environmental improvement programmes. In recent years the Manpower Services Commission has funded numerous schemes, often using the young unemployed, while local government has tried to upgrade city centres by encouraging shopping precincts and pedestrianisation of shopping streets. The identification of Glasgow as an Enterprize Zone in 1980 is an effort on the part of government to stimulate regeneration through the creation of small businesses. This is the only Enterprize Zone in Scotland and emphasises the special problems of Glasgow, as does the GEAR (Glasgow Eastern Area Renewal) Project, co-ordinated by the Scottish Development Agency which also seeks to aid established industries through difficult times and encourage new ventures to succeed.

The older city areas have continued to attract a substantial part of the SDA's available funds but these remain the most difficult areas for its efforts, partly because the co-ordination of the various public and private bodies involved is a complex task. Also the older city areas are ill-prepared to deal with the complicated interaction between the decline of traditional industry, the movement of population and the slow pace of new development, and the fact that it tends to be out of phase with the removal of dereliction and decay.

A major characteristic of the Scottish urban fabric is the very high percentage of municipal housing. Half of Scotland's urban homes are council-owned and in some parts of west central Scotland that figure rises to over 70 per cent. Largely the product of a post-1945 surge to rehouse families living in substandard nineteenth-century housing, the result has been vast expanses of low amenity housing schemes possessing a sad architectural and environmental homogeneity.

Forming broad haloes around the Scottish cities, the council house estates now form one of Scotland's most intransigent urban, social and environmental problems. Rent levels have for various reasons, some political, often been kept at a low level, thus exacerbating problems of adequate funds for maintenance and for amenity and environmental improvement. Such a high municipal tenant population impairs much needed mobility of labour dictated by the changing distribution of employment opportunity.

The 1979 Conservative Government introduced the right of council tenants to buy their homes at discount prices. The Scottish Office hopes that by May 1984, 100,000 council houses will have been sold to the sitting tenants; but, while it reduces the position whereby Scotland has more municipal tenants than most East European countries, it will not substantially alter the character of the Scottish urban fabric. To do this will remain a dominant political, planning and investment challenge for the remainder of the century.

Devolution

The two attempts in the 1970s to change the government of Scotland both foundered. The wave of support for the Scottish National Party, which culminated in the 1974 elections with eleven Nationalist MPs being returned to Parliament, was reversed when all but two of them lost their seats in the 1979 election and in many constituencies, where the SNP had been second in the 1974 polling, they dropped to third place. The other reverse was the failure of the devolution provisions of the Scotland Act 1978 to gain the support of the 40 per cent of the total electorate necessary before the Act could be put into effect.

These two events should not be interpreted as the end to political efforts to change the government of Scotland. The success of the Scottish National Party in the early 1970s, while fuelled by the prospect of substantial North Sea oil revenues, was born of a complex mixture of frustration, a well-cultivated sense of injustice and an emotional bandwagon effect more familiar to Hampden Park or Murrayfield.

The general lack of devolution or nationalistic momentum in the early 1980s may be attributed to the recognition that many other regions in the UK are also suffering during the present recession; internal dissent in the SNP leadership has also made it difficult for them to exploit political opportunities. However, the longer-term possibilities for a revived devolution platform remain, although support for the undiluted SNP separatist cause is less likely to gather pace. In 1974 much of the Nationalist victory could be attributed to dissatisfaction of the electorate with the two main parties of government. Whether or not the Nationalists again provide a major challenge to the Labour and Conservative parties, or compete with the attractions of the SDP/Liberal Alliance, will depend on the general condition of the economy with particular reference to employment, on Scotland's relative position with the UK, and on narrower issues such as the number of major capital projects while oil revenue income remains high, the control and use of land especially in the Highlands, the acceptability of the Common Fishing Policy, the ways in which attitudes develop towards nuclear power and its related issues, and the rate of regeneration and refurbishing of the Scottish cities.

But these, and the other issues discussed above, have more than just a narrow political import, as they are among the main issues which may concern Scotland over the next two decades and which will make a major contribution to the reshaping and fashioning of the human imprint on the Scottish landscape.

Notes, References and Sources

CHAPTER 1

(Pages 15–27)

Scotland's Geological Evolution: Chalmers M. Clapperton

The main sources on which this chapter is based include the following:

Craig, G. Y. (ed.) *The Geology of Scotland* (Oliver and Boyd 1965)

Geological Survey and Museum *British Regional Geology: Northern Highlands* (HMSO 1960); *Scotland: The Tertiary Volcanic Districts* (HMSO 1961); *Grampian Highlands* (HMSO 1966); *Midland Valley of Scotland* (HMSO 1948); *South of Scotland* (HMSO 1971)

Institute of Geological Sciences *Britain before Man* (HMSO 1978)

Lovell, J. P. B. *The British Isles through geological time* (Allen and Unwin 1977)

Owen, T. R. *The Geological Evolution of the British Isles* (Pergamon 1976)

CHAPTER 2

(Pages 28–63)

Scotland's Landforms: Valerie Haynes

1 Geikie, A. *The scenery of Scotland* (Macmillan 1865); Mackinder, H. J. *Britain and the British Seas* (Clarendon 1902); Peach, B. N., and Horne, J. *Chapters on the geology of Scotland* (Oxford UP 1930); Mort, F. W. 'The Rivers of south west Scotland'. *Scot. Geog. Mag.*, 34 (1918), 361–8

2 Bremner, A. 'The origin of the Scottish river system', *Scot. Geog. Mag.*, 48 (1942), 15–20, 54–59, 99–103; Linton, D. L., 'Some aspects of the evolution of the rivers Earn and Tay', *Scot. Geog. Mag.*, 56 (1940), 1–11, 69–79

3 Ramsay, A. C. *The physical geology and geography of Great Britain* (Stanford 1878, 5th edn); Bailey, E. B. 'The interpretation of Scottish scenery', *Scot. Geog. Mag.*, 50 (1934), 308–30

4 Linton, D. L. 'Problems of Scottish scenery', *Scot. Geog. Mag.*, 67 (1951), 65–85

5 George, T. N. 'Drainage in the Southern Uplands, Clyde, Nith and Annan', *Trans. Geol. Soc. Glasg.*, 22 (1955), 1–34; 'The geological growth of Scotland'. In Craig, G. Y. (ed.) *The Geology of Scotland* (Oliver and Boyd 1965); 'Geomorphic evolution in Hebridean Scotland', *Scot. Journ. Geol.*, 2 (1966), 1–34

6 Sissons, J. B. *The evolution of Scotland's scenery* (Oliver and Boyd 1967)

7 Fitzpatrick, E. A. 'Deeply weathered rock in Scotland, its occurrence, age and contribution to the soils', *Journ. Soil Sci.*, 14 (1963), 33–43

8 Thomas, M. F. 'Some geomorphological implications of deep weathering patterns in crystalline rocks in Nigeria', *Trans. Inst. Brit. Geog.*, 40 (1966)

9 Godard, A. *Recherces de géomorphologie en Ecosse du Nord-ouest* (Univ. de Strasbourg. 1965)

10   Linton, D. L. 'The problem of tors', *Geog. Journ.*, 121 (1955), 470–87
11   Sugden, D. E 'The selectivity of glacial erosion in the Cairngorm mountains', *Trans. Inst. Brit. Geog.*, 45 (1968), 79–92
12   Caston, V. N. D. 'A new isopachyte map of the Quaternary of the North Sea', *I.G.S. Rept.*, 77/11 (HMSO 1977)
13   Bowen, D. Q. *Quaternary Geology* (Pergamon 1978)
14   Sissons, J. B. 'The last Scottish ice sheet: a speculative discussion', *Boreas*, 10:1 (1981), 1–17; Connell, E. R., Edwards, K. J. and Hall, A. M. 'Evidence for two pre-Flandrian palaeosols in Buchan, north-east Scotland', *Nature*, 297 (1982), 570–572
15   Gray, J. M. and Lowe, J. J. (eds.) *Studies in the Scottish Late Glacial environment* (Pergamon 1977)
16   Sissons, J. B. *Scotland* (Methuen 1976)
17   Price, R. 'Rates of geomorphological changes in proglacial areas'. In Cullingford, R. A., Davidson, D. A. and Lewin, J. (eds.), *Timescales in geomorphology* (Wiley 1980)
18   Haynes, V. M. 'The modification of valley patterns by ice sheet activity'. *Geogr. Annaler*, 59A (1977), 195–207
19   Linton, D. L. 'The forms of glacial erosion'. *Trans. Inst. Brit. Geog.*, 33 (1963), 1–28
20   Crampton, C. B. *et. al.* 'The Geology of Caithness'. *Mem. Geol. Surv. Scot.* (HMSO 1914)
21   Murdoch, W. 'The geomorphology and glacial deposits of the area around Aberdeen'. In Gemmell, A. M. D. (ed.) *Quaternary Studies in N.E. Scotland* (Aberdeen Geog. Dept. 1975); Chester, K. D., 'Description of the section exposed by the B.P. oil pipeline trench between Stonehaven and the R. Don'. Unpubl Rept. (Aberdeen Geog. Dept. 1974)
22   Burke, M. J. 'The Forth Valley: an ice moulded lowland', *Trans. Inst. Brit. Geog.*, 48 (1969) 51–9; Linton, D. L. 'Glacial erosion on soft rock outcrops in Central Scotland', *Biul. Peryglac.*, 11 (1962) 247–57
23   Thomson, M. E. and Eden, R. A. 'The Quaternary deposits of the Central North Sea 3'. *IGS Rept.* 77/12 (HMSO 1977)
24   Clapperton, C. M. 'Channels formed by the superimposition of glacial meltwater streams, with special reference to the east Cheviot Hills', *Geogr. Annaler.*, 50A (1968), 207–20
25   McCann, S. B. 'The raised beaches of N.E. Islay and W. Jura', *Trans. Inst. Brit. Geogr.*, 35 (1964), 1–16
26   Anderson, F. W. and Dunham, K. C. 'The geology of N. Skye', *Mem. Geol. Surv. Scot.* (HMSO 1966)
27   Ragg, J. M., and Bibby, J. S. 'Frost weathering and solifluction products in S. Scotland', *Geogr. Annaler*, 48A (1966), 12–23
28   Tricker, A. S. and Scott, G. 'Spatial patterns of chemical denudation in the Eden catchment, Fife', *Scot. Geog. Mag.*, 96:2 (1980), 114–120
29   Kirkby, M. *A study of rates of erosion and mass movements on slopes with special reference to Galloway.* Ph.D. thesis (Cambridge 1963)
30   Ward, R. G. W. 'Avalanche hazard in the Cairngorm mountains, Scotland', *Journ. Glaciol.*, 24:96 (1980), 31–42
31   Miller, R., Common, R., and Galloway, R. W. 'Stone stripes and other surface features of Tinto Hill', *Geog. Journ.*, 120 (1954), 216–9

32 Ball, D. F., and Goodier, R. 'Ronas Hill, Shetland: a preliminary account of its ground pattern features resulting from the action of frost and wind'. In Goodier, R. (ed.) *The natural environment of Shetland* (Nature Conservancy Council 1974)

33 Rodda, J. C. 'Rainfall excesses in the United Kingdom', *Trans. Inst. Brit. Geog.*, 49 (1970), 49–60

34 Fairbairn, W. A. 'Erosion in the Findhorn valley', *Scot. Geog. Mag.*, 83:1 (1967), 46–52

35 Baird, P. D., and Lewis, W. V. 'The Cairngorm floods, 1956', *Scot. Geog. Mag.*, 73 (1957), 91–100

36 Common, R. 'A report on the Lochaber, Appin and Benderloch floods' *Scot. Geog. Mag.*, 70 (1954), 6–20

37 Fitzpatrick, E. A. 'An indurated soil horizon formed by permafrost', *Journ. Soil Sci.*, 7 (1956), 248–54

38 Mykura, W. *Orkney and Shetland. British Regional Geology* (HMSO 1976)

39 Steers, J. A. *The coastline of Scotland* (Cambridge UP 1973)

40 Crofts, R. and Mather, A. *The beaches of Wester Ross* (Aberdeen Geog. Dept., Countryside Commission 1972)

41 Buchan, G. and Ritchie, W. 'Aberdeen beach and Donmouth spit: an example of short term coastal dynamics', *Scot. Geog. Mag.*, 95:1 (1977), 27–43

42 Grove, A. T. 'The mouth of the Spey', *Scot. Geog. Mag.*, 71 (1955), 104–7

43 Ritchie, W. *The beaches of Fife* (Aberdeen Geog. Dept. Countryside Commn. 1978)

44 Hollingworth, S. E. 'The recognition and correlation of high level erosion surfaces in Britain: a statistical study', *Quart. Journ. Geol. Soc.*, 94 (1938), 55–84

45 Jardine, W. G. 'River development in Galloway', *Scot. Geog. Mag.*, 75 (1959), 65–74

46 Walton, K. 'Geomorphology'. In O'Dell, A. C., and Mackintosh, J (eds) *The North East of Scotland* (Brit. Association 1963)

47 Soons, J. M. 'Landscape evolution in the Ochil Hills', *Scot. Geog. Mag.*, 74 (1958), 86–97

48 Fleet, H. 'Erosion surfaces in the Grampian Highlands of Scotland', *Rapp. Commiss. Cartog. des Surfaces d'Applanissement Tert.* (I.G.U. 1938)

49 Al Ansari, N. A. and McManus, J. 'Fluvial sediments entering the Tay estuary: sediment discharge from the R. Earn', *Scot. Journ. Geol.*, 15:3 (1979), 169–256

50 Geikie, A. 'On denudation now in progress', *Geol. Mag.*, 5 (1868), 249–54

51 Fleming, G. 'The sediment balance of the Clyde estuary', *Proc. Am. Soc. Civ. Engrs. Hydraul. Divn.*, 96 (1970), 2219–30

52 Ledger, D. C., Lovell, J. P. B., and Cuttle, S. P. 'Rate of sedimentation in Kelly reservoir, Strathclyde', *Scot. Journ. Geol.*, 164 (1980), 281–5; Ledger, D. C., Lovell, J. P. B., and McDonald, A. T. 'Sediment yield studies in upland catchment areas in S. E. Scotland', *Journ. Appl. Ecol.*, 11:1 (1974), 201–6

53 Rapp, A. 'Recent developments of mountain slopes in Kärkevagge and surroundings, N. Scandinavia', *Geogr. Annaler*, 42A (1960), 72–200

CHAPTER 3

(Pages 64–93)

The Bio-climate: Joy Tivy

1   Anderson, M. L. and Fairbairn, W. A. 'Division of Scotland into climatic sub-regions as an aid to silviculture', *Bulletin for Dept. of Forestry, Univ. of Edinburgh*, 1 (1955)

2   Francis, P. E. 'Some climatic factors in land assessment'. In Thomas, M. E. and Coppock, J. T. (eds.) *Land Assessment in Scotland* (Aberdeen UP 1980)

3   Green, F. H. W. 'The Climate of Scotland'. In John H. Burnett (ed.) *The Vegetation of Scotland* (Oliver and Boyd 1964)

4   Miller, Ronald, 'Bioclimatic Characteristics'. In Tivy, Joy (ed.) *The Organic Resources of Scotland: Their Nature and Evaluation* (Oliver and Boyd 1973)

5   Gregory, S. 'Accumulated temperature maps of the British Isles', *Trans. Inst. Brit. Geog.*, 20 (1954), 59–73; 'The Growing Season at Eskdalemuir Observatory, Dumfriesshire, *Meteorol. Mag.*, 102 (1955), 1211

6   Lyall, I. T. 'The growth of barley and the effect of climate', *Weather*, 35 (9) (1980), 271–276; Anderson, R. 'Weather and crop yields in North East Scotland', *Weather*, 31 (1976)

7   Holmes, John C. 'Tillage Crops'. In Tivy *op cit.*

8   Hunt, I. V. 'The Grass Crop'. In Tivy *op. cit.*

9   Green, F. H. W. 'A map of annual average potential water deficit in the British Isles', *Journ. Applied Ecol.*, (1964), 151–8

10 Ledger, D. C. and Thom, A. S. '200 years of potential moisture deficit in S. W. Scotland'. *Weather*, 32 (9) (1978), 342–9

11 O'Riordan, T. 'Spray irrigation and water supply in East Lothian'. *Scott. Geogr. Mag.*, 79 (1963), 170–3

12 Smith, L. P. 'Meteorology and the pattern of British grassland farming'. *Agric. Met.*, 4 (1967), 321–38

13 Francis, P. E. *op. cit.*

14 Pearsall, W. H. *Mountains and Moorlands* (Collins 1952)

15 Fraser, G. K. 'Studies of Scottish Moorlands in Relation to Tree Growth'. *Bulletin For. Commn.*, 15 (1933)

16 Jowsey, Peter C. 'Peatlands'. In Tivy *op. cit.*

17 Conrad, V. 'Usual formulas of continentality and their limits of validity'. *Trans. Am. Geophys. Un.*, 27 (1946), 663–4

18 Burnett, John H. *Vegetation of Scotland* (Oliver and Boyd 1964)

19 McVean, Donald N. and Ratcliffe, Derek, A. *Plant Communities of the Scottish Highlands*, Monograph of the Nature Conservancy No. 1 (HMSO 1962)

20 Mitchell, Joan 'The Bracken Problem'. In Tivy *op. cit.*

21 Russell, G. and Grace, J. 'The effect of shelter on yield of grasses in southern Scotland', *Journ. Appl. Ecol*, 16 (1979), 319

22 Manley, G. 'The effective rate of altitudinal change in temperate Atlantic climates'. *Geogr. Rev.*, 35 (1945), 408–17

23 Mochlinski, K. 'Soil temperature in the U.K.', *Weather*, 25 (1970), 192–200; see also Green, F. H. W. comment in Francis *op. cit.*

24 Hunter, R. F. and Grant, Sheila A. 'The effect of altitude on grass growth in East Scotland', *Journ. Appl. Ecol.*, 8 (1981); Hegarty, T. W. 'Effects of solar radiation and temperature on vegetation growth in the East of Scotland', *Journ. Appl. Ecol*, 10 (1973), 145; Grant, S. 'Temperature and light as factors limiting the growth of hill pasture species', *Proc. Sym. Hill Land Product*, Occ. Symp. No. 4 (British Grassland Society 1968)

25 Pears, Nigel, V. 'Wind as a factor in Mountain Ecology: Some data from the Cairngorm Mountains'. *Scot. Geog. Mag.*, 83 (2) (1967), 118–24

26 Locke, G. M. L. 'Land Assessment for Forestry'. In Thomas and Coppock *op. cit.*

27 Poore, M. E. D. and McVean, D. N. 'A new approach to Scottish Mountain Vegetation'. *Journ. Ecol.*, 45 (1957), 401–439; McVean and Ratcliffe *op. cit.*

28 Spence, D. H. N. 'Studies on the Vegetation of Shetland', *Journ. Ecol.*, 45 (1957), 917

29 Manley, G. 'The mountain snows of Britain', *Weather*, 26 (1971), 192–200; 'Scotland's semi-permanent snows', *Ibid.* 458–71

30 Green, F. H. W. 'The transient snow-line in the Scottish Highlands', *Weather*, 30 (7) (1975), 226–235

31 Green, F. H. W. 'Persistent snow-beds in the Western Cairngorms', *Weather*, 23 (1968), 206–209; 'Changing incidence of snow in the Scottish Highlands', *Weather*, 28 (9) (1973), 386–394

32 Spink, P. C. 'A summary of summer snows in Scotland 1965–74', *Journ. Met.* (Trowbridge), 5 (1980), 105–111

33 McVean and Ratcliffe *op. cit.*; Watt, A. S. and Jones, E. W. 'The Ecology of the Cairngorms', *Journ. Ecol.*, 36 (1948), 283–304

34 Watson, Adam. 'Climate and the antler shedding and performance of red deer in north-east Scotland', *Journ. Applied Ecol.*, 8 (1971), 53; Jackers, A. D. and Watson, A. 'Winter whitening of Scottish Mountain Hares (*Lepus timidus scoticus*) in relation to day-length, temperature and snowline', *Z. Zool.*, 176 (1975), 403–409

35 Watt, A. S. and Jones, E. W. 'The ecology of the Cairngorms. 1. The environment and the altitudinal zonation of the vegetation', *Journ. Ecol*, 36 (1948), 283–240

36 Miller *op. cit.*

37 Manley, G. 'Snowline in Britain', *Geogr. Annaler*, H. (1–2), 31 (1949), 179

38 Durno, S. E. (1973). 'Vegetation Chronology'. In Tivy *op. cit.*; Durno, S. E. and Romans, J. C. C. 'Evidence for variations in the altitudinal zonation of climate in Scotland and Northern England since the Boreal Period', *Scot. Geogr. Mag.*, 85 (1) (1969), 31–33

39 Parry, M. L. 'Secular climatic change and marginal agriculture', *Trans. Inst. Brit. Geog.*, 64 (1975), 1–3; 'The significance of the variability of summer warmth in upland Britain', *Weather*, 31 (7) (1976), 212–217

CHAPTER 4

(Pages 94–115)

Prehistoric Scotland: The Regional Dimension: William Kirk

1 Geikie, A. *The Scenery of Scotland* (Macmillan 1865)

2   Linton, D. L. 'Morphological Contrasts of Eastern and Western Scotland'. In *Geographical Essays in memory of Alan G. Ogilvie* (Nelson 1959)

3   For a general account of the prehistory of Scotland see e.g. Piggott, S. (ed.) *The Prehistoric Peoples of Scotland* (Routledge and Kegan Paul 1962); Piggott, S. and Henderson, K. *Scotland before History* (Nelson 1958); Feachem, R. *A Guide to Prehistoric Scotland* (Batsford 2nd edn. 1976); Richmond, I. A. (ed.) *Roman and Native in North Britain* (Nelson 1958); MacKie, E. W. *Scotland, an Archaeological Guide* (Faber 1975); Megaw, J. V. S. and Simpson, D. D. A. (eds.) *Introduction to British Prehistory* (Leicester UP 1979); and for a concise summary linked to landscape changes, Whittington, G. 'Prehistoric activity and its effects on the Scottish Landscape'. In Parry, M. L. and Slater, T. R. (eds.) *The Making of the Scottish Countryside* (Croom Helm 1980)

4   The most comprehensive survey of recent times is Nicolaisen, W. F. H. *Scottish Place Names; their study and significance* (Batsford 1976). This summarises some twenty years work at the School of Scottish Studies and numerous papers, and all scholars in this field are in his debt. See also, however, Watson, W. J. *The History of Celtic Place-names of Scotland* (Blackwood 1926); and for the *pit-* names Jackson, K. H. 'The Pictish Language'. In Wainwright, F. T. (ed.) *The Problem of the Picts* (Nelson 1955); Whittington, G. 'Place names and the settlement pattern of dark age Scotland', *Proc. Soc. Antiq. Scot.*, 106 (1974–5), 99–110

5   Ekwall, E. *Scandinavians and Celts in Northwest England* (Lund 1918)

6   MacQueen, J. '*Kirk-* and *Kil-* in Galloway Place-names', *Archivum Linguisticum*, 8 (1956), 135–149

7   Nicolaisen, W. F. H. 'Norse Place-names in Southwest Scotland', *Scottish Studies*, 4 (1960), 49–70

8   The *-dalr* and Anglian name distribution is based on Nicolaisen, *Scottish Place Names, op. cit.* Chaps 6 and 5 respectively

9   See particularly Wainwright *op. cit.*

10   See Stevenson, R. B. K. 'Pictish Art'. In Wainwright *op. cit.*

11   See Richmond *op. cit.*

12   See Feachem, R. W. 'Fortifications' in Wainwright *op. cit.*

13   See Scott, L. S. 'The Problem of the Brochs', *Proc. Prehist. Soc.*, 13 (1947), 1–36; Graham, A. 'Some observations on the Brochs', *Proc. Soc. Antiq. Scot.*, 81 (1947), 48–99

14   Hamilton, J. R. C. *Excavations at Jarlshof, Shetland* (HMSO 1956)

15   Hawkes, C. F. C. 'The ABC of the British Iron Age', *Antiquity*, 33 (1958) 170–82

16   Feachem, F. W. at a Conference on the North British Iron Age 1961. In Rivet, A. L. F. 'The Iron Age in Northern Britain', *Antiquity*, 36, 141 (1962), 24–31. The map referred to is Fig 2, p. 29

17   MacKie, E. W. 'Brochs and the Hebridean Iron Age', *Antiquity*, 39 (1965), 266–78

18   Kirk, W. 'The Primary Agricultural Colonisation of Scotland', *Scot. Geog. Mag.*, 73 (1957), 65–90

19   Cf. Lanting, J. N. and Waals, J. D. v.d. 'British Beakers as seen from the Continent', *Helenium*, 12 (1972), 20–46, esp. 29

20   For a major survey see Henshall, A. S. *The Chambered Tombs of Scotland* (Edinburgh UP Vol. I. 1963., Vol. II. 1972)
21   See Lacaille, A. D. *The Stone Age in Scotland* (Oxford UP 1954)
22   See e.g. Durno, S. E. 'Certain aspects of vegetational history in north-east Scotland', *Scot. Geog. Mag.*, 73 (1957), 176–184; Edwards, K. J. 'Aspects of the prehistoric archaeology of the Howe of Cromar'. In Gemmell, A. M. D. (ed.) *Quaternary studies in north-east Scotland* (Aberdeen 1975); O'Sullivan, P. E. 'Radiocarbon dating and prehistoric forest clearance on Speyside', *Proc. Prehist. Soc.*, 40 (1974), 206–8
23   Even at the close of prehistoric times the population of Scotland is not likely to have exceeded 200,000
24   See Robertson, Anne S. *The Antonine Wall* (Glasgow Arch. Soc. 1979)

CHAPTER 5

(Pages 116–27)

Patterns of Rural Settlement from Medieval Times to 1700: James R. Coull

1   Whyte, I. D. 'The Evolution of Rural Settlement in Lowland Scotland in Medieval and Early Modern Times. An Exploration', *Scot. Geog. Mag.*, 97 (1981), 4–15
2   Barrow, G. W. S. 'Rural Settlement in Central and Eastern Scotland: The Medieval Evidence', *Scottish Studies*, 6 (1962), 123–144
3   Dodgshon, R. A. 'Changes in Scottish Township Organisation during the Medieval and Early Modern Periods', *Geog. Annaler*, 59B (1977), 51–65
4   Whittington, G. 'Field Systems in Scotland'. In Baker, A. R. H. and Butlin, R. A. (eds) *Studies of Field Systems in the British Isles* (Cambridge UP 1973), 552–565
5   Information from Dr. J. C. Stone, Department of Geography, University of Aberdeen
6   Parry, M. L. 'Secular Climatic Change and Marginal Agriculture', *Trans. Inst. Brit. Geog.*, 64 (1975), 1–13
7   Dodgshon, R. A. 'Medieval Settlement and Colonisation'. In Parry, M. L. and Slater, T. R. (eds.) *The Making of the Scottish Countryside* (Croom Helm 1980), 62–5
8   Dodgshon, R. A. 'Scandinavian 'Solskifte' and the Sunwise Division of Land in Eastern Scotland', *Scottish Studies*, 19 (1975), 1–14
9   Dodgshon, R. A. 'The nature and development of Infield – Outfield in Scotland', *Trans. Inst. Brit. Geog.*, 59 (1973), 1–23
10   Whyte, I. D. 'Infield – Outfield Farming on a Seventeenth Century Scottish Estate', *Journ. Hist. Geog.*, 5 (1979), 391–401
11   Dodgshon, R. A. 'The Origins of Traditional Field Systems'. In Parry and Slater *op. cit.*, 81–4
12   Whyte, I. D. 'Written Leases and their Impact in Scottish Farming in the Seventeenth Century', *Agric. Hist. Review*, 27 (1979), 1–9
13   Fenton, A. 'The Traditional Pastoral Economy'. In Parry and Slater *op. cit.*, 107
14   Fenton, A. *Ibid.* 95–8

15 Whyte, I. D. 'The Emergence of the New Estate Structure'. In Parry and Slater *op. cit.*, 128

16 Miller, R. 'Land Use in Summer Shielings', *Scottish Studies*, 11 (1967), 196–204

17 Gaffney, V. 'Summer Shealings', *Scot. Hist. Review*, 38 (1959), 27, 28

18 MacSween, M. D. 'Transhumance in North Skye', *Scot. Geog. Mag.*, 75 (1959), 84–5

19 Whyte, I. D. 'Rural Housing in Lowland Scotland in the Seventeenth Century: the Evidence of Estate Papers', *Scottish Studies*, 19 (1975), 55–68

20 Slater, T. R. 'The Mansion and Policy'. In Parry and Slater *op. cit.*, 125

CHAPTER 6

(Pages 128–51)

Patterns of Rural Settlement, 1700–1850: J. B. Caird

1   Adams, I. H. 'The Agents of Agricultural Change'. In Parry, M. L. and Slater, T. R. (eds.) *The Making of the Scottish Countryside* (Croom Helm 1980), 155

2   Skelton, R. A. 'The Military Survey of Scotland, 1947–55', *Scot. Geog. Mag.*, 83 (1967), 5–16

3   See, for example, Third, B. M. W. 'The Significance of Scottish Estate Plans and associated documents', *Scottish Studies*, I (1957), 39–64; Adams, I. H. *Descriptive list of plans in the Scottish Record Office* (HMSO, Edinburgh, Vols. I, II and III, 1966, 1970, 1974)

4   O'Dell, A. C. 'A View of Scotland in the middle of the eighteenth century', *Scot. Geog. Mag.* (1951), 58–63

5   Timperley, L. 'The Pattern of Landholding in Eighteenth Century Scotland'. In Parry and Slater *op. cit.*, 140 and 151

6   Adams, I. H. *loc. cit.*, 171

7   S.R.O. Polwarth Mss: quoted in Campbell, R. H. and Dow, J. B. A. *Scource Book of Scottish Economic and Social History* (Blackwell 1968), 16–17

8   Adams, *loc. cit.* 171

9   Adams, I. H. (ed.) *Papers on Peter May, Land Surveyor, 1749–1793. Scot. Hist. Soc.*, Fourth Series, Vol. 15 (1979), xxi–xxv

10 S.R.O. GD248/3408/6 quoted in Adams, *Ibid.*, xv–xvi

11 Colville, J. (ed.) *Letters of John Cockburn of Ormistoun to his Gardener, 1727–44. Scot. Hist. Soc.*, XLV (1904), 42

12 Adams, I. H. (ed.) *Directory of Scottish Commonties, Scottish Record Society*, New Series, 2, 1971

13 Donaldson, James. *General View of the Agriculture of the Carse of Gowrie, in the County of Perth. With observations on the means of its improvement. Drawn up for the consideration of the Board of Agriculture and Internal Improvement*, London: printed by C. Macrae, 1794

14 Lebon, J. H. G. 'The process of enclosure in the western lowlands', *Scot. Geog. Mag.*, 62 (1946), 100–110

15 Caird, J. B. 'The Reshaped Agricultural Landscape'. In Parry and Slater *op. cit.*, 208–9

16 *Ibid.*, 209–11

17 Maclagan, D. S. 'Stock rearing in the Highlands, 1720–1820', *Trans. Highlands and Agric. Soc. of Scot.*, Sixth Series, 2 (1957), 63–71

18 Cregeen, E. R. (ed.) *The Argyll Estate Instructions, Mull, Morven and Tiree, 1771–1805. Scot. Hist. Soc.* (1964), xviii–xix

19 Dunlop, J. *The British Fisheries Society, 1786–1893* (John Donald 1978), 52–53

20 Crawford, W. *Plan of the Island of Benbecula*, R.H.P. 3028, Scottish Record Office. (This is a reduced copy of William Bald's plan of 1805 (R.H.P. 1039) with tables of contents giving areas of arable, pasture and hill pasture for both 1805 and 1829).

21 McLagan, D. S. *op. cit.*

22 Fairhurst, H. 'The Deserted Settlement at Lix, West Perthshire', *Proc. Soc. Antiq. Scot.*, 101 (1971), 160–99

23 O'Dell, A. C. and Walton, K. *The Highlands and Islands of Scotland* (Nelson 1962), 329–36

24 Tait, A. A. *The Landscape Garden in Scotland, 1735–1835* (Edinburgh UP 1980), 26–7

25 Salaman, R. N. *The History and Social Influences of the Potato* (Cambridge UP 1949), 344–390

26 Douglas, C. 'The origin of the Ayrshire Breed of Cattle', *Trans. Highland and Agric. Soc. Scot.*, Fifth Series, XXI (1919), 133–151

27 Ryder, M. L. 'The Evolution of Scottish Breeds of Sheep', *Scottish Studies*, 12 (1968), 159–61

28 Handley, J. E. *Scottish Farming in the Eighteenth Century* (Faber and Faber 1953), 215, and Fenton, A. *Scottish Country Life* (John Donald 1976), 38–41, 49, 64–68, and 121

29 Walker, B. *Farm buildings of the Grampian Region, an historical exploration* (Countryside Commission for Scotland and Grampian Regional Council 1978)

30 Parry, M. L. 'Changes in the Extent of the Improved Farmland'. In Parry and Slater *op. cit.*, 183 and 195–6

31 Gaffney, V. 'The Lordship of Strathavon', *Third Spalding Club* (1960), 34–61

32 Lockhart, D. G. 'Planned Villages in Aberdeenshire: the evidence from newspaper advertisements', *Scot. Geog. Mag.*, 94 (1978), 99

33 Mowat, W. G. *The Story of Lybster* (Lybster 1959)

CHAPTER 7

(Pages 152–67)

The Urban Scene, 1760–1980: Ian H. Adams

1 Adams, I. H. *The Making of Urban Scotland* (Croom Helm 1978)

2 Houston, J. M. 'Village planning in Scotland, 1745–1845, *Advancement of Science*, 5 (1948), 129–33; Smout, T. C. 'The landowner and the planned village'. In Phillipson, N. T. and Mitchison, Rosalind (eds.) *Scotland in the Age of Improvement* (Edinburgh UP 1970)

3 Youngson, A. J. *The Making of Classical Edinburgh* (Edinburgh UP 1966)

4 Butt, J. (ed.) *Robert Owen, Prince of Cotton Spinners: A Symposium* (David and Charles 1971)

5 Shaw, John, 'The utilization of water power in Scotland 1550–1870' unpublished Ph.D. (Univ. of Edinburgh 1980)
6 Thomson, A. G. *The Paper Industry in Scotland* (Scottish Academic Press 1974)
7 Duckham, B. T. *A History of the Scottish Coal Industry* (David and Charles 1970) vol. 1, 204; also Hassan, John A. 'The supply of coal to Edinburgh 1790–1850', *Transport History*, 5, 2 (July 1972), 125–51
8 Wilson, J. M. (ed.), *The Imperial Gazetteer of Scotland* (T. C. Jack 1883), 755
9 Campbell, R. H. *Scottish Shipbuilding: its rise and progress'*, *Scot. Geog. Mag.*, 80 (1964), 107–13
10 Checkland, S. G. *The Upas Tree, Glasgow 1877–1975: A Study of Growth and Contraction* (Glasgow UP 1976)
11 Campbell, R. H. *Carron Company* (Oliver and Boyd 1961)
12 Warren, K. 'Locational problems of the Scottish Iron and Steel Industry since 1760', *Scot. Geog. Mag.*, 81 (1965), pt 1, 18–37, pt 2, 87–103
13 Morris, R. J. *Cholera 1832* (Croom Helm 1976)
14 Flinn, M. W. (ed.) *Edwin Chadwick's Report on the Sanitary Conditions of the Labouring Population of Great Britain* (Edinburgh UP 1965), 21–31
15 *Royal Commission on the Sewage of Towns* 1st Report 1857–8, 2nd Report 1861, 3rd Report 1865
16 Smith, P. J. 'Foul Burns of Edinburgh: public health attitudes and environmental change', *Scot. Geog. Mag.*, 91, 1 (1975), 25–37
17 Butt, J. 'Working-class housing in Glasgow 1851–1914'. In Chapman, S. D. (ed.), *The History of Working-Class Housing: A Symposium* (David and Charles 1971); also Gauldie, E. *Cruel Habitations: A History of Working Class Housing 1780–1919* (Allen and Unwin 1974)
18 *The Builder*, 26 March 1870, 239–40
19 Gulven, Clifford, *The Tweedmakers: A History of the Scottish Fancy Woollen Industry 1600–1914* (David and Charles 1973), 139
20 Osborn, Frederick, J. and Whittick, Arnold *New Towns, their origins, achievements and progress* (Leonard Hill 1978), 505

CHAPTER 8

(Pages 168–95)

The Development of Transport Systems: J. H. Farrington

1 Haldane, A. R. B. *New Ways Through the Glens* (Nelson 1962), 2–3
2 Lenman, B. *An Economic History of Modern Scotland* (Batsford 1977), 26–7
3 Haldane, A. R. B. *The Drove Roads of Scotland* (Edinburgh UP 1968), 192, 205
4 Haldane, A. R. B. *New Ways Through the Glens, op. cit.* 7
5 *Ibid.* 51
6 Lindsay, J. *The Canals of Scotland* (David and Charles 1968), 94
7 *Ibid.* 218
8 *Ibid.* 167–8, 210
9 Lenman, B. *op. cit.*, 150–1
10 Thomas, J. *A Regional History of the Railways of Great Britain, No. 6 – Scotland: The Lowlands and the Borders* (David and Charles 1971), 123

11   Thomas, J. *op. cit.*; Kellett, J. R. *Railways and Victorian Cities* (Routledge and Kegan Paul 1979); Johnston, C. and Hume, J. R. *Glasgow Stations* (David and Charles 1979)
12   Nock, O. S. *Scottish Railways* (Nelson 1950), 177–8
13   Lenman, B. *op. cit.* 166
14   Thomas, J. *op. cit.* 221–222
15   See Hunter, D. L. G. *Edinburgh's Transport* (Advertiser Press Ltd. 1964)
16   Thomas, J. *op. cit.* 35
17   Based on Hibbs, J. *The History of British Bus Services* (David and Charles 1968)
18   Fresson, E. E. *Air Road to the Isles* (David Randel 1967), 105
19   British Road Federation, *Basic Road Statistics 1980* Table 42
20   For examples of work on the rural transport problem in the Highlands and Islands, see the following: Farrington, J. H. and Stanley, P. A. *Public Transport in Skye and Lochalsh* (Highlands and Islands Development Board (HIDB) 1978); Stanley, P. A. and Farrington, J. H. 'The Need for Rural Public Transport – A Constraints–Based Approach', *Tijdschrift voor Sociale en Economische Geografie*, 1981, 72, 62–80; Farrington, J. H., Stanley, P. A. and Bain, S. M. *Public Transport in North West Sutherland* (HIDB 1981); Stanley, P. A., Farrington, J. H. and MacKenzie, R. *Public Transport in Easter Ross* (HIDB 1981)
21   British Road Federation, *op. cit.* Table 41
22   Brent, J. 'London–Glasgow; Rail versus Air', *Modern Transport*, 6 (Ian Allan, 1979), 118–19
23   Smith, B. S. L. 'Getting North Sea Oil and Gas Ashore', *Modern Transport*, 6, *op. cit.* 120–7
24   *Airports Policy*, Cmnd. 7084 (HMSO 1978), 39

Other information has been obtained from the following:
British Airports Authority (Scottish Airports).
British Rail (Scotland).
Civil Aviation Authority.
Clyde Port Authority.
Forth Ports Authority.

CHAPTER 9

(Pages 196–223)

Rural Land Use: A. S. Mather

General Note: Unless otherwise indicated, statistical information in this chapter on agriculture is drawn from *Agricultural Statistics* (Scotland), *Agricultural Statistics* (UK) and unattributed articles in *Scottish Agricultural Economics*. Similar information on forestry is from Forestry Commission *Annual Reports*.

1   Countryside Commission for Scotland *First Annual Report* (1969)
2   Best, R. H. 'Competition for land between rural and urban uses', *Inst. Br. Geog., Special Publication 1* (1968), 89–100
3   Best, R. H. 'Land-use structure and change in the EEC', *Town Planning Review*, 50 (1979), 395–411

4   Mather, A. S. 'Red deer land use', *Red Deer Commission Annual Report for 1972* (HMSO, Edinburgh 1973)

5   Tivy, J. 'Heather moorland', In J. Tivy (ed.) *The Organic Resources of Scotland* (Oliver and Boyd 1973)

6   Mackenzie, A. M., Martin, P. C. and Scarlett, E. R. 'Agricultural output of Scotland by regions', *Scot. Agric. Econ.*, 25 (1975), 347–369

7   Coppock, J. T. *An agricultural atlas of Scotland* (John Donald 1976)

8   Bowler, I. R. 'Regional variations in Scottish agricultural trends', *Scot. Geog. Mag.*, 91 (1975), 114–122

9   Ministry of Agriculture, Fisheries and Food, Department of Agriculture and Fisheries for Scotland and Department of Agriculture for Northern Ireland *The Changing Structure of Agriculture, 1968–1975* (HMSO 1977)

10 Scarlett, E. R. 'Recent changes in potato production in Scotland', *Scot. Agric. Econ.*, 25 (1975), 376–386

11 Ministry of agriculture, *et al. op. cit.*

12 Dunn, J. M. 'The changing structure of Scottish potato growing', *Scot. Agric. Econ.*, 27 (1977), 98–99

13 Martin, P. C. 'Hay and silage production in Scotland', *Scot. Agric. Econ.*, 26 (1976), 10–17

14 Toulouse, N. F. 'Some aspects of land use changes in relation to sugar beet and peas', *Scot. Agric. Econ.*, 27 (1977), 92–97

15 Dunn, J. M. 'The location and structure of Scottish horticultural production', *Scot. Agric. Econ.*, 21 (1971), 48–56

16 Coppock, J. T. *op. cit.*

17 Beilby, O. J. 'Beef cow numbers in Scotland', *Scot. Agric. Econ.*, 24 (1974), 277–283

18 Cunningham, J. M. M. and Smith, A. D. M. 'The impact of technical advances on hill and upland cattle systems'. In Tranter, R. B., *The future of upland Britain* (Univ. of Reading Centre for Agricultural Strategy 1978)

19 Beilby, O. J. *op. cit.*

20 Ministry of Agriculture, *et al. op. cit.*

21 Federation of UK Milk Marketing Boards *Dairy facts and figures* (1976)

22 Mather, A. S. 'Land-use changes in the Highlands and Islands of Scotland 1946–1975: a statistical review', *Scot. Geog. Mag.*, 95 (1979), 114–22

23 Ministry of Agriculture, *et al. op. cit.*

24 Dunn, J. M. 'Some aspects of the structure of the agricultural labour input', *Scot. Agric. Econ.*, 26 (1976), 7–9

25 Dunn, J. M. 'Some aspects of the structure of Scottish farming', *Scot. Agric. Econ.*, 25 (1975), 373–375

26 Dellaquaglia, A. P. 'Size and efficiency in Scottish agriculture', *Scot. Agric. Econ.*, 28 (1978), 149–58

27 Clark, G. 'Farm amalgamations in Scotland', *Scot. Geog. Mag.*, 95 (1979), 93–107

28 Mather, A. S. *State-aided land settlement in Scotland. O'Dell Memorial Monograph No. 6* (Univ. of Aberdeen 1978)

29 Dunn, J. M. 'Enterprise specialisation in eastern Scotland', *Scot. Agric. Econ.*, 21 (1971), 25–27

30 Locke, G. M. L. *The place of forestry in Scotland. Forestry Commission Research and Development Paper 113* (1976)

31 *Ibid.*

32 Forestry Commissioners *Post-war Forest Policy* (Cmd. 6447) (HMSO 1943)

33 Mather, A. S. 'Patterns of afforestation in Britain since 1945', *Geography*, 63 (1978), 157–66

34 Select Committee on Scottish Affairs *Land resource use in Scotland*, H.C. Paper 51 (HMSO 1972)

35 Departmental Committee appointed in November 1919 to enquire and report with regard to land in Scotland used as deer forests *Report* (Cmd. 1936) (HMSO 1922)

36 Red Deer Commission *Annual Reports* (HMSO)

37 *Ibid.*

38 Picozzi, N. 'Grouse bags in relation to the management and geology of heather moors', *Journ. Appl. Ecol.*, 56 (1968), 483–494

39 Scottish National Parks Committee *National Parks and the Conservation of Nature in Scotland* (Cmd. 7235) (HMSO 1947)

40 Countryside Commission for Scotland *A Park system for Scotland* (1974)

41 Countryside Commission for Scotland *Ninth Annual Report* (1977)

42 Countryside Commission for Scotland *Thirteenth Annual Report* (1981)

43 Watson, A. 'Bird and mammal numbers in relation to human impact at ski lifts on Scottish hills', *Journ. Appl. Ecol.*, 16 (1979), 753–64

44 Countryside Commission for Scotland *Scotland's Scenic Heritage* (1978)

45 Bowman, J. C. 'The land available to agriculture and forestry in Scotland', *Scottish Forestry*, 32 (1978), 116–20

46 Scottish Development Department *National Planning Guidelines* (1977)

47 Forestry Commission *58th Annual Report and Accounts 1977–78* (1979)

48 Forestry Commission *The wood production outlook in Britain* (1977)

49 Eadie, J. and Smith, A. D. M. 'The impact of technical advances on hill and upland sheep production'. In R. B. Tranter (ed.) *The future of upland Britain* (Univ. of Reading Centre for Agricultural Strategy 1978)

50 Red Deer Commission *Annual Report for 1978* (HMSO 1979)

51 Highlands and Islands Development Board *Strath of Kildonan Proposals for Development Special Report No. 5* (1970)

52 Highlands and Islands Development Board *Proposals for changes in the Highlands and Islands Development (Scotland) Act 1965 to allow more effective powers over rural land use* (1978)

CHAPTER 10

(Pages 224–33)

Fisheries: J. R. Coull

1 Mercer, J. 'Glenbatrick Hole, microlithic Flint Site on Jura', *Proc. Soc. Antiq. Scot.*, 105 (1972–74), 9

2 Coull, J. R. 'Fisheries in Scotland in the 16th, 17th and 18th Centuries. The Evidence in MacFarlane's Geographical Collections', *Scot. Geog. Mag.*, 93 (1977), 85–114

3 Leith, J. M. 'Salmon Legislation in Scotland'. In Herbert, D. (ed.) *Fish and Fisheries* (Blackwood 1883), 139–144

4   Elder, J. R. *Royal Fishery Companies of the Seventeenth Century* (Aberdeen UP 1912)
5   Dunlop, J. *The British Fisheries Society 1786–1893* (John Donald 1978)
6   Smith, Adam *An Inquiry into the Nature and Causes of the Wealth of Nations* (Bell and Sons 1896 edn. vol. 2), 24
7   Gray, M. *The Fishing Industries of Scotland 1790–1914. A Study in Regional Adaptation* (Oxford UP 1978)
8   Goodlad, C. A. *Shetland Fishing Saga* (Shetland Times 1971), 90–129
9   Information from Dr Hance D. Smith, Department of Maritime Studies, University of Wales Institute of Science and Technology, Cardiff

CHAPTER 11

(Pages 234–51)

Energy Resources: Keith Chapman

1   Hamilton, H. *The Industrial Revolution in Scotland* (Cass and Co. 1966), 131
2   Scottish Office, *Scottish abstract of statistics*, 9 (1980), 152
3   *Ibid.*
4   Data supplied by National Coal Board
5   National Coal Board, *Report and accounts 1979/80*, 34
6   Compiled from data in annual reports of the North of Scotland Hydro-Electric Board (NSHEB) and SSEB
7   Manners, G. *Coal in Britain: an Uncertain Future* (Allen and Unwin 1981), 39
8   Data supplied by SSEB
9   National Coal Board, *Plan for Coal* (1974)
10 Manners, G. *op. cit.* 47–68
11 National Coal Board, *Plan for Coal op. cit.*
12 North, J. and Spooner, D. 'The great UK coal rush: a progress report to the end of 1976', *Area*, 9, 15–27
13 Department of Energy, *Development of the oil and gas resources of the United Kingdom* (1980), 36–38
14 Department of Energy, *Digest of Energy Statistics, 1980*, 12
15 Pennwell Publishing Co., *International petroleum encyclopedia*, 13 (1980), 224–5
16 Department of Energy, *Development of the oil and gas resources op. cit.* 9
17 Chapman, K. *North Sea Oil and Gas: a geographical perspective* (David and Charles 1976)
18 Department of energy, *Development of the oil and gas resources, op. cit.* 31
19 Scottish Council (Development and Industry), *U.K. North Sea oil: the export potential and its implications* (1974)
20 Jones, T. T. 'Oil refining: an EEC and UK problem of excess capacity', *National Westminster Bank Quarterly Review* (May 1979), 34–42
21 Department of Energy, *Development of the oil and gas resources op cit.* 12
22 Chapman, K. 'The utilization of North Sea hydrocarbons as raw materials for petro-chemical manufacture', *Geoforum*, 8 (1977), 169–182
23 Department of Energy, *A North Sea Gas Gathering System*, Energy Paper No. 44 (1978)

24 Scottish Development Department, *North Sea oil and gas: coastal planning guidelines* (1974)

25 Department of Environment, *Accidental oil pollution of the sea*, Pollution Paper No. 8 (1976)

26 Mackay, G. A. and Trimble, N. F. 'The demand for production platforms and platform sites 1974–1980', *North Sea Study*, Occasional Paper No. 3 (Aberdeen Pol. Econ. Dept. 1975)

27 Scottish Office, 'Recent changes in Scottish unemployment relative', *Scot. Econ. Bull.* (1980), 8–13

28 Scottish Office, 'Employment in companies wholly related to the North Sea oil industry', *Ibid.* 48

29 Mackay, D. and Mackay, G. A. *The political economy of North Sea oil* (Martin Robertson 1975)

30 *The challenge of North Sea oil*, Cmnd 7143 (HMSO 1978)

31 Robertson, R. A. and Jowsey, P. C. 'Peat resources and development in the U.K.', *3rd International Peat Congress* Quebec (1968)

32 Jowsey, P. C. 'Peatlands'. In J. Tivy (ed.), *The organic resources of Scotland* (Oliver and Boyd 1973)

33 Jelly, J. O. and Pearce, D. W. *A pre-feasibility study on the development of Scottish peat as an energy source.* Unpublished report submitted to Science Research Council, 1980

34 Electricity Supply Board of Eire, *Annual Report 1978/1979*

35 Scottish Peat Committee, *Scottish Peat* (HMSO 1962), 54

36 Jelly, and Pearce, *op. cit.* 60

37 Lea, K. J. 'Hydro-electric power generation in the Highlands of Scotland', *Trans. Inst. Brit. Geog.*, 46 (1969), 155–66

38 Scottish Office, *Scottish abstract of statistics, op. cit.* 160

39 North of Scotland Hydro-electric Board, *Report and Accounts 1979/80*, 19

40 Department of Energy, *The prospects for the generation of electricity from wind energy in the United Kingdom*, Energy Paper No. 21 (1977)

41 Department of Energy, *Wave Energy*, Energy Paper No. 42 (1979)

42 See Ryle, M. 'Economics of alternative energy sources', *Nature*, 249 (1977), 117 and Ross, D. *Energy from the Waves* (Pergamon 1979)

43 Department of Energy, *The prospects for the generation of electricity op. cit.*

44 Department of Energy, *Wave Energy, op. cit.* 79

45 Hoare, A. 'Alternative energies: alternative geographies?' *Progress in Human Geography*, 3 (1979), 506–37

46 Rayment, R. 'Wind energy in the UK', *Building Services Engineer*, 44 (1976), 63–9

47 Ross, D. *op. cit.*

CHAPTER 12

(Pages 252–80)

Manufacturing Industry: Michael Cross

1 Slaven, A. *The Development of the West of Scotland, 1750–1960* (Routledge and Kegan Paul 1975), 5

2   Manners, G. 'National Perspectives'. In Manners, G. (ed.) *Regional Development in Britain* (Wiley 1972), 44

3   Slaven, A. *op. cit.* 193: 'The boards of the steel companies and the shipbuilders were shared by many men from both sides. Sir James Lithgow and Henry Lithgow were directors of Colvilles and of James Dunlop & Co., and Sir William Lithgow was chairman of Beardmore's. Sir James Lithgow was also a director of Fairfield Shipbuilding and Engineering Co., and Henry Lithgow, Sir Harold Yarrow and A. M. Stephen sat on the board of the Steel Company of Scotland. Conversely, a steelman like John Craig, chairman and managing director of Colvilles, also sat on the board of Harland and Wolff.'

4   Slaven, A. *op. cit.* 14

5   Slaven, A. *op. cit.* 193. It must not be thought the decline of shipbuilding was totally due to international pressures. In fact, in '. . . the case of shipbuilding the decline up to the mid-70s is more peculiarly English'. Fothergill, S. and Gudgin, G. H., *The Structural Growth and Decline of the U.K. Regions in its International Context.* CES-WN-495. (Centre for Environmental Studies 1978), 28

6   Leser, C. E. V. 'Manufacturing Industry'. In Cairncross, A. K. (ed.) *The Scottish Economy* (Cambridge UP 1954), 121

7   Fogarty, M. P. *Prospects of the Industrial Areas in Great Britain* (Methuen 1945), 165; Leser, C. E. V. and Silvey, A. H. 'Scottish Industries During the Inter-War Period', *Manchester School of Economic and Social Studies*, 18 (1950), 169; Cairncross, A. K. *op. cit.* 220–1; Leser, C. E. V. *op. cit.*, 121; Carter, I. J. *Comparative Studies in the Post-War Industrial Geography of the Clydeside and West Midlands Conurbations.* Unpublished Ph.D. Dissertation (Univ. of Glasgow 1971), 44; and Slaven, A. *op. cit.* 193, 207 and 226

8   Leser, C. E. V. *op. cit.* 121

9   Slaven, A. *op. cit.* 201

10 Thomson, D. *England in the Twentieth Century 1914–63* (Penguin 1965), 67

11 Allen, G. C. *British Industries and Their Organization* (Longman 1959)

12 Leser, C. E. V. *op. cit.* 121

13 Lever, W. F. 'Company-dominated Labour Markets: The British Case', *Tijdschrift voor Econ. en Soc. Geografie*, 69, 5 (1978), 306–12

14 Welch, R. V. 'Immigrant Manufacturing Industry Established in Scotland between 1945 and 1968: Some Structural and Locational Characteristics', *Scot. Geog. Mag.*, 86, 2 (1970), 134–48

15 Because of the National Cash Register plant which is within the city as defined by the Department of Employment

16 'Relative Performance of Incoming and Non-Incoming Industry in Scotland', *Scot. Econ. Bull.*, Autumn. 13 (1977), 14–25. (Units are considered to be incomers and non-incomers in this article according to the following definitions: an incomer is (i) any manufacturing unit opening in Scotland since 1 January 1945 and having its origin outside Scotland; or (ii) any manufacturing unit opening in Scotland having as its origin an incomer, where origin refers to the previous manufacturing unit (in the same enterprise) having the closest ties with the new unit. A non-incomer is any manufacturing unit present in Scotland at some time since 1945, which is not an incomer. Note that non-incomer does not mean

indigenous (wholly Scottish companies) since many English-owned and overseas-owned units present in 1945 and their subsequent branches will be considered to be non-incomers

17 The Department of Employment divides Scotland into a large number of administrative units called 'Local Office Areas'. At June 1977 there were 121 in operation, though this total has now declined due to the combination of adjacent offices

18 Cameron, G. C. 'Intra-Urban Location and the New Plant', *Papers and Proceedings*, Regional Science Association, 31 (1973), 125–144

19 Scottish Development Agency *The Electronics Industry in Scotland: A Proposed Strategy*. Report prepared for the SDA by Booz, Allen and Hamilton (SDA 1979), 96

20 During 1978, 191 new manufacturing enterprises were surveyed (firms set up in Scotland during the 1968–77 period). Of the 31 studied in the Highlands and Islands Region, only 9 were established by local people. The remaining 22 (70.9 per cent) had moved into the area with the express purpose of establishing a new firm. Cross, M. *New Firm Formation and Regional Development* (Gower 1981), 228–31

21 With the decline of many large companies in the inner city areas, new and small firms have been seen as a possibly major source for new employment.

22 Keeble, D. E. *Industrial Location and Planning in the United Kingdom* (Methuen 1976), 317

23 Crawford, M. 'Why Uncle Sam is Heading for Home', *Sunday Times*, 3 September 1978, 62

24 Firn, J. R. *op. cit.*; Hood, N. and Young, S. 'U.S. Investment in Scotland – Aspect of the Branch Factory Syndrome', *Scot. Journ. Pol. Econ.*, 23, 3 (1975), 279–194; McDermott, P. J. 'Multinational Manufacturing Firms and Regional Development: External Control in the Scottish Electronics Industry' *Scot. Journ. Pol. Econ.*, 26, 3 (1979), 287–306; Thwaites, A. T. 'Technological Change, Mobile Plants and Regional Development', *Regional Studies*, 12, 4 (1978), 445–461

25 Cross, M. *op. cit.* 228

26 Henderson, R. A. *An Analysis of Closure Amongst Scottish Manufacturing Plants* Discussion Paper No. 3 (Economics and Statistics Unit, Scottish Economic Planning Department 1979), 39

27 'Grasping the thistle. A Survey of Scotland', *The Economist* 18 February 1978, 24

28 Broadly speaking, the general aid programme has consisted of restricting growth in the South East and Midlands, while offering blanket aid to those companies willing to invest in the assisted regions. These policies have become more finely tuned with time, with aid for specific industries and companies

29 Fronko, E. G. 'One company's cast-off technology is another company's opportunity', *Innovation*, 23 (1971), 53–59

30 Oakey, R. P. *An Analysis of the Spatial Distribution of Significant British Industrial Innovation*. Discussion Paper No. 25, (CURDS, Univ. of Newcastle upon Tyne 1979), 42

31 Branch and subsidiary plants appear rarely to gain more functions after
    being set-up and, if they do, it is over a long time period. See Hood, N. and
    Young, S. *op. cit.* 285 and Scottish Development Agency *op. cit.* 46
32 Policies pursued by the SDA might increase the prosperity, wealth and
    outlook for Scotland, but at the same time act in the opposite direction as
    regards the achievement of national (UK) prosperity and growth
33 The British Steel Corporation, for example, will continue its major
    programme of disinvestment. Such a programme will probably adversely
    affect Scotland, but how far will these effects be allowed to proceed before
    some form of hybrid steel industry is set up in Scotland?
34 Firn, J. R. 'Industrial Policy'. In Mackay, D. (ed.) *Scotland 1980. The
    Economics of Self Government* (Q Press 1977), 76–81

Acknowledgements

THE Editor and the contributors would like to thank the following people for their generous help during the preparation of this book: K. Beeston (NCB), R. Birnie, Morag Clapperton, A. Dawson, A. Gemmell, N. Hubbard, J. Livingston, G. Mathewson (SDA), R. MacKenzie, R. Mellor, I. Ralston, J. Smith, R. Swift (SSEB), C. Tarry (SDA), N. Williams.

Index